INTERNATIONALIZATION – THE PEOPLE DIMENSION

For Erica – my partner through space and time

INTERNATIONALIZATION – THE PEOPLE DIMENSION

HUMAN RESOURCE STRATEGIES FOR GLOBAL EXPANSION

Stephen J. Perkins

KOGAN PAGE

YOURS TO HAVE AND TO HOLD

BUT NOT TO COPY

First published in 1997

Kogan Page Limited
120 Pentonville Road
London N1 9JN

© Stephen J. Perkins 1997

British Library Cataloguing in Publication Data

A CIP record for this book is available from the British Library.

ISBN 0 7494 2464 8

Typeset by Saxon Graphics Ltd, Derby
Printed in England by Clays Ltd, St Ives plc

Contents

Contents

Foreword

The world is changing – frighteningly fast. And, if we simply assume that the future is going to be like the past, we're going to be both surprised and disappointed. Since neither of these emotions is one that any of us particularly enjoys, we'd better do something about it.

The organizations that are going to survive and prosper in this new world are those that understand better than anyone else – and better than their rivals – what's happening. They must also understand sooner than their rivals what's happening, and get ahead of the wave rather than getting buried by it.

The world of organizations and commerce is expanding and shrinking. Expanding into new technologies and new market opportunities; shrinking in the sense of time and distance. The 'global village' is here, populated by a diverse array of communities and personalities. Organization leaders cannot but be a part of the global:local environment if they wish to take their enterprises forward. The smarter ones have long since recognized that they can only succeed by building communities of interest. These encompass their financial investors, their business partners (sometimes involving government institutions), their suppliers and their workforces. The common thread is the dimension represented by people. It is people who make and execute decisions; people whom we look to for innovation and flexibility – across boundaries of structure and geography and culture

I first met Stephen Perkins when I joined the Board of National Power, and he was looking after the Remuneration Committee of which I became Chairman. Since that time, he has embarked on an initiative to build bridges between the worlds of academia and business, through the foundation and leadership of a unique research institute, which is exploring the strategic role of reward as the symbolic and practical nexus of the new employment relationship. The Strategic Remuneration Research Centre is working to uncover what it is that really motivates people, rather than following the traditional pathways of pseudo-economics in this important aspect of organizations' capital investment.

This book draws on Stephen's first-hand observation and experience, both as a researcher and an adviser to a cross-section of major organizations (both government- and privately-owned) in different parts of the world. All are seeking to come to terms with the imperative to internationalize – at the very least in terms of best competitive operational practice. He has captured and written down some of the practical learning which such organizations have been going through. These lessons are worthy of passing on to a wider audience. Some of the models the book contains will challenge conventional wisdom as we enter the 21st century. As such, I am very happy to welcome and commend his book as a novel and significant contribution to the sum of our knowledge of internationalization and its critical people dimension.

Sir John Banham

Preface

I began this book in the hope that the lessons I have learned, painfully, over the past few years may, be passed on to similar HR travellers. It is intended as a practical handbook, for dipping into at will, when considering a particular people challenge in supporting internationalization initiatives, or when examining such issues in an educational setting. The offering is decidedly practical, with an emphasis on passing on experience and some models and processes which I have found helpful in a variety of settings. They owe much to friends and colleagues with whom I have collaborated over a lot of years. I thank them all for sharing these riches.

I have, I am sure, done insufficient justice to all those scholars who have explored conceptually, approaches to motivating and leading people as part of business expansion around the world. However, where I have encountered writings which I have found constructively influential, I have made reference to them at various stages as the narrative develops. In the main, however, I have simply shared conclusions based on facing up to the threats and opportunities of playing the international game. I thought I should capture these in a systematic text, before they evaporate from my recollection.

I hope the result of my endeavours will be of practical benefit to the reader. It is my wish that you also may experience some of the colour, and pleasure, I have encountered, both as a corporate practitioner of the HR art form, and as a researcher and adviser to corporations as a strategic partner on the outside. Perhaps you will let me have your views; you can visit me at www.srrc.com. The journey starts here . . .

Stephen J. Perkins

Acknowledgements

I am indebted to a network of special people, who inspired and contributed to the development of this book in a myriad different ways. First, to Pauline Goodwin of Kogan Page, without whose early and consistent support and guidance, the text would not have appeared in print. Secondly, to all those friends and colleagues in my international network. Among them, special thanks go to:

The Americas: Bob Chiste, Paul T. Hansen, David Rhoads, Joe and Ellen Shupack, Ken Zdunich, Lorraine de Zuleta.

Europe, Middle East and South Africa: Michael Armstrong, Richard Moss-Blundell, Jorge Moreira, Scott Eversman, Hugh Feldon, John Smith, John Verster, Geoff Stapley, Mark Geary, Volker Rennert, Chris Hendry, Paola Bradley, Mike Redhouse, Phil Wills, Martin Day, Philip Mayer, Frank V. Sharp, Janus Piétras, Tony McNulty, Neal Wagner.

Asia Pacific: John S. Maxwell, Vaqar Khan, Ooi Chwee Hoon, Henry Yung, Kusum Sahdev, Andrew Gordon, Rebecca Taylor.

Finally, let me pay tribute to the manual dexterity of Laraine Reynolds, in preparing the manuscripts. And, of course, my inspiration and life force – my understanding family: Erica, Marie-Louise and Matthew.

Thank you all.

Chapter 1

Introduction –
a 21st Century
Frame of Reference

From its inception, this book has been intended to operate as a practical guide for human resource directors and other business executives, engaged in the challenging issues which organizations everywhere face, of competing to win in a global market environment.

Many businesses, particularly the major corporations whose home base forms part of the western world, have been operating in various international markets over many years. Other major businesses from those same parts of the world, who previously have been able to develop and grow exclusively within their home markets, are now finding they must turn their face to the world, as well as those that have emerged from the thriving developing countries. In all cases, I believe that the models of international deployment, particularly those surrounding the western expatriate, and traditional approaches to the employment of local national staff, which have dominated corporate thinking for many years, are no longer fit for purpose in the turbulent global market place, as we enter the 21st century.

For that reason, I believe it is important for existing multinationals to revisit some of their long-practised methodologies, and for the aspirant internationalists not to tread traditional paths because of the pitfalls they contain. All this, as they approach the key issue of attracting, developing, retaining, and deploying for sustained high performance the people who will form the lifeblood of the truly global corporations of the future. This book, with an emphasis on practical experience-based learning, is intended to contribute to that new thinking and reworking of established principles.

In that context, I have attempted to structure the book so that it follows an evolving course, which I hope will assist the reader both in gaining a useful overview of the strategic human resources issues which require solutions, and also to have a reference guide, broken into a number of relevant steps.

These will cover the strategic business imperative of internationalization. They will explore issues concerning the organization of business units for success in international markets. The question of understanding and then building and maintaining international capabilities will be explored. Issues surrounding the terms and conditions on which internationalists will need to be engaged for the future will be examined. An HRM due diligence model for supporting business development will be offered. Questions surrounding performance management in an internationalizing business will be reviewed. And, drawing threads together, the role of the global human resource professional will be considered, pointing up the challenge of developing this critical business role as *an holistic navigator*.

Throughout, case study examples from real life situations will be to the fore in supporting the narrative. Despite the need for this categorization, it is important that compartmentalization does not take over, clouding issues which need to be understood within the wider picture of internationalization as a business strategy in its own right. Each one of the areas described under the various headings needs to be seen in terms of its linkages with the other parts. It is only through examining every one of the relevant aspects as part of a wider frame of reference that a core capability, derived from strategic human resource management, can effectively be leveraged.

The intention is that, in this way, readers will be able to review issues overall, while then having a reference text which they can dip into as they are constructing and reviewing the constituent parts of their international human resource strategies as these evolve over time.

There have been a number of attempts to examine various aspects of deploying people in an international context which, while making a worthy contribution to the sum of knowledge in this area, have tended to explore the issues which arise only as of academic interest in themselves. On the whole, these works have either been highly generalized in exploring international human resources themes, or else they have been focused on some specific aspects; for example the problems of managing international alliances.

As one who has been wrestling with the trials of developing profitable business across the major continents of the world, both in a corporate role and in that of an external strategic adviser, it seemed to me there would be merit in developing a practitioner's 'how to' guide, capturing and passing on for the benefit of others engaging in the global challenge, the lessons of hard won experience. There also seemed potential advantage in writing such a book which would draw together a number of perspectives seen through a practitioner's eye, to provide an holistic overview of the issues to which those engaged in business internationalization typically have to face up.

The book has been prepared with the benefit of insights and experiences which have been shared with me, both in on-job situations, as well as from my global network of friends and colleagues (all of whom are senior practitioners in their own right, and have a powerful story to share from their various vantage points around the world).

ORDER OF PLAY

In order to provide a fuller map with which to navigate the book, drawing on the generic chapter headlines as summarized above, I shall now set out in summary form some of the issues I propose to develop in the chapters to follow. This synopsis will sketch out some of the questions to be addressed, as well as providing a context for subsequent discussion, and the style which I propose to adopt.

Internationalization – the strategic business context

At the end of the 20th century, internationalization is not an optional extra. The dynamics of global business development need to be explored, to be anticipated. Further, we must understand the problems of history; 'custom and practice' will not do in setting a future context. Finally, let us highlight the issue of 'making a difference', why HR should be at the forefront in global business development.

The context for the HR management activity described is one in which growth through internationalization is not a luxury add-on, but a business imperative. It is about examining significant business investment opportunities and the maximization of returns. It is about doing this in both the greenfield development and brownfield acquisition environment. It is about operating in both the developed and the developing countries of the world, with the differences that they throw up in meeting the challenge of the people dimension.

Issues of organization

There are no right answers – developing an organizational evaluation framework is a critical aspect of strategic international HRM. The future is federated – strategic alliances and joint ventures are a pre-requisite for leveraging core capability to manage the value chain. We need to create frameworks for avoiding 'people pitfalls'.

Tensions between 'the centre' and its satellites are inevitable. We will discuss new rules of the game for strategic business units to interrelate for corporate business advantage, both with 'HQ' and with one another.

The cultural factor – developing and applying new organizational models which put diversity (structural, geographic and philosophical) to commercial advantage – is a key area for attention in creating workable organization forms on a global basis.

Smart human resource management – policies for designing business units around people, creating the right climate for this core resource – acts as the 'corporate glue', to leverage financial, information, materials and technological resources for maximum sustained shareholder value creation, wherever the organization conducts its business. (We will look at examples of how the various approaches have been developed and applied in practice, and tensions anticipated and managed.)

Capabilities development

In the competitive global economy, only people really do 'differentiate'. We shall examine how enterprises of all kinds can recognize and exploit this fact.

The categories of international capability need to be considered, including:

❑ organizational partnering
❑ acquisition of relevant business units to make up capability shortfalls
❑ talent spotting and attraction – leadership and know-how capabilities
❑ potential identification and rounded capabilities development from within.

Models are required for evaluating existing capability against that required for international business success. Successful internationalizing enterprises perform a 'gap' analysis to identify capability shortfalls. Emphasis is placed on winning top management approval and support for capabilities development programmes.

To make it 'real' and build understanding and ownership throughout the corporation, the 'development centre' approach and Personal International Development Plan management is invaluable. Equally important are policies for integrating relevant new capability in a global business setting, avoiding rejections by the business 'host organism'. Lack of attention here has undermined the most able commercial strategies.

International terms and conditions

We shall outline and review the 'EXPAT' model – an approach which deals with the fact that the expatriate of yesteryear and *his* employment package just won't meet the demands of turn of the century 'internationalist' postings. Further, we shall look beyond the 'balance sheet' – at destination centred assignment terms, where line management justify the added value over the added cost of an expatriate assignment compared with a 'local national' appointment. The 'package' envelope is determined by line and HR partnering, then handing flexibility over to the assignee, to personalize its detailed application against individual and family requirements.

Successful global players are getting smart at leveraging the intangible rewards of international career paths in 21st century organizations. With the increasing commercial and political imperative to reduce the expatriate: local balance, they are also developing relevant local reward strategies which align with corporate mission and reward philosophies, while respecting national and inter-cultural differences. This means they are also managing corporate and local tensions in establishing the employment package necessary to attract, retain and motivate high calibre talent.

Business development – a model for HRM due diligence

Evaluating options and frameworks required to ensure profitable business development in both *greenfield* and *brownfield* (ie, new business build and acquisition/redevelopment) situations, in both developed and underdeveloped/developing territories has become a must for international HR professionals.

Human resource management is increasingly positioned at the centre of commercial business development and harvesting return on investments; anticipating the 'big ticket' risks and designing and implementing strategies tailored to the cultural and structural circumstances of international ventures.

Performance management in an internationalizing business

Novel thinking is required to align the efforts of 'home and away' teams for sustained shareholder value creation. Performance measures need to be evolved in partnership with line managers and other professional stakeholders which reflect the realities of deploying various groups of people in novel multi-cultural, global business situations.

The HR professional's role is that of business partner, interpreting key business drivers, and linking these to objectives which align people capabilities with the goals of strategic business units, as well as corporate critical success factors. The 'motivation factor' is a vital component; performance management processes need to be designed and implemented mindful of the messages they communicate both to managers and staff about the priorities and values of the enterprise and its top management. This needs especially careful handling when messages need to be 'translated' across multiple languages, cultures and traditions.

The global HR manager – an holistic navigator

The role of the HR professional in internationalizing businesses then, is distinctly different to that of his or her counterpart in the domestically bound corporation, or even the 'home-centred' personnel executive overseeing traditional expatriate assignments. The role must be seen in an holistic context, operating as the *navigator* in partnership with both commercial and operational management colleagues, coaching, counselling and informing them about the essentials of business success internationally, drawing on the talents of people.

SUMMARY AND CHECKLIST

One of the difficulties often experienced across the whole spectrum of Human Resource Management is a tendency of specialists to compartmentalize issues. Is this or that policy the property of organization development, career management specialists, employee relations or remuneration specialists? In practice, only by taking an holistic approach can the various elements of the international people management strategy produce successful results. Each of the constituent parts of a strategic approach to international HR management needs to be developed and applied so as to achieve maximum synergy across 'the corporation', however that organization is defined in the novel environment which international business challenges necessitate.

For me, the conclusion is that the approach to international people management should be seen as a journey. The approach companies adopt should recognize the fact that no two ventures and no two management and professional teams are alike. It is essential that relevant line management is informed and required to endorse the excess cost, compared with the excess value to be derived from international initiatives; to evaluate international people management decisions on the same basis as any other strategic investment decisions. The participants should be judging –

and be judged on – maximizing the returns against a quantified level of risk.

The approach adopted needs to be flexible, but openly performance driven. It must be competitive in the international market place, if talented people are to be attracted and secured with 'world-wide capabilities'. The approach itself must evolve continuously in parallel with the evolving business strategy. It must strive to keep the *strategy* = *execution* = *people* equation in balance.

The following questions need to be addressed in making use of this book as part of strategic thinking around the people dimension of business internationalization. Do the lessons learned and conclusions offered:

- ❑ Provide a framework against which, as a human resource professional or other business executive, you can frame the questions top management need to answer, in order that a tailored human resource strategy can be produced which matches your organization's management style and culture, and medium to long-term business plans?
- ❑ Offer a basis on which to undertake focused research both with a corporate perspective and for specific regional and local environments to assist in developing, monitoring and refining people plans?
- ❑ Enable a better informed basis for tapping into global information and advisory networks, and framing strategic questions which are matched to your own organization's strategic goals?

Checklists like this will appear at the end of each chapter of the book, in an attempt to draw out key issues; as an *aide mémoire* to what you have read, on subsequent dips back into the book; and as a basis for questioning the way in which you may apply some of the principles and lessons illustrated in your own business setting.

Chapter 2

Internationalization – the Strategic Business Context

The internationalization of business – or 'going global' – is an inescapable fact of life for most organizations these days. The signs are that the pressures to function in an international context, even where an organization is unlikely to transact its primary business beyond a domestic base, are likely to be overwhelming whatever enterprise you are conducting.

Writing in a recent edition of *The Economist* magazine, Jeffrey Sachs (1997), a professor of international trade at Harvard University, pointed out that:

> For the first time in history, almost all of the world's people are bound together in a global capitalist system. This momentous development forces us to think anew about the world economy. In the past, differences in policies across regions of the world resulted in vast differences in economic performance; in the future, policies are likely to be more similar. As a result, large parts of the developing world will narrow the income gap between themselves and richer nations.

In its 1996–97 world employment report, the International Labour Office comments on trade and investment flows.

> A key aspect of globalization has been the rapid growth in world trade. Since 1984 the volume of world trade has grown faster than world output. As a result export to GDP ratios have increased in the majority of OECD countries and in

developing countries in Asia and Latin America. The growth of exports, especially of manufactured goods, from developing countries has been particularly rapid. This trend has been fuelled by the wave of trade and liberalization across the world and the development of regional trade liberalization arrangements. It is a trend that can be expected to continue with the completion of the Uruguay Round of GATT and the establishment of the world trade organization ...

At the same time flows of foreign direct investment (FDI) have also increased sharply, especially to developing countries. The average annual flows have increased more than three-fold since the early 1980s for the world as a whole, while for developing countries it had increased five-fold by 1993. These increasing flows of direct investment have been accompanied by the growth of globally integrated production systems characterized by the rapid expansion of intra-firm trade in intermediate products and of subcontracting, licensing and franchising arrangements, including new forms of outsourcing work across national frontiers. The value of global sales of the foreign affiliates of multinational enterprises now exceeds that of conventional arms-length trade. These developments have been facilitated by a worldwide move towards more liberal legislation on foreign direct investment.

Other financial flows have also increased with the globalization of financial markets. This has included massive increases in the volume of trading in foreign exchange and in new financial instruments such as derivatives. Cross-border trading in bond and equity markets has also increased rapidly. A striking new development has been the large flows of equity investment towards emerging markets.

In the UK, the average company in the FTSE 100 index now earns more than half its revenue overseas. This means that investors are taking international equities extremely seriously. Table 2.1, developed by BZW Equity Research, sets out an interesting picture of companies now earning at least 90 per cent of their revenues abroad.

In its latest World Economic Outlook, the IMF describes this phenomenon as 'the growing economic inter-dependence of countries worldwide through the increasing volume and variety of cross-border transactions in goods and services and of international capital flows, and also through the more rapid and widespread diffusion of technology'.

Table 2.1 *Where in the world the money is earned*

Companies earning at least 90% of their revenue abroad			Highest exposure to continental Europe		
Company (% of total sales)	UK exposure	Non-UK exposure	Company (% of total sales)	UK exposure	Europe exposure
Std Chartered	7	93	RMC	25	61
RTZ-CRA	7	93	British Vita	34	59
Charter	7	93	Redland	19	57
Zeneca	7	93	Arjo Wiggins	17	55
SmithKline Beecham	7	93	BPB Industries	31	49
Invesco	7	93	Shell Transport	10	47
Vendome	8	92	Hepworth	44	46
Burmah Castrol	8	92	Sage Group	39	44
Siebe	8	92	Sema	33	44
Williams Hldg	8	92	Laird	27	43
English China Clays	8	92			
Glaxo Wellcome	9	91			
Cookson Group	9	91			
British Airways	10	90			
Shell Transport	10	90			
Grand Met	10	90			
BBA	10	90			

Highest North American exposure			Highest exposure to Asia Pacific		
Company (% of total sales)	UK exposure	North American exposure	Company (% of total sales)	UK exposure	Asian Pacific exposure
Invesco	7	78	Std Chartered	7	63
Medeva	16	72	HSBC	31	54
FKI	14	63	Cable and Wireless	30	45
Premier Farnell	23	63	Lasmo	47	41
Grand Met	10	60	Vendome	8	40
Tomkins	32	60	RTZ-CRA	7	38
Wolseley	24	53	Ocean	26	34
Bunzl	23	53	Inchcape	33	33
Willis Corroon	26	53	BOC	24	32
Cookson Group	9	50	Burmah Castrol	8	31

Source: BZW Equity Research

Of course, it is technology which makes globalization feasible. Improved communications have lead to an organization of innovation – the multinational company – a superb mechanism for transferring technology across frontiers. Liberalization, however, is the dynamic which makes globalization happen. Martin Wolf (1997), observed recently, writing in the *Financial Times*, that 'globalization was not inevitable. Nor does it merely reflect the march of technology. It marks the successful worldwide spread of the economic liberalization that began nearly fifty years ago in western Europe with the Marshall plan. It is now bringing unprecedented opportunities to billions of people throughout the world.'

Peter Drucker (1995), has reminded us that

> twenty years ago no one talked of the 'world economy'. The term then was 'international trade'. The change in term – and everybody now talks of the world economy – bespeaks a profound change in economic reality. Twenty or 30 years ago the economy outside the borders of a nation – and especially outside the borders of a middle-sized or large nation – could still be seen as different, as separate, and as something that could be safely ignored in dealing with the domestic economy and in domestic economic policy. That, as the evidence makes unambiguously clear, is sheer delusion today . . .

Drucker goes on to discuss the question of where new markets for global trade are likely to be located. His conclusion is that the new markets, which will be the source of focus by internationalizing businesses, are not consumer-goods markets. Nor are they, he says, traditional producer-goods markets (ie markets for machinery and factories). 'Rather, three of the new markets are for various kinds of "infrastructure", that is, for facilities that serve both producers and consumers. And the fourth new market is for things that are neither "products" nor "services" in any traditional meaning of those terms.'

In Drucker's view, the most immediately accessible of the new markets involves communication and information.

> Demand for telephone service in third world countries and the countries of the former Soviet Bloc is practically insatiable. There is no greater impediment to economic development than poor telephone service and no greater spur than good telephone service . . . In the developed world, the information and communications market may be even larger. Both the office of tomorrow and the school of tomorrow are likely to built around information and communication.

Drucker goes on to describe three additional new markets; one relating to the environment, which includes agro-biology and energy; another, the growth of the existing market in developed and developing countries alike to repair, replenish and upgrade visible infrastructure, and a final market, created, he says, by demography, for investment 'products' to finance survival into old age. Drucker links the growing world of privatization initiatives with these material developments, particularly in relation to infrastructure. He concludes that no government in the world today is solvent enough to manage this process on its own, whether through taxation or through borrowing. 'Yet,' he says, 'the capital is there, and in abundance, and so are the opportunities for profitable investment'.

It is in this context then that many domestically bound organizations, facing increasing pressure within their home markets, are examining their core capabilities and the opportunities to expand their businesses on a global scale. This may be summarized as the 'pull' and 'push' to internationalize. Given the intensification of competition from without the domestic economy as well as within, there really is no alternative for major corporations who wish to survive and prosper into the 21st century.

In most cases, it is not the technical or commercial issues, however complex they may appear, which will cause organizations the greatest difficulty. It will be those issues which relate to their people. This can be summed up in the phrase: *We've got the kit, we've got the cash – it's the people that will make the difference!*

A STRATEGIC BUSINESS IMPERATIVE

There are many businesses which have, of course, operated on an international basis for many years. However, in people terms, this can be part of the problem which HR professionals face at the present time, in translating their domestically bound operations into ones competent to operate on a global basis. Many of the organizations who have had international employees in the past were operating in a very different business environment to the one which prevails today, and which certainly will apply in the future.

In his book, *Human Resource Strategies for International Growth*, Chris Hendry (1994), comprehensively reviews the considerable body of literature which has been concerned with identifying the methods by which a firm can penetrate a foreign market and the reasons for adopting one solution rather than another. He says a basic framework is to consider market entry in terms of three generic methods: exporting, licensing, or foreign direct investment. These categories, he says, are complicated by a variety of collaborative arrangements between firms, especially with the emergence in recent years of new forms of strategic alliance. Chris Hendry comments that:

> when a firm first embarks on international trade through export, managers may well perceive this as a technical and knowledge problem. They would have specific concerns about getting to know particular markets; setting up distributions channels; regulations and standards they need to meet; export documentation and formalities to be completed; what currency they should trade in; how to deal with exchange rate fluctuations; and so forth ... In many cases, there will be direct training and recruitment implications concerned with specific areas of expertise: for example, on documentation procedures involving clerical staff and, of course, languages.
>
> However, from a human resources point of view, the issues are rather more profound. They centre on the process of learning about specific customers within foreign markets. Trade does not take place through the operation of price mechanisms alone. It entails the matching of a number of activities to customer needs and capabilities, adapting products and production processes, scheduling, delivery routines and logistical systems. This requires considerable knowledge by supplier and customer about one another, and implies the best way to establish these requirements is through direct, personal experience and contact. Recognizing this, industrial marketing puts particular emphasis on buyer/seller relationships ... The importance of the buyer/seller relationship, however, extends beyond the particular character of 'industrial'-type products to marketing generally, and provides a model of inter-firm relationships within internationalization at large.

Chris Hendry opines that, in one sense, internationalization is about leveraging resources and competencies from the domestic into the international arena. He says this requires many kinds of adjustment, however. 'Internationalization is not a process simply of transferring domestic strengths, but of adapting product functionalities, technologies, and marketing approaches to situations which are subtly and sometimes substantially different. It begins in learning about specific customers in other markets, but it is likely then to require change in accustomed ways of doing things domestically.' Chris Hendry identifies a number of organizational weaknesses which stand in the way of such development. These include blocks to thinking internationally and specific changes that have to be made in the domestic organization to implement an international commitment.

> Human resource management in its formal, functional sense has a role to play in undoing blocks and assisting implementation. More broadly, however, its relevance lies in the fact that internationalization is a 'social process'. Networking is a social skill, while organizational phenomena such as attitudes to risk, patterns of power and control, and culture are fundamentally social in character. Overcoming or confronting problems of this kind which inhibit internationalization is a human resource issue centred on learning.

As Chris Hendry observes, the imperative to internationalize is frequently complicated by the requirement to enter into joint ventures and alliances, in order to build the bridge between local domestic capability and relevant business opportunity identification and exploitation in new territories. For this reason, a disciplined process is required for the selection of partners and engaging in collaborative operations with them. International business consultants Booz Allen & Hamilton, have developed a methodology which they apply in their own alliance work, and which they recommend to clients. My interpretation of this is reproduced diagrammatically in Figure 2.1.

As the work of Nancy Adler (1991), in the US (summarized in Figure 2.2) amply demonstrates, in the past, international operations frequently were not the primary focus of a business's growth potential. It was often the case that individuals were sent overseas either as part of their preparations for 'early retirement', or because the organization simply did not know what to do with them. Therefore, international assignments frequently acquired a tag of being for those individuals who were not the most able in corporations. This tended to mean an HR 'policy', in effect, of 'bribing' individuals in many cases to undertake an international assignment, often identifying individuals with characteristics *not* best suited for successful operation on an international basis! It also meant that 'throwing money at the problem' tended to reinforce many of the behavioural deficiencies among certain expatriates, rather than address the problem at its core.

The new business context means that none of this will do anymore. Opportunities to grow major organizations are likely to be almost exclusively international. Therefore, only the brightest individuals will be selected for international assignments. With the end of conventional

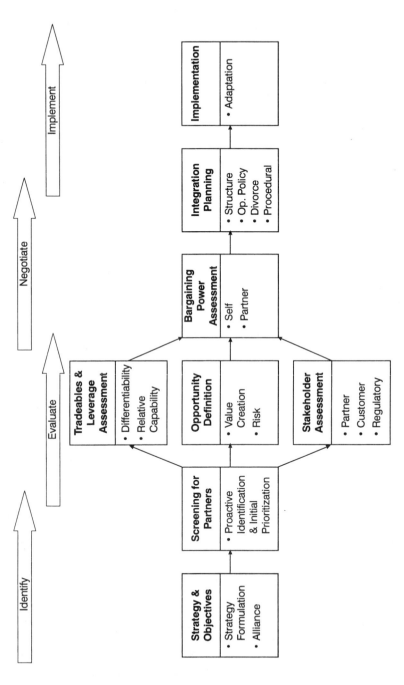

Figure 2.1 *Alliance formulation methodology.*

	Export	International	Transnational	Global
Business focus	Domestic	Domestic with some developed economies	Multinational	Global
Significance of world business	Minimal	Moderate	Important	Critical
Global strategy	Representation of product/ service	Business development and the control/ transfer of technology	Manage and expand global business efforts	Borderless management and the leverage of internal capabilities
Level of global competition	None	Some	Increasing	Significant

Figure 2.2 *Overseas business opportunities are transforming corporations into global identities.*
Source: Nancy Adler, McGill University

careers, for the majority, the opportunity to be part of a growing business on an international footing will it be an intrinsic reward in itself.

However, precedents have been set. It is easy even for this new breed of international manager to have expectations which are not realistic in the more commercially robust situation in which most organizations now find themselves. The objective will be to secure the *right* talent, on terms which are cost-effective and suited to the future business context. This will mean avoiding one-off deals, which could easily serve no purpose other than to demotivate the increasingly critical local national employee population, who compare themselves adversely with the over-expensive 'expat' in his ghetto.

LOCALIZATION OF THE TALENT PORTFOLIO

Equally, the emphasis is more and more on securing expertise – for business development and operations – which can only be found within the territories in question. In some instances, this is the result of regulation, limiting the number of work permits available to foreigners entering a country and its employment market. Even more significantly, local market opportunities frequently can be identified and opened up only by those with long-established networks in a particular region or country. And with the in-built cultural conditioning to win in competitive developing markets, sensitive to 'how we do business here'.

This is a major challenge for HR managers. It is one which we can grasp by some clear thinking, by the ability to stand by professional expertise, and by resolution. Or, it is one which could easily overwhelm the function.

In order to help organizations build a systematic approach to developing their international business operations, there is merit in creating a framework against which steps along the way can be set, and then measured in practice. There are benefits in establishing strategic milestones which provide relevant markers for monitoring purposes. Figure 2.3 suggests one approach to doing this with the issue of internationalizing human resource management strategy to the fore.

	Milestone 1: a company that delivers	Milestone 2: a major player	Milestone 3: a world leader
External Positioning	Establish a reputation for responsiveness and effectively closing/ launching projects	Dominate a few country regional markets or investment project 'types'	Be sought out by governments, banks and partners for serious consideration on all major projects in the sector
Tasks	• Identify, assemble and integrate capabilities required to win • Adjust business development process for focus on winning internationally (and for internal consistency) • Modify behaviour, build teams to support strategy • Expertly launch initial projects	• Confirm/modify winning capabilities • Demonstrate success of initial projects • Begin to build scale (logistical, HR, technical, reputation, capital) • Test and implement global leadership model • Learn from mistakes/ successes and refine processes/organization • Establish major new business units • Form enduring partnerships	• Achieve most profit and revenue from international business – become 'the international XYZ company' • Achieve scale in all key capabilities through internal development, alliances, and acquisitions • Institutionalize a learning process to guarantee continuing evolution
Number of International Projects	1–2 Successfully launched	3–10 Successfully completed	10+ Successfully completed
Time frame years	0–2	3–5	5–10

Figure 2.3   *Internationalization milestones.*

A good example of an organization which recognized the imperative and opportunity presented by internationalization is Texas Instruments. Peter Stirling, the firm's Vice-President, Human Resources, Europe, offered a pen-portrait at the 1994 Annual Conference of the UK's Institute of Personnel and Development.

Texas Instruments, as the name suggests, is a multinational electronics company headquartered in Dallas, Texas. Founded in 1930 as 'Geophysical Services Inc' and providing geophysical exploration services to the petroleum industry using the reflection seismograph, it rapidly developed as a manufacturer of electronic equipment for the US forces. In 1951, the corporate name-change to 'Texas Instruments' signified the company's move into mainstream electronics, and a few years later the invention of the integrated circuit by TI heralded the start of the semiconductor age.

TI's position as a world leader in electronics is founded on a long tradition of transforming leading edge technologies into useful products and services. Other firsts include:

❑ the commercial pocket radio
❑ the commercial silicon transistor
❑ terrain-following airborne radar
❑ the handheld calculator
❑ the single-chip microcomputer which squeezed all the logic circuits and memory cells of a computer on to a single piece of silicon.

In the late 1950s TI began expanding into international markets, and establishing manufacturing and trading entities outside the US. In 1994, the company had annual revenues of over $8bn, operations in 30 countries worldwide, and employed some 60,000 people; less than half of those being US based.

TI can immediately be recognized as a company with a strong pervading culture. That is to say there are a set of attitudes, values and beliefs that are shared widely throughout the organization. In such circumstances it is invariably the case that company founders are men or women possessing drive, charisma and a vision of 'how things ought to be' which becomes woven into the fabric of the enterprise in its formative years. TI is no exception.

Not so exceptional today, but in the early 1960s a company which operated on first name terms, single status employment conditions, paid above the market, used teams to solve problems and drive improvement, and emphasized communication including face to face appraisal practices, was rather revolutionary. In moving into the international arena, TI exported many of its Texan values and, with other American multinational corporations, started to influence the way other nationalities approached work. The basic formula persists today, but in each country of operation trade-offs have been made to accommodate local norms, preferences and cultures.

TI regards its diversity as a strength. By integrating globally it is possible to take advantage of:

❏ local customer interfaces
❏ low manufacturing costs and high output from the Asia Pacific region
❏ the engineering prowess of the Germans, combined with the marketing ability of the Italians.
❏ the software design talents of TI's centre in Bangalore, India,

all linked by a satellite communications network that allows instantaneous communication.

The strong global culture has supported the evolution to a well integrated and networked 'matrix' organization which is TI today. Different sites and businesses must support one another to serve the customer, products can be designed in France, produced in Dallas or Japan, sold in Germany, and distributed through Holland to a tight specification of quality and delivery, but all these interconnections are invisible to the end customer. This can only be accomplished if all parties to the process have a shared view of what is important and trust the 'upstream' link in the supply chain.

In this example it appears a strong company culture is good. However, the culture must be relevant to the business condition. Many companies are successful by organizing as autonomous profit centres with considerable local empowerment, and little reliance on a central structure. In these cases the culture which develops in the unit is the most important determinant of business success – corporate culture is non-existent or irrelevant!

Within a multinational organization there are subcultures. TI's observation of its own situation leads Peter Stirling to believe there are three important cultural vectors:

1. The corporate culture
2. The national culture
3. The operational culture. (eg sales organization versus R & D, group versus manufacturing line).

Managing culture then, in TI's view, is to do with managing the inter-relationship of these three forces in a way that is appropriate to one's particular business aims.

In fact, in many ways it is a misconception to imagine that undertaking human resource management activities on an international basis, at least at the philosophical, or strategy-making level, is fundamentally different to any other form of high quality human resource management activity. Organizations with sound corporate HR policies and practices in place will be those most likely to be successful in applying them wherever they do business, both domestically and on a global scale. This is not to deny there are special features associated with taking a domestic business activity and growing it across geographical and cultural boundaries. Therefore, there is a need to assess HR strategy in the context of: 'Will it deliver the expected results irrespective of the environment in which it is to be implemented?' We need new models for evaluating key options. We shall attempt to frame some of these questions in the chapters which follow.

SUMMARY AND CHECKLIST

There is no doubt that the economic imperatives now driving the great majority of businesses who wish to expand and thrive into the 21st century, are to take their core capabilities and grow them internationally. There is often a 'push', in the sense of core capabilities which the organization recognizes, that with suitable adaptation will be capable of deployment for business advantage in different territories around the world. This is accompanied by the 'pull', frequently based upon the requirement of domestically bound organizations to compete more effectively in deregulated markets, where both domestic and global competition has hotted up dramatically. Overseas business opportunities and the accompanying necessities are therefore transforming corporations into global entities.

All this is calling for a different breed of organizational form and employee type in order to exploit the opportunities which are available, winning against fierce global competition, particularly in the developing markets around the world. The internationalizing firm must, therefore, both leverage its existing resources and capabilities from the domestic into the international arena, and also begin to learn about specific customers in other markets, in order to activate organizational changes to the way in which domestic operations are carried out, in order to compete successfully within the new business and market conditions. Many of those markets are in infrastructure development, an area where many of those organizations which, in the developed world, have been forced to adapt from regulated to deregulated markets, are well positioned, and indeed find a strategic necessity, to respond to.

The challenge for human resources professionals will be to stand back and undertake some clear thinking about the ways in which domestic excellence in human resources management and modelling can be deployed within this different and dynamic environment. In particular, to develop new frames of reference against which alternative courses of action can be quickly assimilated and adaptation put into place at rates which are superior to those being adopted by the competition.

Does your organization:

❏ Have a clear perspective throughout the business on the requirement to internationalize?
❏ Have a series of milestones for monitoring progress?
❏ Recognize that internationalization involves not only leveraging domestic capabilities abroad, but also developing sensing mechanisms for collecting and interpreting diverse global customer priorities?
❏ Devote strategic management attention to the identification and assessment of new market opportunities internationally?
❏ Accept that people types and the associated people policies for 21st century international success necessitate new models of HRM, and consequently will demand material managerial investment in developing those tailored to organization circumstances, to provide a competitive edge?

Chapter 3

Issues of Organization

Wherever you see references to people in organizations these days, they are portrayed as 'our greatest asset'. This is nowhere more true than for businesses trying to succeed internationally, but it's really the case that it is how you *organize* your people, rather than the individuals themselves which will make the difference in the competitive market place. The intellectual capital which people represent is highly mobile, people are less willing to be 'owned' by their organizations, and they may not be 'employed' in the conventional sense of the term.

So, the company setting out to develop business, or to improve its existing performance, on an international scale needs to think very carefully about how its people are organized, led and *empowered*. There are also some critical issues which the human resources function needs to ask itself too, regarding how it can best shape central and business unit focused activity to meet 'customer' needs.

AN ORGANIZATIONAL EVALUATION FRAMEWORK

The simple conclusion, in my experience, is that there are no right and wrong answers. There is certainly no panacea for addressing this critical business development factor. However, it is possible to create a framework within which relevant questions on organization and leadership can be asked and results assessed.

I have found it useful to draw on a ten point checklist for evaluating the pros and cons of alternative organization forms for international business units. The original design for the checklist has been refined and tested out in evaluating proposed organizational approaches in the USA, in Southern and Eastern Europe, in the Indian subcontinent, in South-East Asia, and China.

The checklist has been used to assess both strategic business development, marketing and administration units, and operational installations. It has been applied whether the units are an extension of existing domestic facilities; for subsidiaries; as well as in relation to strategic alliances and joint ventures. The accent is on evaluating the effect of organizational change, particularly relevant when embarking on a new venture or undertaking due diligence before a business acquisition. The object, following a simple framework of questions, is to build an integrated picture of the 'winners and losers' in alternative organizational contexts, and to build an action plan for anticipating and resolving any potential conflict.

Clearly, the intention is to ensure fitness for purpose, flexibility to accommodate market place dynamics and consequent change requirement, and to keep teams of people focused on achieving a common purpose for organizational success, instead of being distracted by inconsistencies at the interface between individuals and teams. It also may help to minimize the debilitating effects of organizational politics and conflicting interests. The checklist appears as Figure 3.1.

MANAGEMENT AT THE CENTRE AND DEVOLVED

In many internationalizing enterprises there appears to be a magnet which draws them outwards, away from a centralized domestic organization over time. More and more, the day-to-day business decisions need to be made in full knowledge and sympathy with the local cultural and business environments in which they operate. In truly cosmopolitan multinationals, the fact that strategic business units (SBUs) are geographically bound means there is unlikely to be as strong a pull towards functional or product line management. More innovative ways need to be found to exploit synergies on a global basis. In the current context, frequently the primary area to secure synergy, at least in the medium term, will come from the application of a business's core capabilities.

What is best for the business?

Experience suggests a logic, at the earliest feasible stage, for adopting working arrangements within which SBU leaders take the lead in establishing focal points for business development and ongoing operations, and calling for resources, in the context of a strategic framework determined on the basis of what approaches will most likely add to shareholder value.

	Yes/No	Action Plan
1 Does the current or proposed design in any way inhibit the organization from accomplishing its objectives?		
2 Are the lines of communication, authority and responsibility clear? Are they in support of the overall purpose and strategic goals of the organization?		
3 Have layers of management been minimized to allow for rapid, efficient and accurate information flow?		
4 Is authority and responsibility well placed in terms or being with the person most knowledgeable about matters to be decided upon?		
5 Are these areas of under-utilization or unnecessary duplication which could be addressed via organizational process changes? Are all available resources of the organization deployed in the most effective way?		
6 Have any unnecessary organizational and/or cultural conflicts been created as a result of the current or proposed structure and supporting processes?		
7 How much flexibility and adaptability is built into the structure? What is the likely impact of the structure on operations, culture and morale?		
8 Are the activities of the various 'units' of the organisation grouped appropriately? • by function specialization? • by specialization of skills? • by geographic location? • by groupings having responsibility for a product, project, or end-result?		
9 Who are the 'winners' and 'losers' in the current or proposed organization? Are any of the 'losers' vital to the successful implementation of the new grouping(s), and if so, what steps should be taken to ensure their retention and commitment?		
10. Are the organization's values best supported by and achieved through this organization approach and its processes?		

Figure 3.1 *Organisational design checklist.*
Source: After A. McNulty, 1994 (unpublished)

Therefore, under this model, the centre – defined to include both 'International' divisional 'central' functions, where these exist, and the corporate centre – sets the overall parameters in which SBUs are set up (and possibly merged/expanded over time), and determines the appointment of key international staff. The centre will approve budgetary proposals, set and measure performance standards, and, where appropriate, determine the allocation of investment funds. The centre will also determine standards against which individual SBU performance and actions will be judged. Given the recognition, especially in multinational corporations that *people make the difference,* it also makes sense for there to be a central overview of talent. The object is, of course, to ensure the right people with the right skills are available to do business when and where needed.

These arrangements tend to create the right motivational climate, so that SBU teams feel empowered to build profitable new business – rather than just representative offices, or manufacturing plants – in their territories. In giving the SBUs the authority for building their territory businesses, all concerned recognize that SBU management will be judged on how well they make use of the services and resources available to them within the corporation. In addition, they are accountable for influencing the centre, for instance keeping central functions informed about relevant changes and developments which need to be taken into account in setting corporate priorities.

Where and how can central services add value?

This does not mean a diminished role for the centre. On the contrary, its *different* role, evolving with the internationalization programme, creates a powerful new corporate *raison d'être.*

The issues most frequently highlighted, where a material well-received corporate centre contribution is vital, are:

❏ to determine which aspects are best undertaken on a group-wide basis
❏ how they can be influenced to meet real SBU needs on a cost-effective basis
❏ how they can ensure the group remains greater than just a sum of the parts
❏ to ensure SBU leaders get the opportunity to add value to the development of group strategy.

Figure 3.2 summarizes under four generic headings, the issues which it has been found help focus organizational development thinking by top management in this area of internationalization strategy.

Summary of issues

Four issues, which experience suggests are critical in building a successful international organisation, have been arranged as a tool to facilitate further considerartion of (a) what are the possible structural 'end' points, (b) what are the likely steps along the way, and (c) what, if any, changes to process are needed immediately or in the near future?

Communications	Management
A shared vision is critical: SBUs have an obligation to contribute to development of common purpose – if they ignore rest of business, own unit will suffer eventually too Once a common vision exists, then SBUs can network to share among other things market intelligence Mechanics for building a framework in which team leaders can participate in and take collective responsibility for key strategic decisions *Round table gatherings – two aspects:* (i) An annual (several days) forum for strategy review, in the light of market messages, framework for capital allocation – to ensure level playing field – and key succession and resource allocation planning (including need for centralized services). (ii) Complement to ongoing bilateral meetings to set priorities (use of tele-conferencing to keep in regular touch, but not for debate on major decisions).	Think global act local – scope for subsidiarity principle to operate? Avoid situation where there is too much central input to what should be localized and too little local input to what must be centralized *Central role* • strategy, quality • consistency • selection/retention of key people • capital allocation • monitoring/measuring performance against objectives *Local role* Everything else (no micro management by centre, otherwise best people will leave, and others will not 'own' decisions). Team leaders to take decisions/make recommendations on the ground. Corporate overview, to ensure team leaders are acting in ways which will contribute, in sum, to the development of overall international business.
Planning	**Growth**
Two stage process – first short SBU/ regional strategy statements for testing against corporate framework. Once agreed, build detail. SBUs have to say whether they believe the corporate strategy is deliverable. SBU leaders need to input to corporate strategic framework for determining allocation of capital and resources Use of round table meetings for strategic development purposes – see 'Communications' section.	Essential for a coherent business strategy and disciplined framework for enacting it to be in place (which has gained confidence of corporate business). Future trend should be the gradual migration of activities into regions, as a critical mass develops in specific SBUs. Local recruitment will give a local 'face' to the business Migration strategy needs to be developed: away from mostly centrally resourced project development and management, to a more and more devolved structure. Progressive decentralization: SBUs will develop along this path at differing speeds – and some may eventually be absorbed by others as regional business units emerge, managing assets as well as developing new business.

Figure 3.2 *Management at the centre and devolved.*

ORGANIZATION FOR TRANSFORMATION

In a number of cases, businesses expanding internationally do so by taking an equity stake – often as part of a consortium – in organizations situated in emerging markets, where governments are seeking to introduce private capital into previously state owned and operated assets.

Many organizations have had some 'de-nationalization' experience, either as part of the business undergoing 'privatization', or via institutions making strategic investments. The UK government's Private Finance Initiative has been set up to encourage the further transfer of major capital expenditure away from the Treasury, bringing together construction, facilities management companies and investment banks, while maintaining the delivery of core services within the public domain.

These transformations have not been without their own challenges, as I know from personal experience in the UK energy and transport sectors. However, a whole array of different problems and stumbling blocks are brought into play, when the investor is operating outside the developed, Anglo-Saxon world. Far sighted organization leaders have developed novel organizational forms specifically in response to such demands.

Anglo-Saxon characteristics

De-regulation of markets and privatization have become a global phenomenon. However, it needs to be borne in mind that the successful experience of such transformations in the Anglo-Saxon economies had a distinctive politico-economic context, which made it easier to drive the changes through, particularly as they affected the people working in such industries.

In the UK, for example, from the mid-1980s the governing political party was motivated by a particular brand of Conservative ideology, intended to roll back the state sector, and to expand the free market economy. The government were determined to tackle collectivism in all its forms, and thus presided over the decline in traditional 'heavy' industry, introducing a new legislative framework to underpin a drive to more 'flexible' labour markets. This meant reforms of long-standing regulation and practice in the conduct of industrial relations. The drive by managements and the shareholders they served to achieve fundamental 'downsizing' in industrial employment, and a move to a service-based economy was relatively unopposed.

The entire climate of public opinion, shaped by the economic depression in the early 1980s, which followed a period in which industrial strife, and trade union influence over the economy was generally perceived as having got out of hand, was encouragement for or acquiescence in industrial restructuring at all levels, and a more individualized employment relationship, all led by a populist right wing parliamentary executive.

Enterprises attempting to develop new investment-focused business interests in the emerging markets, many of whom remain collectivist in nature, with powerful labour interests exercising political influence at the centre, will have to achieve the improvements in manning and working practices they need for business efficiency gains without that supportive infrastructure for management freedoms.

In countries such as Portugal, for example, government lacks the necessary impetus to drive through the relevant political reforms. A more socialist ethos from the 1970s still remains implicit in those industries ripe for privatization, despite the liberalization rhetoric among political leaders.

In eastern Europe, the whole character and expectations of people remain influenced by 70 years of Communism. One-party rule still exists in China, with its influence on the control by the state of all aspects of its people's lives including employment and the lifestyle which accompanies it. And, in the Indian subcontinent, the bureaucracy and instability among central and – highly influential – regional government means that Anglo-Saxon flexibility of organization form and style are not capable of simply being imposed by capital interests and their management stewards who believe 'there is no alternative'.

Fit-for-purpose forms

A firm grasp of these contrasting realities, and the historical rationale behind them, is essential to those leading global business expansion, particularly through investment in major infrastructure projects, if their endeavours are to be successful.

The discriminating business professionals, both those involved in leading change from within the emerging markets, as well as those providing capital and commercial and technological core capability, are finding novel organizational forms fit for purpose in the circumstances in which they find they must manage.

In a number of cases, this involves adopting a long term perspective regarding the complete transformation of their inherited work forces. However, labour costs are often such that additional investment to bridge the old and the new is not especially onerous in relative terms to the gains which can be realized by successfully transforming the future basis on which previously state-owned organizations can operate and create wealth for investors and the local economy alike.

It has been found that one of the most effective organizational options is to create two organizations operating in parallel, one a new and fully commercial operation, where the best and brightest – as well as generally the generation with shorter memories of the past – can be re-deployed, and led by the champions of the investors, transferring know-how to the local professional and 'operator' community. A speedy transition can be effected in one step to more efficient 'modern' leadership and working styles, and resourcing levels.

The second organization, shadowing the first, is a 'social enterprise', representing the gradually shrinking shell of the former state enterprise. This organization:

❑ enables the residual labour, unwilling or incapable of change, to be accommodated until they are either persuaded to 'retire', or leave through natural wastage

❑ contains and manages bureaucratic and trade union resistance, on the basis that no one is any worse off than previously, and that a socially responsible approach is being taken to achieve the organization and business transformation.

Adopting such an organizational design strategy also demonstrates that – albeit with generally less of a collectivist focus – the smaller, more flexible labour force is becoming more technologically adept, creating improved morale, and a greater acceptance of the need to manage self-development for working life and beyond, than state-dependant populations in such parts of the world, have been traditionally.

An added advantage over the experience of massive downsizing in the Anglo-Saxon countries is being found to be the second chance employers gain to review skills potential among inherited work people, and the level of such resource needed continually to re-invent the business, leveraging core capability which is increasingly vested in the intellectual capital of the organization (its people); some of whom are the longest serving employees (and hence traditionally the first to be 'outplaced').

These approaches obviously need to be tailored to the specific circumstances of the industry sector and territories concerned; for example, the regulation surrounding employment in whatever organizational form of local nationals in China. But, a more fundamental approach to re-formation, while preserving the old form intact, but with a diminishing role, as a generic model has much to commend it.

Let us look at this aspect of international organizational development through two specific case cameos. First, the electricity supply industry co-ordinators in Poland. Secondly, the ship-building industry in Portugal.

Steps toward privatization in the Polish electricity supply industry (ESI)

Some six years ago, the World Bank insisted that Poland restructure its electricity supply industry. They offered a number of models, including that which was then being introduced in the UK. The Poles decided to follow the UK approach, and restructured their ESI into 33 distribution companies, one national grid and a series of independent generating businesses. Power stations are all, at present, separate companies.

All these enterprises have remained state owned; they have been transformed into state plc's, to enable them to be privatized or developed along some other form of commercial lines.

A major problem currently being experienced in Poland, is the absence of a competitive market place for electricity. Therefore, it is recognized that, for a successful privatization, the first element which must be established is market competition. It is judged that a competitive market place in electricity will address many of the fears governments tend to have about the impact of restructuring and the introduction of foreign investment into infrastructure projects.

This however is the key to bringing about change. In the UK, having created the conditions where a competitive market would transform the structure of the industry, the government was able to step back and let matters take a natural course.

There was a significant period of planning for privatization, with much of the latter half of the 1980s set aside for this purpose. However, once the companies were formed, and a brief period of 'shadow' running, a fully competitive market was put into operation to coincide with the stock market flotations. In Poland, in contrast, while the planning took less time, and the restructuring was in place by the turn of the 1980s, little has since occurred to set competitive forces at play.

In essence, then, quick *actualization* of the restructured industry with a free/competitive market has meant no turning back. Whereas privatization recently appeared to have stalled in Poland, because of their piecemeal approach, in the UK it is now the accepted wisdom.

At the present time there is a great deal of fear among those involved in the Polish ESI about the likely implications of large slices being acquired by foreign investors. The big question is: 'What will they do to cut costs? Does this mean massive unemployment?'.

Many of the new leaders running key parts of the Polish ESI have returned to their country after being educated and having initial career experience abroad. They bring with them many Anglo-Saxon lessons of business restructuring into 'lean and mean' organizational forms. They are impatient to effect a change, to secure the necessary capital investment to improve operating efficiency and to create new capacity to meet future demand as the economy develops. But they are anxious to do so in a manner which does not leave them dominated by a handful of foreign paymasters.

Equally, they are poorly supplied with management at support levels; not in terms of potential (this exists in almost unlimited supply), but with the technological and commercial know-how, and the management confidence and resolution to take individual responsibility for the consequences of their actions. This is a hang-over from the state-controlled past, where accountability was shunned by the average functionary: personal initiative was unwise.

So, creating new units, led and manned by the new generation of more confident professionals, as a commercialization vanguard, has been seen as one way in which to create change which the over-bureaucratic institutions which have been inherited could not achieve from within. At the same time, the existing institutions have the core physical asset base which can be used to attract new investment, while a more commercial and competitive market place offers some protection against being annexed by a wealthy foreign investor.

Restructuring for commercial success in the Portuguese shipyards

In 1975, during its era of revolutionary socialist dictatorship, in common with many others, the Portuguese ship-building industry was nationalized. The subsequent period saw the development of a monolithic organization, becoming increasingly inefficient and unprofitable.

As part of its modernization and commercialization programme, the Portuguese Government is in the process of restructuring the industry, and has granted approval to consortia of private interests to secure the equity in the various companies which comprise the industry. One consortium is formed of an overseas investment group and a Portuguese family business with long-standing interest in the sector. Indeed, they were the owners pre-nationalization.

The difficulties facing the organization this group is acquiring are enormous. The business is almost bankrupt; it has failed to settle creditors' bills (and even government social security obligations) for some time. Its labour force is low skilled and poorly motivated. The workforce is at least twice the size required for competitive performance. Restrictive working practices abound, and its employment terms and conditions are over-complicated and outdated. For example, individuals receive an 'on-board' salary premium, under some obscure negotiated custom, dating back some twenty years, even when a ship is undergoing maintenance in dry dock!

The labour force is represented by a communist-dominated trade union, with strong central political connections and influence in Lisbon. Despite the company's status, they continue to claim what management regard as outrageous increases in employment rates and associated conditions.

In order to address the issues, and to avoid unnecessary industrial strife, the new owners have resolved to take a long-term approach to securing improved commercial and workforce performance. In this way, they hope to generate sufficient new funds to invest in reshaping the business and the skill sets of its people. They are creating a new business to which a hand-picked core workforce will transfer, which will take the goodwill and business prospects of the existing organization as a basis for a future commercial operation to be financed and developed.

The employees will be encouraged to make the transfer by reassurance that their existing living standards will remain unaffected by the transfer. They will receive enhancements on transfer to accept a more streamlined set of terms and conditions of employment. Future salaries and benefits will be determined by reference to competitive local markets in sectors where the organization might reasonably recruit from or lose employees to. A performance culture will be installed by the gradual linkage between individual and team reward, and the profitability of the organization. Stress will be placed on fair and transparent performance assessment and recognition, and only those managers who have been trained and received accreditation in performance management will be eligible to assess staff and award resulting remuneration enhancements. A gainshare plan will be considered to encourage initiative at all levels to achieve lowest cost operator status.

Underpinning this new ethos, investment will be made in developing staff in new skill sets which will ensure they have the core capability to innovate for future business advantage. They will also gain from the fact that this will increase their own market worth and employability.

A 'social enterprise' will be maintained within the shell of the existing business. This will accommodate the generally more long-serving, less flexible members of the workforce. It will offer collectively-determined rates and honour long-standing pension and social security commitments, guaranteed and funded by the government. It will create the necessary 'firebreak' between the past and its increasingly untenable status as a going concern, and the new fully commercial operation.

Much remains to be clarified and 'sold' to the workforce by their new parent organization. The union wild-card has yet to be played and countered. However, the enterprise and their advisers are more confident of success over the medium term under this organizational framework than if they had attempted to operate within the complex institutionalized maze which might have been inherited.

CULTURAL DIVERSITY IN CONSORTIA FORMATIONS

Appreciation of the approach outlined above, and its rationale, can also help in achieving the blend between the cultural diversity which characterizes increasingly important strategic alliance working, partnerships of international and local consortia (a local partner tends to be a prerequisite in the East, for reasons of local political management, as well as access to the most profitable opportunities via a complex web of long-standing commercial and familial relationships), and joint venture business development and operation.

Most joint ventures and strategic alliances are doomed to failure. This tends to be the result of the parties' failing to recognize each others' agendas and needs within the partnership beyond the strict commercial terms. The successful ones – like any other medium- to long-term partnership of individuals and groups of people – are those where the parties continue to work at building and refining the relationship over time.

The situation becomes even more complex where there is a cross-cultural dimension involving the construction and development of relationships across geographical borders. There is much which contractual and other legal frameworks cannot resolve, and it comes down to each side taking time and trouble to understand and accommodate one another. This socio-political dimension is the 'softer' side of alliance and joint venture working.

Diffuse versus specific cultures

This area of working, which may involve exposing emotions in dealing with other people, is particularly troublesome to national cultures where 'task relationships', in business and other formal or institutional areas of life, are meticulously segregated out from other dealings with people, say, in domestic and recreational settings. There are a numbers of parts of the world where every life space and every level of personality tends to permeate all others, however. The 'culture guru' Fons Trompenaars, in his book *Riding the Waves of Culture* (1993), refers to this phenomenon as the degree to which we engage others in *specific* areas of life and single levels of personality, or *diffusely* in multiple areas of our lives, and at several levels of personality at the same time.

To illustrate the point, he tells a story about a Swedish company which beat an American company who had a technically superior product for a contract with an Argentinian customer. The Swedes recognized that, in this cultural setting, an upfront investment in building relationships was as important, if not more so, than the deal.

The Swedes invested a whole week in the selling trip, the first five days of which were not related to the business at all. They just shared the 'diffuse life spaces' of their hosts, talking about common interests. Only *after* a 'private space' relationship had been established were the Argentinians willing to talk business. And that had to include several life spaces not just one.

In contrast, the Americans invested only two days in the trip, knowing they had a superior product and presentation, and were turned down. They found themselves continually interrupted in their presentation with 'personal' questions and 'social distractions' and, when the corporate jet arrived on schedule to take them home, they had not adequately covered the business agenda. Fons concludes: 'The Argentinians, to the Americans, seemed unable or unwilling to stick to the point. The Argentinians, for their part, found the Americans too direct, impersonal and pushy. They were surprised by the Americans' apparent belief that you could use logic to force someone to agree with you.'

So when, in developing organizational forms which involve two or more parties from different regional and cultural backgrounds, one's partner asks to know where you went to school, who your friends are, what you think of life, politics, art, literature and music, this is not 'a waste of time', because such preferences reveal character and form friendships. They also make deception nearly impossible.

Friendship and trust precedes business relations

A few years back, I spent the day in the company of the managing director of a Singapore-based head-hunting firm. I asked him, at the end, how he was prepared to take time from a busy schedule to be my host for a day, with no apparent purpose other than to offer hospitality. He patiently explained that his company's ethos was to take quality time for developing friendships. They were confident these would result in business benefits in the longer term: I would return in time, as a candidate maybe, or as a client, and then the process would no doubt repeat itself several times over. 'Time spent in deciding whether we can get to like one another in my culture, in all walks of business life', he said, was 'far more important than in high powered negotiation. Why would I do business with someone I'm not sure I like and can trust? If we build a friendship, mutual commercial gain will follow naturally. And we leave the detail to subordinates while we take time to drink tea.'

47

The need for cross-cultural tolerance is critical not only between the partners to establishment of an alliance or joint venture organization. There is an additional dimension. That is for the culture which develops naturally, with its associated allegiances and value sets, within the partnership formation itself. Even the most inter-culturally adept business leaders sometimes forget that, in deploying often their best people to set up and lead collaborative ventures outside the parent company, these people will take on a new team culture. The parent may find it must tolerate decisions and behaviour from its offspring which traditionally has been interpreted as the representative group 'going native' on the project.

Assessed over the long term, all parties to the venture may see their investment returns enhanced by allowing this freedom to their respective teams, who will be close to the context and customer setting for the conduct of this business operation, rather than feeling the need to rein them in, purely in the service of individual partners' short term local organizational politics. So often this is the case, however. And so often one observes the demise of 'rising stars' from businesses, deployed on a critical international venture, unable to return to the fold, because their loyalties to the firm did not 'pass challenge', and their value sets have become 'incompatible'.

As an illustration of how problems can arise, let us consider an example of an organizational scenario where a major infrastructure project, based on non-recourse project finance was set in place in the Iberian Peninsular.

A spiced cultural cocktail

The partners were drawn from France, Portugal, Spain and the UK. The project was formed into two distinct but, at least in theory, complementary strategic business units; one acting as the holding company, managing the commercial contract and holding the equity; the other an operational unit.

The partners were each represented on each of the organizational units in the top management roles. Parent business top management were also represented on the boards in non-executive capacities. The roles of the two bodies were: Holding Company – to manage the relationship with the financing institutions over a long-term repayment cycle, and with the state-owned customer over the terms of a parallel long-term supply contract; Operating Company – to extract the maximum efficiencies from the assets, and deliver under an operating contract with the holding company, against a sophisticated and highly lucrative supply contract, to the end customer.

It was clear to objective observers that interests of the holding and operating companies were closely interwoven, and the emphasis should have been on team collaboration. However, the fact of an organization arrangement which placed the operator in a contractual relationship with the holding company, but still required the former to play a subsidiary role to its 'customer', who expected continuous micro-level information flows and sought to drive the operator to increasing resourcing constraints, created growing tensions.

The technical director of the equity company was also the president of the board of the operating business. This individual seemed able to play dual but potentially adversarial roles depending in which location he was at the time! The operating company was located in a remote site, with not particularly sound access and communications. The holding company was located in an attractive capital city, where the top management could establish themselves as leading corporate citizens, mingling with the country's top politicians, and enjoying an apparently high expatriate lifestyle.

The individual selected to lead the asset owning company made the transition to this new lifestyle with ease, was able to surround himself with an inner cabinet team of familiar high calibre professionals, and managed the inter-cultural politics in a statesmanlike manner.

He stood in stark contrast to the individual selected (from the same parent company) as asset operations manager, a career 'technician' engineer-manager, ill at ease in the new cultural surroundings, and quickly feeling cut off from the traditional corporate support network enjoyed by peers in the domestic business environment. There were language barriers, complicated further by the four nationalities involved on site, including the commissioning agents, acting on behalf of the financing institutions. There were significant local tensions over the most basic aspects of technical operations and management style.

The organization, while brilliantly conceived by the deal makers who handled the contract negotiations and financial engineering, left a dangerous vacuum.

It encouraged tensions of a cross-organizational unit nature, as well as reinforcing the conflicting ideologies among the partners and the local nationals retained to operate the acquired assets. In short, while the project had been structured in a manner which delivered significant short term returns to the investors, this sacrificed potential long term co-operation between the partners as a result of local tensions which then transferred back to the respective headquarters. Thus, major commercial learning could not be leveraged for subsequent international collaborative projects.

It also potentially led to a break-down by the asset manager, and his early return to a role which was on the face of it of a lesser status. It again meant that international capability acquisition in a key business leader was lost to the organization over the longer term. As for the equity business managing director, while significant personal wealth enhancement resulted, the home organization had become disenchanted with the high level of success attributed to one key individual on what was held to be a flagship project. As such, internal manoeuvring took place to ensure that the promised parent company main board role which would have enhanced the parent company in its aspirations to achieve material global success, as well as the individual's career, was denied. What might have distinguished the group in the international community was in fact a source of negative comment which the company had to paper over.

One step forward . . . two steps back

So, the lesson from the perspective of long-term international business success is one of ensuring commercial 'cleverness' in setting organizational arrangements in place for short-term gain does not negate the benefits to the parent group in terms of its ability to leverage international learning for long-term strategic advantage. There is merit in arguing for the organization to be matched as far as possible to the key people – the intellectual assets of the business – who will ensure the long-term success of a venture once the developers and their commercial advisers have moved on to the next 'deal'.

The intuitive voice of the human resource director in this context may be a key business tool in securing competitive advantage for the corporation in developing an international asset portfolio, with the capabilities to transfer organizational learning and enhance core skills – distinguished from the market competition – for sustained wealth creation on behalf of corporate shareholders.

A useful working model for understanding the needs for inter-cultural respect and collaboration when working in international alliances or joint ventures is offered in Figure 3.3. This illustrates the fact that either culture collision or cohesion will result from organization and leadership styles which ignore or accommodate the combination of two or more 'parent' organization cultures; a third, geographically determined culture; and a fourth, in the form of the venture organization itself.

Hierarchy versus flat structure working

Organizations in the developed countries of the world have gone through major restructuring and de-layering exercises over the past two decades,

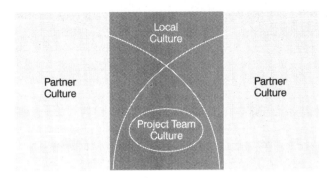

Figure 3.3 *The cross-cultural environment: trans-national alliances and joint ventures.*

to the point where it is now being argued in some quarters that 'corporate anorexia' has set in.

Internationalizing businesses will wish to take these design principles into their new ventures, in the interests of operating efficiency. In my experience, it is possible to follow 'best international practice' in shaping organizational forms in most parts of the world. But, for sustained success; for the increasingly critical local organizational leaders to 'own' it once the expatriate developers have moved on, sensitivity to cultural norms and expectations and an ability to avoid the quick fix option is important in organization design.

This applies both to 'greenfield' development, as well as to the 'brownfield' acquisition and restructuring of existing business units.

Organization badge makes the individual

In some cultures what they are called is far more important to the motivation and general morale of managers and professionals than what they receive in tangible rewards from their employment.

In Southern and Eastern Europe and in the Indian subcontinent, for example, there are myriad levels of supervisors, assistant- and deputy-managers, directors and controllers. The differential in salary terms between such layers is frequently negligible. However, in terms of feelings of self worth and personal esteem, the differentiation is of vital importance. Recognition of *who you are* rather than *what you contribute* is a major factor in people's thinking. Seniority, or length of service is equally regarded as a distinguishing factor among the population of an organization.

In my experience, it is perfectly possible to create organizational forms which conform to the requirements of western shareholders. But, it is imperative that, before embarking on wholesale changes, the internation-alizing business leaders take time out to form an appreciation of the cul-tural undertones, and how best to accommodate them by some form of compromise; at the very least to invest heavily in communicating and explaining the benefits to all concerned of streamlining; that no loss of face is involved; and to develop locally respected champions who can be seen to have 'crossed the divide' with positive rather than negative conse-quences.

To assist in determining answers and possible alternative courses for action in this area of organization and leadership strategy for interna-tionalizing businesses, I have developed a *Four Quadrants* tool (see Figure 3.4). This builds on research undertaken by Professor Amin Rajan (1995), at the Centre for Research in Employment and Technology in Europe, and helps international business managers avoid saying one thing and doing another, as they approach the design and reconfiguration of organ-izational formations. Simple in construction and layout, the model invites managers to audit the organization against four generic factors, or 'the way we do things here'.

The quadrants cover, first, the 'relationships-driven' organizational context. This type of setting can be very important in those areas of the world where who you are, what your connections may be, and how you interface with significant others inside and outside the organization are taken as a guide to the way in which strategic business formations are likely to operate.

Then there is the 'bureaucratic' or rules-driven context. This environ-ment is particularly prevalent in parts of Central and Eastern Europe – where uncertainty about how business outcomes will be reached is not welcomed; planning and precision are favoured – and in a number of emerging markets (eg India, where traditional bureaucracies continue to function much as they have done since the days of British colonial rule). The organization depends on systems and rigidly applied 'ways of getting things done' which may be perceived as inefficient and time-wasting in a modern business context.

Paternalistic: relationship-driven	Bureaucratic: rules-driven
Anarchic: excellence-driven	Democratic: performance-driven

Figure 3.4 *Cultural quadrants – 'the way we do things here'.*
Source: adapted from *Winning People* report – Professor Amin Rajan, 1995

There is the 'anarchic' or excellence-driven environment, in which to the uninitiated, organizational chaos reigns. However, to the insider, this environment is one in which much occurs below the surface. It tends to be highly creative, often operating on a campus-style basis, in high-tech or leading-edge research-focused operations in those areas of the world (or a particular group itself) where innovative outcomes with long-term benefits are what is prized, rather than conformity with today's norms.

The fourth quadrant is manifested by a 'democratic', results oriented organizational environment. This context is particularly associated with liberal societies, where what you achieve – particularly in terms of commercial and material success – rather than what you are, is the basis on which individuals and groups are both judged and motivated. Organizations in the modern Anglo-Saxon world tend to conform to this type, in particular where the focus is on marketing and sales of products and services for commercial advantage.

An organizational matrix

The quadrants offer a means to work with managers and professionals and other employee groups in strategic business units in different cultural zones, and to determine through dialogue 'where we are' and 'where we would like to be'. The answers can be revealing, They can also prompt the conclusion that in the same organization, depending on its phase of development, and the people involved, it may be necessary to accept that a variety of different organization and cultural styles will need to be adopted and integrated to achieve business aims and value over time.

So, an appreciation of managing across organizational and geographical boundaries is a pre-requisite for the high performance international business leader. We shall see later, in the chapter on developing world-class capabilities for international success, how such core competence can be acquired and nurtured, as part of the personnel directors' internationalization support strategy.

THE PROJECT-BASED ORGANIZATION

Project teams are an increasingly familiar organizational form in the more flexible business enterprise. In an internationalization context, they are an essential tool for understanding and developing new markets, for negotiating investment and operational opportunities, for assembling finances (frequently working in project-specific consortia blending commercial, technical, legal and investment banking professionals), and then designing, building, commissioning and operating manufacturing and service organizations for commercial return.

I recently conducted a survey of international project management, among a representative sample of 'blue chip' enterprises, to report on the ways in which a number of construction-related businesses are now organizing their capabilities in the increasingly competitive global business environment for turnkey plant construction and transfer.

A number of the conclusions are instructive generally in gaining an understanding of the manner in which project teams need to be organized and led for competitive commercial advantage.

While there are instances where, by definition, activities are exclusively site-based, the majority of respondents stressed the development of matrix taskforce partnership working. There is an emphasis on a working philosophy which has been referred to as 'alliancing'. This represents the need for project-driven organizations to form improved partnerships not only within their own organizations, but with clients and sub-contractors. It is felt repeat business opportunities will only arise in such instances. In the past, profits were frequently made either by exploiting subcontractors or by cutting corners in relation to perceived client requirements. In all cases now, it has been recognized that the role of the project manager in particular is to deliver *win win* benefits for all players.

Internally, the matrix operation reflects the importance of building balanced teams with complementary skills. Where in the past, for example, in a technology or construction business project managers may have been drawn exclusively from an engineering background, often they will now have a commercial track record. This means the formation of project teams requires the balancing of complementary skills; eg strong technical/engineering skills at the support level, where the project leadership is commercial; or vice versa when the project manager's skills are mainly technical. Team development, and team building is getting more and more attention.

In reality, flexibility is the key: rigid reward boundaries do not reflect the fact that project managers may have to accept they will be moving between large and small projects. It is impossible to secure such flexibility without integrating the organization development process with all other people strategy factors (eg avoiding any adverse impact on on-going compensation levels).

Companies are also accepting the need – without guaranteeing jobs – to absorb people between projects, in order to flatten the peaks and troughs and to offer some security so as to retain the best people.

There are lessons learned here for building the professional resources and intellectual capital, which require further examination when considering international capability development, as we shall do later.

PROJECT ORGANIZATION AND CONTROL

The size and complexity of international business projects can mean roles for a project manager and a 'supervisory' project director, although this does not imply an extra layer of management. The organizational structure needs to be responsive to the project needs, and there needs to be greater consideration of individual accountabilities from the outset. A typical model format is set out in the table below.

The project manager and representatives from participating functions must be empowered to respond to project requirements. It is also necessary to recognize the need to segregate certain joint venture to corporate activities and report and co-ordinate work accordingly.

Improved communication of progress on projects to senior management across the parent company can be expected to facilitate confidence in the organizations activities. This will then lead to reduced management involvement in decision making properly within the authority of the project director/project manager.

Joint ventures

The project management structure is influenced by the role of and

Table 3.1 *Organization structures for projects*

Phase	Concept/Evaluation	Offer/Negotiation/ Financial Close	Implementation/ Operation
Ownership	Parent company	Partners	Partners
Guidance/ Approval	International division	JV Steering committee	JV Board
Strategic Direction	SBU Team leader	Project director	Managing director
Project Management	Business dev manager	Project manager + support	Other managers + support
Activities	Functional roles	Work packages	Contracts
	Assessment for provision of parent services	O & M/Raw materials	Plant
	Development assistance	Finance team	Raw materials

interface with partners in joint ventures. Establishing other partners' confidence in an organization's technical and commercial judgement is essential to exercising effective control or influencing their project development.

Staff assigned to joint ventures may well need to go 'native' and appear segregated from corporate interests. It is necessary, therefore, to define roles and structures within both the joint venture and the partner company to ensure effective working, management and resourcing of such projects.

It has been found beneficial to appoint a senior 'career manager' for all project managers who may have to go 'native' in the Company's interests. A 'career manager' will ensure that individuals' career interests are not affected by virtue of the stance they may sometimes have to take in the course of delivering a project.

ORGANIZING HUMAN RESOURCES FOR INTERNATIONALIZATION

The successful expansion of business on an international basis, I believe, necessitates some changes in the way we organize the provision of professional personnel management support to the business.

In order to support an internationalizing organization, I have found it useful to shape the HR activities into a set of *Roundtable* professional team roles (see Figure 3.5). These are then capable of translation into a variety of services and 'HR products' customized to the needs of the specific business at its various stages of global development.

All the roles will be required, to ensure the business development and operational leaders can access comprehensive specialist know-how and support in discharging their own critical roles in organizing, developing, motivating and evaluating teams of people. These roles need themselves to be organized and developed over time in a fully integrated fashion, aligned with the development of the corporation and its constituent parts.

To discharge the professional roles successfully in an international context, it is necessary to have HR professionals available both on the ground in the various territories in which the enterprise seeks to conduct business. Also to have a strategically positioned, tightly resourced central grouping which can provide the corporate 'glue', assisting business leaders to achieve their long-term aims through the people they acquire and deploy to maximum effect.

Figure 3.5 *HR partnering – the roundtable.*

Services and products

The human resources function needs to develop and educate internal clients in the use of a raft of services tailored specifically to the needs of the business and in particular its SBUs at their particular stage of development. As illustrated in Figure 3.5, these can include: human resource planning and forecasting, and matching supply with demand; gathering intelligence on the ground regarding employment practice and regulation; expert guidance to line managers and to international assignees; and ensuring ongoing organization and project team development.

The services are underscored by a number of customized human resources 'products' including: international development plans (IDPs) for individuals and teams; capabilities development initiatives to improve core competence in specific differentiating areas of the company's international business practice (financing, design, operations and refurbishment, informations systems etc); development centres, intended to act as a capabilities 'gaps' screening process; performance alignment system support (PAS); and associated policies, processes and intelligence.

Strategies for actualizing aspects headlined here as services and products will be explored in depth in later chapters.

SUMMARY AND CHECKLIST

Organizing for international effectiveness represents a major strategic challenge. World class businesses are becoming increasingly sophisticated in tackling the issues for leadership which result. This involves being ready to study in some detail the multiplicity of interests involved – particularly where cultures outside the parent business combined with geographically and philosophically distinct cultures come into play.

Frequently there is a complex web of strategic challenges for those intent on investing in non-domestic operations, and/or offering goods and services on a global scale. There is a need to take time out to understand and reflect on the differences between the various stakeholders, at all levels.

There is a requirement to explore imaginative ways of turning diversity to competitive advantage over others competing in the international market place. There is a clear requirement to refine the basis on which teams are formed, developed and re-deployed in a manner which serves a number of – possibly conflicting – agendas. It will be essential to leave behind a sense of well-being on the part of partners, backers and customers alike, as well as to have the means to carry forward key lessons learned as part of the corporate memory, to be leveraged for future business advantage.

There is a need for balance; between long-term and short-term interests; between tangible and intangible factors which influence the perspectives various parties carry with them about the organization of which they are a part and/or affiliated to; and between the world we know, and that which appears alien.

This will inevitably involve compromise and trade-offs. Human resources directors and the organizations they are supporting must be clear about this before proceeding.

The following questions need to be addressed in planning an organization strategy for internationalization. Does the proposed organization:

❑ Reinforce and focus energies on achievement of business purpose?
❑ Release the full potential of all resources?
❑ Ensure optimum balance between the 'centre' and devolved SBUs?
❑ Accommodate change management issues which demand time sensitivity and may need more than one organizational 'shell' to do the job?
❑ Encourage a fitting blend of structural, political and cultural factors to leverage diversity for commercial market advantage?
❑ Provide a natural channel and repository for project team know-how transfer?
❑ Include an HR function matched to the unique needs of the internationalizing enterprise?

Chapter 4

Capabilities Development for International Business

Everyone wants to win in the global market. But only those who understand and can 'commercialize' their core capabilities will break out from the pack. Also, the ability to recognize capability gaps and find imaginative ways to plug them is critical. Closing the gaps must be done so as to enhance, not disturb, the core organism which is the business entity. Capabilities identification and development is therefore a pivotal aspect of internationalization – it demands a strategic approach. The way businesses organize their human capital is a point of differentiation with which to create competitive advantage. Organizations need to develop the skill and sensitivity to recognize and exploit this fact.

International capability can be created drawing on a variety of sources, including:

- Organizational partnering.
- Acquisition of relevant business units who possess the talent to make up capability shortfalls.
- Talent spotting and attraction – leadership and know-how capabilities.
- Potential identification and holistic capabilities development from within.

Organizations need to develop models which will help them in assessing the capabilities they will require, by acquisition, alliancing or development, as an intrinsic part of actualizing international business strategy. This process will require clarity in forecasting not only the activity areas and markets into which organizations wish to grow their interests and the capacity to exploit opportunities. It will also be necessary to gauge the comparative capability advantages being developed by competitors. Moreover, aspirant international businesses will need to identify where over the short-, medium- and long-term they can leverage the capability of talented individuals and work-groups to win an advantage in their target markets and sectors.

The matrix in Figure 4.1 provides a useful guide to addressing some of the questions which will come to light in trying to align capabilities with business objectives.

In their book, *Strategy Formulation: Analytical Concepts*, C W Hofer and D E Schendel (1978), suggest several theoretical business strategies which business units can follow, ranging from aggressive market share growth through to consolidation, exit and liquidation. For the sake of simplicity in developing the matrix in Figure 4.1, I have used three generic stages: growth, sustain, and harvest.

1. In the *growth phase*, internationalizing businesses are at the early stages of their life-cycle. They have products or services whose growth potential is significant. To realize this potential, considerable resources may have to be committed to develop and enhance the new products and services, and to create an operational and distribution infrastructure which will support local and global relationships with partners, suppliers and customers.

2. International businesses in the *sustain phase* will still require investment and re-investment, but are expected to earn sustained high returns on the capital which investors have supplied. Management focus will be on enhancing continuous improvement in market share and operational efficiency, rather than the long payback and growth resourcing investments necessary during the first (growth) phase. This is where the majority of businesses will be in their domestic operations and will expect to move into as soon as possible during their international expansion.

3. The *harvest phase* will apply to business units which have reached a mature phase of their life-cycle. Investors will be seeking payback on the capital programmes during the two earlier phases. Such SBUs no longer warrant significant investment, simply enough to maintain equipment and capabilities rather than to create new ones. The main financial goal is to maximize cash-flow back to the corporation.

Facing up to the reality of matching international business development aspirations with the current capability pool, organizations find benefit in defining a programme to cover distinct but interrelated phases.

Business Unit Strategy	Strategic Themes			
	Market Development: building local network + opportunity identification	**Deal Making**	**Long-term Market Development**	**Business Operations**
Growth	Strategic alliance with local partners – hire local business development team	Acquire local company with in-house business deal making talent	Short-term expertise import – /long-term capabilities development	Expatriate expertise for skills transfer
Sustain	Joint venture – marketing operation – local agency	Hire specialist 'internationalists' (expats) + key local expertise if available	Local team with corporate capability developed in-house with 'centre' coaching	Local team recruitment
Harvest	Mature JV – expansion opportunities – exit strategy/ asset realisation group from 'centre'	Core business team (in Joint Venture with local partners?) combining limited expatriate input with mainly locally developed key capability	Host team transferring know-how locally and as corporate memory to other projects in region and globally	O & M distribution using own local team or agency: limit operations to residual capital investment repatriation

Figure 4.1 *Matching capabilities to strategic business requirements, retaining core capabilities which differentiate the business to win, and outsourcing non-core activities.*

Following their business forecasting exercises, internationalizing businesses will identify a number of priorities. These will include the requirement to improve both the management process for business development and execution, and the capabilities deployed on international projects. As experience is gained, further issues will emerge of a behavioural and cultural kind. For instance, some organizations in benchmarking their capability with advisers, clients and customers have feedback that sometimes 'we talk down overseas'. Despite the best efforts of those involved, in developing from a long-standing domestic business, organizations often find there remains the feeling in some quarters that they retain a 'two business' culture. Such businesses have much to learn about developing and managing overseas projects, and especially joint ventures, in a way which continues to give both the investment community and their boards confidence that their long-term interests are secure.

In assessments which have been undertaken of organizations attempting to internationalize through the development of a portfolio of investments overseas, the need for clear lines of responsibility within the project management process has been emphasized. The roles of key individuals and functions need to be clearly defined and understood.

Increasing importance is being placed on the part played by project managers during both development and operational phases in leading and coaching multi-disciplinary teams. Cross-cultural sensitivities must be recognized and managed to ensure project objectives are met. Also, the project manager has a key 'corporate' function; namely, ensuring lessons learned on a specific exercise are distilled and captured, so they may be transferred within the sponsoring organization, as a source of competitive advantage in approaching new or repeat business opportunities.

Reporting controls are also necessary so that executive and functional management have the information they need to be assured that the quality is right and projects are on track. Organizations also need to develop a 'corporate memory', setting down in a more structured and formal way best practices, so that these can become common practices. This will reduce the risks inherent in having valuable project knowledge and expertise residing solely with a small number of individuals.

DEFINING THE INTERNATIONAL CADRE

The next century will be the age of the multinational employee, emerging in parallel with the global corporation or federation. Every successful major business will invest heavily in the development of a distinctive *International Cadre* of executives, capable of transferring the enterprise's commercial and operational philosophies and systems into every location in which they wish to do business. This group – capable of thinking global, acting local, and vice versa – will be among the premium capital any organization will wish to have access to.

But, the shortage of talented executives with the abilities and background to run global businesses will soon become one of the most significant challenges facing business everywhere. Most multinational employers are, at present, embarked on the process of finding a distinctive framework within which they can adequately describe their present or future internationally mobile executive grouping.

A few years ago, a US-based telecommunications company undertook an exercise to determine what steps were necessary to form a pan-European executive cadre. After much deliberation by a cross-functional management group, they resolved that their European workforce could best be categorized on the basis of career trajectories. This was an important departure from previous practice, where international assignment duration tended to be the measure against which individuals were differentiated. The new approach created a simple model against which people can be identified, and for those not in 'the cadre' something possibly to aspire to. It also legitimized inequity of treatment between different categories of staff, which is accepted throughout the organization. Therefore, the model which emerged is not only simple to apply, it also makes sound business sense.

Building on this work, it seems to me most helpful to approach the task of defining the *International Cadre* by reference to these career paths. In my experience, three distinct career paths can be identified which characterize various types of executive groupings.
These are as follows:

Domestic Staff hired locally and whose career is unlikely to take them outside the domestic market other than in the most infrequent and unusual of circumstances; eg a one-off project, or for training.
Parent Parent company staff who may be deployed at some point in their career to an overseas location for 'skills transfer' reasons, but who are likely to return to the domestic operation subsequently (and certainly to 'retire' in their country of origin).
International Staff who may begin a career with a multinational organization from anywhere in the world, and whose professional skills can be used in a variety of markets; who accept that their next posting location cannot be predicted; and accept this condition of employment; and who have no preconceptions about where they may 'retire' at the end of their career.

Studies have shown that there are particular tensions often surrounding the categorization of corporate or 'Headquarters' executives. In practice, there are clear indicators which will assist in placing individuals. Those supporting international business activity as a fundamental part of their job definition (with the need for frequent travel with its impact on lifestyle which differentiates such individuals from their domestically bound colleagues), and who accept they are obvious candidates for postings outside their 'home' country at some stage in their professional careers, usually may properly be placed in the *International Cadre* category.

Finally, consideration needs to be given, in each instance, to the manner in which the *International Cadre* concept may be launched and institutionalized. Some organizations have found that a high visibility launch, and a transparent statement regarding the different basis on which members of the cadre will be measured and rewarded is necessary to avoid the 'just another initiative' syndrome. At BP, the fanfares were, however, a little too loud for general taste. Then Chairman Robert Horton personally led a particularly lavish programme launch, which fell foul of the recessionary times. However, although scaled back, the BP internationalist programme remains a key plank of their business strategy.

IDENTIFYING INTERNATIONAL EXECUTIVES

Although the appropriate mix of capabilities can be secured in the short term through acquisition (by recruitment of individuals who already possess such skills, or through alliances and partnerships), existing resources must be developed over the medium to longer term, by structured training, and by career development (planned experience).

My experience of working with organizations attempting to *internationalize* their businesses, has led me to a simple conclusion. Very few of us really know our executives well. It may be acceptable for domestic career development purposes to have only a two dimensional, exclusively career-orientated view of our executive population. The challenges which individuals face when deployed on international assignments, mean that a more rounded or '3D' perspective is required.

We need to know whether the executives can cope with the very different working environment to that for which their training and past experience may have equipped them. Moreover, when deploying the mature executive overseas, the job does not stop at the office or factory door. It is part and parcel of the domestic environment. When put to the test, there are few companies who would claim to know intimately the full domestic circumstances of an individual employee; indeed efforts to do so might be deemed to be intrusive under normal circumstances. However, before inviting individuals to step on a plane to develop careers outside their domestic environment, companies are learning to have a more comprehensive understanding of their key executive group and their families.

The situation may in time be addressed by virtue of the fact that executives with potential are being deployed on a multinational basis from the earliest stage of their careers. In this way, individuals will be acclimatized to the implications of international working throughout their employment, and will normally form relationships which reflect those circumstances. (This has long been the case, for example, in global oil businesses.)

However, developing new international business as a strategic priority means experienced executives are needed to spearhead development and implementation, as a matter of urgency. Globalizing organizations often find it essential to learn from early mistakes which result from acting in haste in deploying capabilities. In my experience, mistakes arose by virtue of the fact that we had picked 'winners'! These were individuals who had had a track record of continued success in developing technical and/or commercial careers within the United Kingdom. Such winners in many cases quickly became dubbed 'losers' when deployed on new ventures around the world.

CAPABILITIES DEFINITION

As a result of this 'early learning', we embarked on a process to develop a new set of capabilities against which we could assess individual potential for overseas deployment. These fell into both technical capabilities and behavioural capabilities.

Surveys on the characteristics of the 'international manager', as conducted in different countries with major multinationals, came to the following order of priority in importance of competencies (*source*: The Ashridge Survey, 1989–90):

❏ Strategic awareness (global view)
❏ Adaptability to new situations
❏ Sensitivity to different cultures
❏ Ability to work in international teams
❏ Language skills
❏ Understanding international marketing
❏ Relationship skills
❏ International negotiating skills
❏ Self-reliance
❏ High task-orientation

❏ Open, non-judgemental personality
❏ Understanding international finance
❏ Awareness of cultural background

Furthermore, executives are characterized by the following pattern:

❏ Subjective, flexible and relative in their perception and assessment; seeing themselves and their impressions as changing.
❏ Use of cultural stereotypes in a self-consciousness and tentative way.
❏ Forward-thinking in trying to understanding *what* is going on and not *why* things occur as they do in different cultures.
❏ Flexibility to re-frame fields of reference (as opposed to looking for certainty, tidiness and rationality).

Other surveys stress:

❏ Intellectual ability
❏ Self-esteem: realistic and thorough degree of self-knowledge, self-confidence and self-acceptance
❏ People-orientation: respect for others, trust in people
❏ Perspective
❏ Result-orientation

Psychological research on international adaptation

The theoretical model of psychological research on cultural adaptation focuses on life events, change and potential stress. The basic assumption is that working in a different country/culture puts high demands on the individual and, depending on personality and external factors, could result in maladaptation and psychological disturbance. Psychologically, international assignments fall into the category of 'life events'. Life events are defined as major life changes requiring modification of one's behaviour, ie, adaptational skills. Life events, especially negative events, can put the individual at risk of psychological difficulties, such as depression, anxiety disorders, or alcoholism. Research in this area has shown that there is a definite link between the number and severity of life events (ie, moving house, loss of a loved one, unemployment, etc.) and psychological disorders.

Individuals deployed as expatriates are exposed to several such life events: changing country, changing job, and changing house; consequently, there is a high risk to their psychological well-being, and hence a risk of deteriorating job performance and company profitability. Moreover, these changes are not restricted to the individual, but usually concern the entire family. Spouses may give up high-powered jobs with no prospect of finding interesting employment abroad, children are uprooted, losing their friends and having to cope with new educational systems, etc.

The following factors influence the extent of stress an individual experiences and these factors ought to be considered in selection situations:

❑ *Personality factors:*
  — general personality profile
  — stress vulnerability: predisposition to react strongly to difficult situations (in an emotional sense)
  — internal versus external locus of control (ie, whether a person believes that events are influenced by him/her own behaviour or by powerful others or fate)
  — self-efficacy and mastery
  — motivation for expatriation
❑ *Predominant coping styles*
❑ *Social support system* (with the assumption that strong social support – of affective, instrumental and informative nature – can buffer potential stressors and thereby facilitate emotional well-being and adaptation).

Taking account of the research findings, we recognized that, in order to capture these factors, a person- *and* situation-oriented assessment ought to be considered at different stages of the selection process.

Following a series of interviews and workshops with experienced line executives from right across the business, these issues were evaluated within the strategic business development framework, to pinpoint the business 'technical' and business 'behavioural' capabilities that would assist in matching individuals to organizational needs. Once gathered, sifted and tested, these new capabilities became the basis for an ongoing programme of development centres, in which executives who had been nominated or had volunteered for international assignments could test their potential in a non threatening and systematic way.

The results were to provide not only greater confidence on behalf of the organization that we could find round pegs to fit into round holes in our international operations. It also provided the individuals with an opportunity to *deselect* themselves from direct involvement with the international programme, without loss of face, if they recognized when faced with simulated reality that they would simply be uncomfortable in such an environment.

The main areas of internationalist capability for development centre construction, can be summarized under nine headings as follows:

1. *An open approach to contrasting cultures*
   Proof of interest through travel, or study, in other business or geographic cultures; recognition of different, or conflicting, moral standards; an enquiring, yet objectively analytical, intellect.

2. *Individual motivation level*
   What are the individual's true aspirations; how can they be met? What is the benefit to the organization?
3. *Balance between open/closed behaviour*
   Independent, good judgement; recognition of host business unit culture and expectations.
4. *Ability to listen, analyse, persuade, motivate and direct.*
   Total, persistent, communication; consensus normally the ideal (dependent on business unit culture) but confidence to provide direction.
5. *Constant, yet responsive style*
   Even temperament; provides recognizable, consistent role model in adverse, or favourable, circumstances; recognizes and responds to significant changes, yet rides minor deviations.
6. *Creating teams; being player and leader*
   Sensitive, balanced behaviour; *confidence to allow experts to lead*; ability to contribute factual as well as managerial skills, sustaining team aims above those of individual.
7. *Self confident and decisive*
   Able to operate when isolated, both by distance and host culture; independent intellect, confident of corporate core values.
8. *Reliable*
   Resilient; able to retain a separate sense of perspective.
9. *Being in control*
   Establishing credibility; providing an effective influence.

Development centres, run by a cross-section of senior line managers with specialist HR support, tested individual potential against the foregoing criteria. A battery of assessments were created and deployed, drawing on assistance from a professional psychologist.

DEVELOPING INTERNATIONAL EXECUTIVES

The outcome of each development centre was the preparation, for each individual who wished to proceed, of a personalized *international development plan*. The plan was supported by the individual, his or her line management, and those responsible for international business development and operations. It meant that, well before any decisions were taken regarding any particular international assignment, individuals were honing their strengths, and addressing development needs which had been identified in this systematic way. It also provided an excellent opportunity for the organization better to get to know the executive concerned, both through information gathering and by opening a dialogue with the family. In this way recommendations for particular postings would be avoided which, based on the evidence, would clearly not produce the kind of results any of the parties to this 'new contract' would be satisfied with. We were, therefore, developing human capital for business success.

This process works best when it is part of a wider capabilities development programme for international business. From my experience, this is a process whereby corporate memory can be built and transferred across the executive population via a variety of formal and informal means. It also allows a programme covering both internal and external inputs. In order to maintain ownership of the programme right across the internationalizing business, I have found it helpful to identify a series of *Champions*, experts or functional leaders in their field, each of whom takes responsibility for a particular element of the programme. Its application can range between informal exchanges to pass on experience and learning points – eg working lunches with individuals who have just completed successful international ventures – to more formal sessions.

In the latter case, individuals can gain both know-how critical to the advancement of capabilities giving the organization a competitive edge in the global market place (eg industry-specific contractural and commercial factors) and specific skill sets, deployed as modules relevant to the overall business development process (eg negotiating skills or communications skills), all set within the context of intercultural understanding.

The identification of a group of Champions gives momentum to such a programme. It also provides a network within which feedback on the programme, its strengths and weaknesses can be shared, in order to strengthen and improve the ongoing conduct of the programme, in all its constituent parts, over time.

The Champions, properly co-ordinated, become a capabilities development fraternity, collectively transferring know-how and experience – honing their own expertise in the process – and providing the life-blood of a continuously learning organization.

Developing Global General Managers

One international hotels group has developed a sophisticated, powerful and, at the same time, highly cost effective means of developing its talent to fill general manager positions for the medium to long term future.

The group have recognized that the changing nature of the hotel business requires a different category of individual to fill hotel general manager positions now and in the competitive global markets of the future. They have recognized that the old style hotelier, whose interest is 'in deep pile carpet and sucking up to the bosses', is no longer relevant in the changing world of the hotel business where their properties become, in essence, 'hospitality centres'. What they need are individuals who can spot business opportunities and manage their affairs in a rounded business sense. They continue to need to serve their clients locally and regionally to the best of their ability; they need to continue to be able to manage the complex technical, creative and significant staffing issues faced by a hotel, 24 hours a day, 365 days a year. But they also need to serve the interests of the shareholders in the business, who require above average returns on their investments, continuously growing. The analogy which is used is that of a three-legged stool. One leg represents the staff the second the sources of financial investment, the third the customers. It is not possible to reduce the dimensions of any one without unbalancing the stool as a whole.

The group have developed a sophisticated set of psychometrics, which underpin their development centre approach to identifying talent for general manager positions. They are also looking beyond the traditional hotel colleges for sources of graduate level talent to fill general manager positions ten years following entry. The psychometrics have been developed working in partnership with the currently most forward-thinking general managers of the business, in order to distil their collective learning about the role and challenges they face, and to provide the necessary buy-in to the programme.

The individuals identified early in their careers are put on an international fast-track. In order to continue their mix of theoretical with practical learning they are placed on a customized MBA programme. However, recognizing that they will be in individual positions and locations for no more than 18 months at a time, the programme has been specially designed with a business school in order to have it completed on the basis of distance learning. In essence, the package itself is totally portable, reflecting the needs of a fast moving international business.

One of the aspects tested and demanded as part of the initial assessment process is the capability to develop up to three additional languages. Also the willingness and attributes to be deployed on a truly global scale working across cultures, while still delivering the core business requirements of the hotels group.

The essence of the roving general manager population, and those being developed to join it, is in itself distinctive. Rather than being comprised of individuals who are engaging in secondments from their domestic parent base, this group of individuals are true career internationalists – they may not have 'home country' appointment for the whole of their career – they join the organization fully understanding that.

The individuals are then placed under the watchful eye of mentors drawn from area managers who are seasoned business professionals in the hotel trade, who will observe and monitor the progress of individuals over the years. Their placements are also carefully selected in order that they are put into hotels run by general managers who themselves are forward thinking, in order that relevant forward thinking business experience rubs off them, rather than the more backward looking old style hotel management.

To ensure that this cadre becomes a truly integrated global source of talent for general management positions throughout the world in future, great store is placed upon building the intake each year into a community itself. They have regular gatherings, both in the context of their hands-on MBA training, but also for general trading and sharing of learning experiences. In addition they publish a regular newsletter for the fast-trackers edited on a rotating basis by the fast-trackers themselves. In this way, strategic learning points are captured, and a corporate memory is built up. This group also provide the future 'corporate glue' to serve the mission of the hotel group as a whole, in terms of its core principles around the world, in the short and longer term. While these individuals, during their training, may indeed provide some turbulence to the local population – hence it is important to place them with seasoned general managers who know how to resolve such issues, both with their own staff and the fast-trackers – they are also a source of new ideas and stimulus to those people who form the core of the particular hotel or group of hotels in the domestic environment.

People often wonder whether this programme – attractive as it may be, in investing in the development of future talent for the business – is incredibly expensive, running to millions of pounds. The reality is the budget in 1996/7 was £35,000. This annual cost simply covers the cost of running the assessment centres, and supporting the MBA programme corporately. The corporate HR function does not hold any further budget than this. Individual general managers own the costs, and hence have a vested interest in maximizing the practical benefits of having fast-trackers placed with them, including the cost of airfares as well as their salaries, for the duration of the assignment. They will tend, for example, to provide a fast-tracker with a placement, say on the front desk alongside the local appointee not included on the international programme. In this way there will be a balance, creating an environment where the fast-tracker can make mistakes but learn from them, complemented by his or her local partner. The local partner in return gains the benefit of ideas and creativity as well as business acumen which rubs off from his or her fast-track colleague.

The other benefit of maintaining the global community of fast-trackers is that, over the years, this developing senior management cadre will build relationships which have practical business benefits. When facing particular difficulties in one part of the world or another, they feel able (in a non-competitive way) to make contact to share experience. Engaging in long-term learning means being able to ask how someone else has resolved a problem they will probably have encountered in the past, to avoid 're-inventing the wheel' continuously when the individual faces, what appear to him, a unique set of circumstances. This is another way also of making sure the corporation flies its corporate flag around the world

The notion in many ways is similar to that adopted historically by the Jesuits. These individuals were indoctrinated; ie, thoroughly developed in core principles (doctrines) of the Roman Catholic Church. When they were then sent literally to the far corners of the earth, the Jesuit leaders could be confident that the credo would not be sacrificed, when it was necessary to interpret the scriptures in specific local settings. This concept of a 'credo' has been practiced with great success around the world by US firm Johnson & Johnson. This is their system of corporate values, regarded by insiders as 'the heart of J & J'. Recent internal review has concluded that the *credo* has been a determining factor in their retaining place number six in the 'Fortune 500' listing of companies. Individuals being considered as potential recruits to J & J in one of their various world-wide business units, are in part judged on their potential to fit in with this system of core values.

One particular issue the hotel group has been having to face up to recently with its programme is that of regional impacts, in the context of extended family relationships which apply. Africa, Middle East and the Asian countries are particular examples. For this reason, the group, has introduced a further, regional fast-track programme. As it is a major issue for many of these locally recruited candidates to move between countries, let alone embark on a truly global career, easing them gently through deployment across a region means that many of the benefits of the international fast-track programme can still be obtained, with the benefits to the hotel group which thus accrues from developing regional general managers for the future. Arrangements are being made with regional institutions for MBA programmes to be provided in order that this aspect of the programme is not watered down, and there is still an opportunity for a regional cadre to develop and to build a learning culture and working set of relationships between them.

A further benefit is that there are some regions where less of a high profile general management is required. That is simply coming to terms with the local business reality. Countries such as Africa are obvious examples, according to the Vice-President – Human Resources of the hotels group. Consequently, regionally developed individuals who may not have the potential for deployment on the truly global programme can nevertheless provide totally satisfactory business-oriented general management capability within the country or region which this applies to.

This means that the true global managers are able to be deployed in those territories where value-added business is available, and high quality and service and management is pre-requisite, to win against stiff competition.

In order to ensure that this programme is owned – and, as noted above, budgeted for – by the area and general management population, group human resources have gone to great lengths to ensure they understand those general managers who will be open to the programme, and wish to support the corporation by mentoring and managing these fast-trackers as the programme unfolds. Efforts are made therefore to ensure the programme is truly sold to the general managers, and that they buy-in to the consequences to them, and take the matter very seriously. It is after all something of bottom-line significance to each of them. A secondary benefit for the group, arising from this, is developing a shared sense of future-facing mission among the existing cadre of general managers who are involved in this coaching, mentoring and development programme for the talent of the future. It gives them a stake in the group and in its long term development.

Wastage from the programme is extremely low. The group believe that, having gone to the lengths they have to develop psychometrics and associated testing and development, they are able to screen out from the outset individuals unlikely to meet the requirements long-term. In instances where it is found, through a process of 360° appraisal – local manager, mentor, and among peer groups at the regular fast-tracker meetings – an individual is unlikely to meet the full rigour of the fast-track programme, they are faced with some options. The first is to leave the organization, having had the benefit of the experience to date. Secondly, to move into a functional area, such as finance. The organization therefore retains its investment in developing an individual; and the function itself has the benefit of individuals who have been through a stretching and broadening general business experience. In this way corporate learning benefits again as individuals bring the lessons learned to the functional areas of supporting the business from a corporate perspective.

The programme is also being tested in the context of what will happen to the hotels business in the future. What kinds of general management will it demand, in order to remain competitively successful? Increasingly, 'hospitality centres' are turning into either business centres, with business support in the fullest sense of the word, or leisure centres. In the former sense, business support networks are the first priority, in terms of the room accommodation available to executives, where they may be prepared to sacrifice 'home comforts' for meeting facilities, and the ability to maintain contact with their business. New infra-red sensor keyboards are being provided to individuals, offering personalized e-mail addresses where they can be reached anywhere within the hotel group world-wide, and via the TV set retrieve their messages and initiate appropriate action. In addition, suitable points are being provided for laptop computers to be plugged in, in individual rooms, with the commercial benefits, including the lower cost of using the service, the internet can provide. For the 'leisure' customers, clearly benefits available in the hotel include leisure facilities and room comforts, tailored to family or singles use.

Lateral thinkers among the new business-oriented general managers have already identified certain benefits of having business centres at the core of the hotel, which provides, for example, word processing and administrative capability for the hotel itself, as well as the business community among the guest population.

Hence, a series of cultural achievements have been made by this group with its innovative and cost effective approach to senior management development. They have understood the need to develop new skills relevant to changing business dynamics and the competitive market. They have gone out and attracted a new calibre of individual to join the fast-track development programme. They have found a willingness and built on the development of a truly global group, but who build a corporate memory through the academic support that they receive and also the simple building of relationships between those on the programme. The group have also recognized the need to take a regional perspective, taking account of those cultural norms and values in regions of the world where, in the early stages, it is not relevant or acceptable to individuals to become part of a truly global cadre. Having said that, it is understood that, working with their colleagues from across the world, those of the highest potential who may wish to develop a global career will be eligible to be included in that programme, if they demonstrate the necessary potential and capability over the medium to long term. In every sense this is a group who are thinking global, acting local and vice-versa. Their own term for it is the *GLocal School of Management Development!*

PROJECT TEAM CAPABILITIES

A successful project is crucially dependent on the calibre and experience of the project manager and his or her team. The manner in which appointment of key personnel is made must be on the basis of need and not of expediency.

Benchmarking a number of aspirant internationalizing businesses, key features for winning were:

❑ *Deploying well a number of significant company strengths*: eg, technical skills; operational capability; reputation; commercial understanding; the commitment of people; and its ability in the management of critical raw materials procurement.

❑ *Technical people who ask the best questions.* The strength of technical due diligence can be definitive in winning 'bankable' projects. Better definition of risk means a more informed basis for bidding on price.

❑ *Handling aspects of the local element on some projects:* eg, the setting up of a local company and the deployment of local nationals in the project can contribute strongly to success.

❑ *Efficient, cost effective use of external advisers*

A set of competencies required of key project management team members needs to be established, drawing strength from benchmarking outcomes. Company HR systems need to be utilized to identify potential project team leaders and in team formation.

The 'Project Manager Model' illustrated in Figure 4.2, traces two distinct career paths, one leading to the management of an international greenfield project, the other to an international acquisition. It is possible to start from either the technical or the commercial box in early career, passing through the management of a domestic project in mid-career. For each stage, the model sets out the basic competency and know-how requirements.

Organizations can profitably draw on the model, under the aegis of their corporate management development programmes, to guide the identification and development of international project managers over the medium/longer term. Figure 4.3 illustrates how international capabilities may be grouped with associated functional capabilities, and integrated with performance planning and development. In order to achieve this integration, management development initiatives should be planned accordingly, drawing on the common database of assessment material. It will be necessary to consider and plan for assignments and redeployments well in advance, in order that proper selection and preparatory actions can be taken.

75

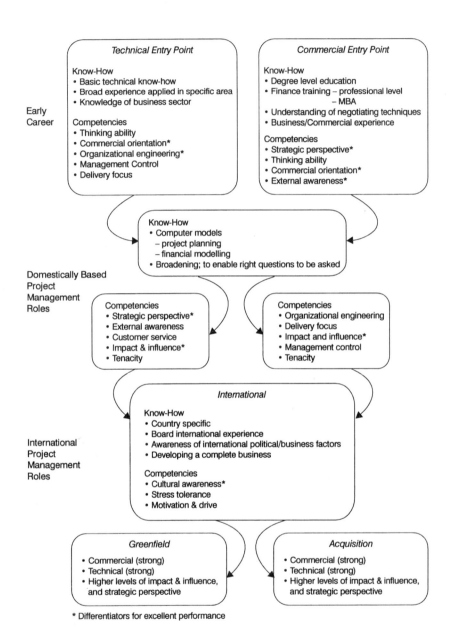

Figure 4.2 *Project manager model for two distinct career paths.*

There are three key deliverables:

1. *Cadre of internationalists* – identified and then developed through work assignments, capabilities development and skills training.
2. *Capabilities development programme* – a series of modules to introduce awareness and knowledge, and develop appropriate know-how and expertise, aligned to common goals for global business expansion.
3. *Corporate memory build* – in areas of critical international business development and execution, knowledge recorded and made available through briefing and training modules and for reference.

CAPABILITIES DEVELOPMENT FROM WITHIN

The objectives of a successful programme of capabilities development are the creation of well balanced international teams, operating to maximum effectiveness, sharing common goals (linked to strategic business plans). There will be recognition of cross-cultural sensitivities, an evolution of demonstrable international business skills, including interpersonal and negotiating skills, deal structuring and financial engineering, communication and project management skills.

In addition, the process will be carried out with the involvement of key individuals within the parent corporation, affording the opportunity of a wide pool of talent and experience, while enhancing communication links and understanding between domestic and other parts of the internationalizing business entity.

To be successful, a programme of capabilities development must target the right population. It is critical, therefore, not only to define this population correctly, but to have a good understanding of their strengths, weaknesses, aspirations and development needs so that the right training can be targeted at the right person at the right time. Furthermore, the programme should contain some distinct but interrelated components; assimilation of knowledge/information; acquisition of business (technical) skills and business (behavioural) skills, giving a mix of 'hard' topics and 'softer' skills.

A menu of capabilities development modules may be constructed around four levels, converging from a general assimilation of knowledge and information to generating specific targeted skills. An illustration of a menu I formulated with a business developing internationally through major infrastructure project investment is given in Figure 4.4, together with some sample training modules.

Internationalization – The People Dimension

Area	Functional Capability	Comments on Performance	Development Needs
Partnership arrangements	Memorandum of understanding Joint venture agreements Confidentiality Shareholders agreement Alliances/conflicting objectives Letter of intent Heads of terms		
Sales/supply agreements	Legal implications Product/service availability Transport connections Knowledge and understanding of contract settlement processes Non-conventional supply/purchase agreements Duration, shape, flexibility and financing of agreements		
Financial arrangements	Develop and maintain an in-depth knowledge of financial management systems Maintain an understanding of financial planning techniques Develop an understanding of project evaluation and cost control techniques Maintain detailed knowledge of domestic and overseas statutory accounting practices Corporate structures Non-recourse finance Lending agencies/sources Tax implications Risk mitigation		
O & M arrangements	O & M strategies O & M agreements Develop an ability to plan and co-ordinate the operation and maintenance of overseas plants Maintain a thorough knowledge of optimal operating systems for new developments Responsibilities Maintenance philosophies Turnkey approaches Conflicts with ownership		
Plant contracts	Develop a thorough knowledge and understanding of contract management Technology selection Contract strategy		

Capabilities Development for International Business

Area	Functional Capability	Comments on Performance	Development Needs
Plant contracts (*continued*)	Tendering process Procurement Economies of scale Customer 'partnering' contracts		
Human resources	Identify and understand the implications of cultural differences during the resourcing of projects Be adaptable to new situations Demonstrate communication/ relationship skills having an affinity with people generally Demonstrate self-reliance and a resistance to stress Demonstrate a high degree of action and result orientation Responsibilities Organizational design Manpower strategies Selection/development/mentoring Employee relations		
Project management	Develop and maintain an ability to co-ordinate the technical and commercial inputs Costing Planning Cost control Task allocation Risk assessment Due diligence Insurance Investment appraisal		
Project evaluation	Develop an ability to evaluate investment proposals Strategic fit		
Raw materials	Develop and maintain an understanding of raw materials supply contracts Maintain a detailed knowledge of the alternative options for raw materials supply Raw materials availability International vs Domestic supply Supply logistics Contract strategy Product/service supply contracts interface Constraints		

Figure 4.3 *International capabilities.*

Capabilities Development Module Levels and Target Population.

Levels
1. The first level seminar creates a general understanding of what is involved in setting up and running (sector specific) business entities.
2. The second level 'Knowledge Modules' offer a more detailed subset of the first level and focus on the creation of an understanding of the elements of the project development process (project finance, investment appraisal, product or service supply agreements, the realities of manufacturing and distribution in a commercial environment). These would normally last one day per module, and be led by internal expert 'champions'.
3. The third level 'Business Skills' are targeted at the creation of specific skills (negotiation, project management, cultural awareness etc), introducing customized courses – probably externally led.
4. The fourth level 'Expertise' involves the creation of in-house experts in project specific areas, generally a combination of project assignments and complementary on-job training. This, by definition, will be a medium- to long-term aspect of the programme. It will require careful co-ordination at a high level, and be a key aspect of strategic management of the international business development process. It will form a core of the corporate memory building programme.

	Seminar	Knowledge	Skills	Experience
1. Corporate Management	✓	Part	Specific	
2. Project Managers	✓	✓	Specific	
3. Business Development Managers	✓	✓	Specific	Specific
4. Project Core/Service Participants	✓	✓	Specific	Specific
5. Functional Participants	✓	Part	Specific	Specific

Capabilities Development Training

Level Two – 'Knowledge' Modules

Learning Area	Overview of Content
Product/Service/Supply Agreements	Legal Frequency/Availability Logistics Billing and Settlement Non-conventional Agreements Duration, Shape, Flexibility, Financing
Partnership Arrangements	Memoranda of Understanding JV Agreements Confidentiality Shareholders Agreement Alliances/Conflicting Objectives Letter of Intent Heads of Terms

Level Two – 'Knowledge' Modules (*continued*)

Learning Area	Overview of Content
Project Evaluation and Quality Control	Costs Risk Assessment Due Diligence Insurance Strategic Fit Investment Appraisal
Financial Arrangements	Corporate Structures Non-recourse Finance Lending Agencies/Sources Tax Implications Risk Mitigation
O & M Arrangements	Strategies The Agreement Databases Responsibilities Maintenance Philosophies Turnkey Approaches Conflicts with Ownership Local IR Climate
Plant Contracts	Technology Selection Contract Strategy Tendering Process Procurement Economies of Scale/Modulars
Project Resourcing	Responsibilities Inter-Cultural Factors Organizational Design Manpower Strategies Selection/Development/Mentoring Employee Relations
Project Management	Accountabilities Planning Cost Control Task Allocation Function Roles Deliverables Co-ordination Project Experience (Corporate Memory)
Raw Materials/Components	Sourcing Options Supply Main Management Risks Contracts – Off-sets on Supply Agreements Logistics Management

Figure 4.4 *An example menu of capabilities development modules.*

SUMMARY AND CHECKLIST

A successful capabilities development programme is designed to meet the strategic needs of the internationalizing corporation and to reflect the framework and process for business development and operational management. It forms part of an holistic HRM framework incorporating establishment of an internal talent pool for international business development; a recruitment and selection process for key team members; and team building techniques and process to facilitate information flow and understanding within project teams and corporate management.

These capabilities – development from within initiatives – must be integrated with those designed to augment capability by other means, including targeted recruitment, alliances and joint ventures and SBU acquisitions. These efforts will generally assist in providing internationalizing businesses with a 'kick-start', providing an injection of targeted capability to complement existing core organizational competence. They also provide the time needed to grow one's own over the medium term.

The following questions need to be addressed in planning a capabilities development strategy for internationalization. Does the proposed programme:

❑ Follow a systematic process whereby capabilities needs have been matched to projected strategic business requirements?

❑ Reflect judgements over the sources of winning capabilities (via acquisition or development) over the short, medium and long term?

❑ Fit the model selected against which an *International Cadre* is to be defined?

❑ Draw on a comprehensive knowledge fund covering the attributes and potential of the executive and professional workforce, secured through self-directed development centres?

❑ Provide comprehensive development programmes for individuals and teams, covering technical and behavioural capabilities formed from a combination of 'briefing', 'training' and 'doing'?

❑ Have top level support and a capabilities development fraternity of expert champions?

❑ Form a core element of a definitive global corporate memory?

Chapter 5

Internationalization – the Rewards

People in all parts of the world are the same in almost every way. In a few ways they are different. It is critical that, in approaching reward management in an international context, human resource professionals appreciate both the similarities and the differences. In going global, a significant error frequently made by HR professionals, wherever they are starting from, is to believe that they have all the answers. They tend to conclude that what has worked in their home environment will work anywhere – they believe all they have to do is export well-honed practices to the less enlightened countries of the world. On the other hand, we sometimes make the mistake of believing we have nothing to offer. We simply accept that what we find in other countries are givens. In these ways approaches to international compensation tend to be cost ineffective at best – and a disaster at worst.

SOME DEFINITIONS

In international companies there are two major categories of employee: local nationals and expatriates. Local nationals are people recruited as contracted employees in the country in which they are resident. Generally, they are citizens of that country. Expatriates are employees sent from their 'home' countries by their employer to another country – 'host' country – on a temporary assignment (generally one to five years).

Expatriates can be sub-divided into three principal categories:

❑ Headquarters expatriates – those sent overseas from the headquarters country of the organization (often called simply 'expatriates')

❑ Inpatriates – those sent to the headquarters country from another country
❑ Third Country Nationals (TCNs); those working temporarily in a second country for an employer headquartered in a third country.

Quite a lot has been written about compensation and benefits practice in an international context. There are suppliers of intelligence on international – particularly expatriate – compensation trends (notably, Organization Resource Counsellors, and Employment Conditions Abroad). In this chapter, we will try to reflect on some of the issues surrounding the determination of rewards for an internationalizing business. This will obviously take account of the trends in expatriate compensation, among other things, drawing on my own participation in a programme combining inputs from a variety of major multinational companies, sponsored by the US National Foreign Trade Council. This initiative was taken in response to the increasing concern among multinationals (predominantly US-based) about the spiralling costs of expatriate compensation, set against the growing international competitiveness and cost pressures they were having to face up to. Figure 5.1 sets out participants' views on expatriate programme elements which they have found problematic. Figure 5.2 then summarizes their views on what their companies believe to be the most critical factors. The consensus was that something had to be done from a strategic perspective.

In this chapter, we will also begin to look at some of the issues surrounding the compensation solutions for the increasingly critical category of local national employees and third country nationals. This will examine the requirement to view international reward policy from a corporate perspective through two lenses. The first is one of seeing

❑ Repatriation
❑ Expatriate/family support
❑ Dual career issues
❑ Cultural training/orientation
❑ Too much hand-holding
❑ Selection (does not consider cultural sensitivity)
❑ Rules too restrictive/inflexible
❑ Relocation
❑ Programme too expensive/generous
❑ Career value of assignments/career development
❑ Assignment planning

Figure 5.1 *Sponsored NFTC study. The participants listed the programme elements that have worked poorly for their companies.*
Source: NFTC/Towers Perrin

❑ Selection
❑ Schooling
❑ Repatriation
❑ Career development/opportunities
❑ Cost containment
❑ Expatriate support
❑ Minimize tax; increase tax planning
❑ Communication of policies and compensation
❑ Orientation; cultural and language programmes
❑ Dual career/spouse issues
❑ Compensation equity
❑ Assignment planning; assignment goals and roles defined in advance
❑ Programme simplicity and flexibility

Figure 5.2 *Sponsored NFTC study. The participants listed the programme elements that they considered to be the most critical.*
Source: NFTC/Towers Perrin

employee compensation and performance management in the context of cross-cultural implications; the second is through the lens of the corporation itself. We shall also have the opportunity to review one or two practical examples of where an internationalizing organization has to face up to the challenges of setting appropriate international compensation levels – but often experiences internal pressures and paradoxes in doing so.

It has been estimated that all but ten per cent of the total payroll for multinational enterprises comprises compensation for local nationals. While it may be understandable, it is not entirely appropriate, then, that most of the writing on international reward focuses on expatriate staff – and by implication concerns organizations with ethnocentric staffing policies. No doubt this has been because of the proportionally high cost of such individuals to multinational corporations. However, this over-focus on expatriate issues has tended to distort treatments of international human resource management generally and, increasingly, organizations are looking to reform their approach to international reward strategy; to design compensation programmes appropriate for specific cultural traditions. It has been suggested (Bradley *et al.*, 1997) that the issues are similar in some respects to those in marketing, when decisions are made to adopt either global or multilocal marketing strategies. From the point of view of simplification, global policies on reward would be ideal. But, there are undoubtedly some cultural aspects that make implementation, understanding and effectiveness different between countries. Increasingly, therefore, practitioners and commentators alike are concluding that the exportability of management theories and practices is determined by the comparability of the cultural values between the importing and exporting nation. Any internationalizing business, then, needs to concern itself with the broad question of reward strategies in the context of how local cultural values impact on the delivery of corporate performance. Reward strategy, after all, has as its very essence the requirement to encourage and deliver superior levels of corporate performance, sustained over time.

REWARD STRATEGIES FOR INTERNATIONAL EXECUTIVES

I explained in an earlier chapter that my experience of working with organizations attempting to internationalize their businesses, had led me to the conclusion, that very few of us really know our executives well. Not only do we, as HR people, need better to understand our *International Cadre*, it is fundamental that we engage the attention of our senior line management in this process too. In the past it has often been the case that managing an expatriate group has been something which the line have sought to shuffle-off to the HR professional, as too complex or too emotive an issue for them to become embroiled in. The result has been that the HR professional has found him or herself with the worst of all worlds. On the one hand, they have frequently had employees – possibly those who have not been identified with the degree of clarity required fully to appreciate the demands and the benefits implicit in an international assignment – angling for the best possible 'deal' which they can strike. And on the other, they have line management impatient to 'get the individual (frequently with his or her family in tow) on the plane as quickly as possible'. In my experience, it is only when senior line management responsible for deploying individuals on international assignments accept their true role as the *pilot* of the exercise, with the expatriate the *co-pilot* – and with a new value-added role for HR as the *navigator* - that the process can be effectively managed with all parties signing on to the strategy.

PRINCIPLES FOR DEVELOPING INTERNATIONAL ASSIGNMENT POLICIES

From my experience in supporting organizations in managing expatriates, and attempting to deliver the strategic objective of internationalizing, full recognition has been given that this naturally will entail the employment of local national staff wherever possible. But, in all cases, organizations conclude there are specific circumstances where the deployment of internationally mobile expatriate staff will be the preferred option. Deployment of core capabilities and skills transfer at the early stages of an international investment initiative provides a source of competitive advantage.

This experience has revealed four key messages:

1. No two assignments and no two assignees are alike.
2. It is critical that line managers are informed, in a timely manner, of the excess cost and value equations associated with expatriate postings, and their endorsement is secured.
3. A flexible and responsive policy must be in place which provides both incentives and rewards for the successful completion of overseas assignments and their associated objectives.
4. Organizations need to remain competitive with their employment offering in the international market place, to attract and retain high quality staff with worldwide capabilities.

TYPES OF ASSIGNMENT

I have found that assignments typically fall within three separate and distinct categories:

1. Business trip (less than 31 days duration per single trip)

This scenario is generally covered by established company policy, contained within their standard 'Guide to Business Travel and Expenses'.

2. Short-term assignment (over 31 days but less than 12 months)

During this period, the assignee moves on to the headcount/budget of the project, with selected assignment terms applied, matched to individual circumstances. Career management remains the responsibility of the employee's home department, while performance management may be a shared responsibility.

3. Full assignment (over 12 months)

During this period, the above conditions apply, but with career management embraced by the appropriate manager and any 'corporate' mentor.

Stages in the process

I have evolved a philosophy in guiding organizations in these circumstances, on the basis of a 'Ten Stage Journey' of assignee management. The objective is to:

1. Support business strategy

Organizations need to recognize the reasons for using expatriate staff including:

- ❑ ensuring corporate business objectives are met
- ❑ providing managerial and technical expertise aimed at long-term development of national staff to assume responsibilities
- ❑ as a part of a structured process, enhancing and developing the capabilities of the firm's international cadre of staff
- ❑ allowing time to identify, recruit and develop local nationals.

2. Manage costs as appropriate

A key feature in the determination of an assignee's package should be the 'excess cost/excess value' equation; ie 'what does an expatriate deliver in terms of skills transfer in return for the cost of the assignment?' Each assignment should therefore reflect considerations of:

- ❑ an expatriate assignment versus local recruitment
- ❑ a corporate philosophy of providing flexible incentives and reimbursing costs, necessarily incurred
- ❑ the local culture or custom and practice
- ❑ the rationale behind the costs.

3 Involve line management

The process should play a critical supporting role to line management of the business venture and it is important jointly to:
- ❑ understand and clearly define the requirement to mobilize an expatriate
- ❑ understand any specific issues or problems relating to the assignment that could impact on the final selection of the assignee
- ❑ recognize and get agreement on the cost implications and justification.

4. Communicate the value of international assignments

The importance of any international role should be communicated:

- ❑ by clearly defining the roles and responsibilities of the posting

❏ in terms of both the individual's growth and achievement of company objectives

❏ as contributing to the development of an 'International Cadre'.

5. Select the right expatriate

The cost and complexities associated with international assignments combine to create a need for a high quality identification and selection process, aimed at:

❏ establishing the specific competencies required for the post and matching them to potential assignees

❏ ensuring that potential candidates are progressed through an appropriate development centre before any commitments or decisions are made on either side

❏ ensuring that the motivational and personal/domestic aspects related to the individual are fully recognized and understood.

6. Set realistic expectations

The objectives of the assignment should be clearly stated at the outset:

❏ depending on the category of the assignment, performance objectives should be set by the appropriate manager(s)

❏ setting realistic requirements will also assist in the identification and selection of the best candidate(s)

❏ the personal and career development issues will be able to be more accurately defined as a result.

7. Prepare the expatriate for the move

Fundamental to the planning and preparation phase will be the design and implementation of a programme which takes the individual (and family, as appropriate) through a carefully prepared series of events and discussions. This approach seeks to reduce the likelihood of assignment failure due to personal/family problems:

❏ to include full cultural, language and orientation briefings/training

❏ consideration of all health/medical issues

❏ arrangements for visas, work permits, residence permits, passports

❏ taxation and social security advice/guidance

❏ schooling, accommodation, transport, insurance should be covered in pre-assignment briefings, and form part of the assignment conditions

❏ wherever possible, a comprehensive range of services should be provided to the assignee covering the above areas, but 'personalized' to reflect the individual circumstances.

8. Manage career development

The assignment should:

❏ be part of a structured framework within which line management should ensure that the assignment represents a valuable element of the individual's personal and career development

❏ be reflected in the creation of an *International Development Plan* for the individual, aligned to the company's career management process

❏ provide for early consideration of any redeployment issues to be established, recognizing both 'home' country management requirements as well as the potential for further international assignments upon successful completion

❏ consider the appointment of a mentor as part of the process.

9. Communicate well

Effective communication will enhance the application of assignment policy with regard to:

❏ an understanding of the company's approach to international assignments, and the structure of the programme

❏ communication links, which must be established at the outset, to maintain the channels between the company and the assignee whilst he/she is away from the 'home' country, keeping abreast of 'home' company developments and assisting in any subsequent redeployment issues; (mentoring will be important here).

10. Apply consistent policies

An expatriate policy management suite should instil consistency and co-ordination into the process, while still remaining capable of meeting the varying agendas of the assignee and line management by its inherent flexibility.

PATHWAYS TO SUCCESS

Through the application, and continued refinement of the *Ten Stage Journey*, to match their unique, evolving circumstances, organizations may continue to utilize their staff in a manner which provides real competitive advantage to the organization in its international push, while providing genuine personal and career development opportunities to flourish.

Gathering information about the employees' expectations and needs, set very firmly in the domestic circumstances as well as the business case circumstances which will apply, is a fundamental part of developing reward management arrangements for individuals operating internationally. I must say that, in recent times, it has been far more straightforward securing the full involvement of line management in the process, as they have come more fully to understand the need to keep costs carefully under control. In the days before intensive international business competition and the rather careless way sometimes in which expatriates were identified and deployed, money often appeared to be no object. Nowadays, the need to show value-added deployment engages the attention of the line manager responsible for managing project costs, and keeping the customer happy, overall.

THE EXPAT APPROACH

Future-effective expatriate reward management needs to balance a number of factors, encompassing strategic business goals and employee aspirations. There are five key components to successful expatriate management (see Figure 5.3).

Fundamentally, organizations must be confident that, in deploying expatriate personnel, they will bring value to the assignment greater than the cost of their employment and support outside their country of origin, compared with the alternative of engaging local talent. The expense of expatriates is acceptable in the short term since, for a while, they can create greater value than a local can. This issue is illustrated in Figure 5.4.

Organizations are increasingly moving away from an approach to expatriate rewards based on 'topping up' home-based compensation without any reference to local market conditions. This is especially pronounced in 'developed' countries; in 'developing' countries expatriates at middle and senior executive levels still tend to expect some compensation for 'hardship'.

E	Excess cost/excess value
X	'X' marks the spot
P	Participative process
A	Attractive deal
T	Totality of approach

Figure 5.3 *The five key components to successful expatriate management.*

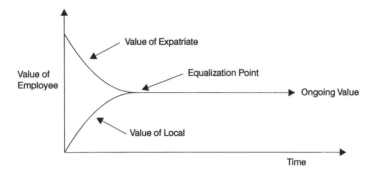

Figure 5.4 *Excess cost versus excess value of using expatriates.*

Among the new generation of globally mobile professionals (a 'trainee executive' group), even in the latter territories a more 'bare-bones' approach is beginning to prevail. The NFTC study group concluded that a destination-based approach ('x' marks the spot), where expatriate rewards used the local assignment market context as a platform, was more appropriate.

This new emphasis requires far more involvement of all the parties to the expatriate reward contract; individuals, their families and corporate and local management. Participation in the detail in this way means a more efficient system is called for, and more effective HR guidance to accompany it.

Nonetheless, as with any aspect of talent acquisition, retention and motivation, an attractive total 'deal' is called for. The interpretation of 'reward' is likely to be more imaginative, than in the past, however. A new generation of internationalists place weight on development opportunities and early responsibility allocation as a feature of their assignments, as a constituent part of their overall contract.

This totality of approach means too that, having determined explicit and implicit expatriation terms, individuals wish to be given greater flexibility to customize the organization's investment in them, tailored to their own diverse needs and expectations.

To complement this, I worked on the development of an approach starting with the rate for the job and then delivering additional components flexibly and cost-effectively, as illustrated in Figure 5.5. This represents a flexible 'pot' available to an expatriate, capturing the overall investment available for financing their deployment, signed on to by the relevant line manager, with particular reference to the comparisons between what an expatriate would cost and a similar local employee (assuming one was available). The line formally accepts accountability for delivering the excess value from the assignment in return for the excess cost to the company involved.

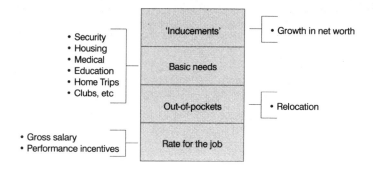

Figure 5.5 *The 'expat' approach.*

In this way, the development of expatriate terms is better informed, is owned by line management as well as the individual being deployed, and is more of a partnership arrangement, rather than one party seeking exclusively to negotiate with HR, to get a better deal over the other. An example of the application of this approach, with associated notes of guidance, appears in Figure 5.6.

As far as possible, accountability for determining the value and make-up of international assignment terms and conditions should rest with the line manager on whose budget any costs will fall. A matrix of responsibilities for determining expat packages is provided in Figure 5.7. This shows the balance between aspects such as salary and incentives which need to be centrally determined to ensure maximum group-wide mobility of assignees, and aspects which properly fall to local management discretion.

HUMAN RESOURCES IMPLICATIONS ASSOCIATED WITH EMPLOYING EXPATRIATES VIA A GLOBAL EMPLOYMENT COMPANY (GEC)

In order to tackle the issues surrounding employment terms for a truly international cadre of expatriated professionals, some organizations are considering whether to form a Global Employment Company (GEC) which could become the legal employer of managers and professional staff during periods of international secondment.

There are a number of implications associated with employing expatriates via a Global Employment Company (GEC). Key aspects are summarized below.

	$

SALARY

BONUS (if applicable)

Hypothetical 'Home' Income Tax and Social Insurance deduction (1)

NET BASE AND INCENTIVE PAY

'Location Mark up' incentive payment for assignment to . . . (2)

NET CASH PAYMENTS (NO TAX)

Flexible 'pot' which can be drawn-on up to this maximum figure, at the individual's discretion, to cover 'rest and recreation' trips, flights for leave, club membership etc. (3)

Housing and transport costs

Tax free 'Inducement' payment at start and conclusion of assignment, linked to whole-assignment performance achievements

TOTAL NET VALUE OF PACKAGE (4)

Estimated additional tax charge to employer's account (5)
Total annual cost to employer, before addition of 'hidden' costs (6)

Estimated total cost to employer of the assignment, once 'hidden' costs are included

This compares with the total market-assessed cost of employing an individual on *local* terms to perform an *equivalent* role of $ . . . . per annum approximately. The comparison is intended to assist line management's decision to approve or vary the expatriate package from an informed viewpoint, and to judge the excess *value*/excess *cost* of the expatriate against the alternative of recruiting an equivalent local candidate, if available.

Approved: **Line Manager**

Notes to the Above

1. Assessment of income tax and Social Insurance contribution which would be payable (on salary and any bonus payable) if the post was based in 'home' country. Tax advisors to confirm figure, once they have all relevant information on the individual's tax circumstances.
2. Recommended payment method/timing will be that which is tax efficient for the employer.
3. Sum calculated based on research into circumstances/costs relevant to status of accompanied/unaccompanied assignment. Provides scope for individual to apportion the budget maximum customized to own preferences, trading one 'standard' item value off against another. There remains an audit trail of budget make-up justification and draw-down.
4. This value is increased once 'hidden' benefits (pension funding, international health care, insurance premiums, utilities charges (all company paid direct) plus shipping and other miscellaneous costs reimbursements are accounted for.
5. Additional tax burden is adjusted to reflect costs of assignment benefits (including any location 'mark-up' cash lump sums for example).
6. 'Hidden costs' = 'hidden benefits' – see note (4).

Figure 5.6 *An example of the generic 'flexible pot' approach.*

94

Item	Where paid	Corporate	Local
Assignment salary	Home	Determine	Administer
Incentive pay	Home	Determine	Administer
Expat premium/mark-up	Home	Determine	***
Disturbance payment	Home	Determine	
Reconnaissance visit	Home (via expenses)	Determine	Support
Freight/storage	Home	Determine	***
Travel to host location	Home	Determine	
Settling-in assistance	Host		Determine
Accomodation**	Host	Guide	Determine
Utilities	Host	Guide	Determine
Domestic help**	Host	Guide	Determine
Personal transport**	Host	Guide	Determine
Education assistance/children's visits	Host#	Determine	Administer
Club membership**	Host	Guide	Determine
R&R + leave travel**	Host	Determine	Administer
Return to home location	Home	Determine	

**   Paid as part of pre-assignment budget 'pot'
***   Host location to provide regular intelligence to assist review of appropriate levels in each location.
\#   Home if children remain in that country for boarding schooling.

Figure 5.7 *Responsibilities for determining expat packages.*

Standardization of contracts

It is important to determine to what extent contracts of employment should be standardized for all employees. Factors to consider are:

❑ Where the company will be registered and what law will govern in the event of a dispute?
❑ What contractual rights will apply?
❑ What existing 'home' contractual rights will be preserved?
❑ Where existing contracts of employment must be terminated, how will variation of rights be handled? What action, such as compensatory measures, will be taken to avoid disadvantaging employees as a result of a change of employer?
❑ Whether employees will be granted continuity of service and what the effect will be upon service related benefits; eg, pensions, holidays and redundancy entitlements?

Relationship of GEC with the home firm

Factors to consider include:

❑ Who will have the right to 'hire' and 'fire'?
❑ Who will be responsible for handling disciplinary and grievance matters?

95

❑ How will appeals be handled?

❑ What support services will be available; eg, employee assistance programmes?

Statutory rights

A key issue is determination of what statutory or mandatory rights should apply, so as to guarantee employees a certain level of protection regardless of where they are assigned.

Employee population

It will be necessary to agree the target employee population at the outset. For example:

❑ Will the GEC employ only the 'brightest and best'?

❑ If so, what will be the relationship of this 'elite' global cadre with the rest of the organization?

Pension implications

This is perhaps the most complex area and includes such questions as:

❑ What pension arrangements will apply? Is it possible and practicable to establish a pension scheme, provident fund, or other deferred compensation arrangement, which transcends country-specific legislation?

❑ How portable will such a scheme be?

❑ What will be the effect upon home country pension schemes; eg, what will happen to accrued pension rights in the home country?

❑ What will be the tax implications on contributions and what will be the effect on any tax-free elements of the pension?

Medical cover and life assurance

Key issues to consider include:

❑ Will be feasible to establish a global provider?

❑ If so, what standard and level of medical cover will apply?

❑ How will variations of medical cover be handled?

Career development

Employability is now a major feature in the 'reward' package expected by knowledge workers. If it is a long term intention that international assignments are to be viewed as career enhancing then it will be important to ensure that there is a clearly defined policy and infrastructure for career development. The key issues include:

❑ Who will be responsible for managing the process?

❑ How will development needs be identified?
❑ How will training be delivered and who will meet the cost?
❑ How will any mentoring scheme work?
❑ Who will meet specific training costs?

The international hotels group example in Chapter 4 provides some possible insights here into the manner in which global businesses are responding practically to this issue.

Performance management
Core issues to consider include:

❑ How will performance be monitored?
❑ How will performance be rewarded?
❑ Who will determine the capability and readiness of an individual to take on new assignments?
❑ How will the GEC ensure that the reward structure is competitive?

Tax and social security
Tax and social security provisions will be major issues. The key considerations from an employee's perspective include:

❑ What tax regulations will apply?
❑ Will employees always be required to pay host country tax or will 'hypothetical tax' be applied?
❑ Will employees receive 'equalization' treatment if the host country tax liability is greater than a figure agreed at the outset and, if so, how will this be determined?
❑ Who will be responsible for tax planning activities?
❑ What will be the impact upon home country social security benefits?
❑ What will be the contribution requirements on the part of the employer and employee and how will these be made?

Administration
This covers such matters as:

❑ How will employees be paid; eg, via an international bank account?
❑ In what currency will employees be paid?
❑ Will employees receive protection for exchange rate fluctuations; ie, should a rate be agreed at the beginning of each year and any differences reconciled at year end?
❑ How will the payroll be administered: who will resolve issues such as missing and/or late transfers?

POTENTIAL BARRIERS

Certain issues have been identified by international organizations, reviewing policy options in this area, as potential barriers to the harmonization of expatriate remuneration policies and packages.

❑ The present diversity of expatriate remuneration policies and practices used among a group's strategic business units (SBUs) means that a harmonized approach may be more difficult for certain organizations to implement initially than for others. A phased approach to implementation may be required.

❑ A lack of effective administrative and human resources management systems may well hinder the implementation of a successful international secondment programme for the 'brightest and best'. Senior management commitment to support the programme is therefore essential.

❑ The potential costs associated with harmonizing expatriate remuneration packages, and the allocation of these costs, may seem prohibitive to some SBUs. Group-wide funding may therefore need to be considered, to pump-prime GEC initiatives.

OVERVIEW OF APPROACHES TO EXPATRIATE REWARD

Drawing on three internationally recognized sources of data, based on comprehensive survey activity, it is possible to construct a picture of current organization practice in relation to expatriate reward.

It is possible, drawing on the same sources, to summarize benchmark information on core components which currently feature in expatriate reward packages.

A MODEL EXPATRIATE REWARD POLICY

Table 5.3 sets out a possible model policy framework on expatriate assignment terms and conditions, which may be deployed in conjunction with the 'flexible pot' concept displayed earlier. This approach provides guidance on systematically evaluating all aspects relevant to an expatriate package, and in determining a gross value. The elemental approach facilitates the dialogue required to assist line managers and expatriate staff alike in understanding what is involved and how. It also guides an appreciation of the cumulative costs to the organization, and total value to the individual, before offering choices surrounding trade-offs between the size of each element in application.

Table 5.1 *Expatriate reward – current practices*

General Approach	Definition	Trends
Home Country based	Expatriate pay is related to that of peers in the home country. Expatriates are therefore treated the same regardless of country of assignment.	**ECA** • 63% of companies surveyed used this approach **ORC** • Most companies seek 'to provide equivalent purchasing power to help maintain home lifestyle' **PW** • Most common
Host Country based	Salary is related to that of peers in the host country; this will result in different living standards from country to country	**ECA** • Less than 10% of companies use this approach • 95% of companies using this approach, provide additional allowances **PW** • In developed countries, one in three companies delivers the total salary to the assignee in the host country
Dual Home/Host Country based	Salary is either the higher of home or host country based	**ECA** • 24% of companies use this approach **PW** • 17% of companies divide the salary between home and host currencies as requested by the employee
Select Country	Expatriate compensation is based on a single salary structure, regardless of the the expatriate's home country base	**PW** • An International or Regional salary structure was found to be the least popular system
Hybrid	There are two components – one is designed to produce equity between different expatriate nationalities in the host country, and the other to ensure equity with the employee's home country	**PW** • Nearly as many companies use this approach as use a home based approach for intra-regional assignments

Sources: See Table 5.2

Table 5.2 *Benchmark data - core expatriate packages*

Component	ECA	ORC	PW
Cost of Living Allowances (COLA)	For those companies who apply the index to a fixed percentage of home net, the average percentage of net is 66% For those companies who apply the index to a fixed percentage of home gross, the average percentage is 50%	96% pay a separate goods and service' allowance: 92% look for comparability with home country living standards: 87% take family size into account	49% pay a separately identified COLA: 35% pay a COLA but not as a separate item Circa 80% set no limit on the COLA Majority use external sources to calculate the COLA
	47% separately express the COLA as an allowance and 53% combine it with the home country spendable income to give host country spendable income		
	56% make a negative adjustment to the home spendable income where the index is below a certain level	53% do not apply a negative index if the cost of living is lower in the host country	54% take no action where there are negative indices
Benefits and allowances	95% of companies which base expatriate pay on local salary scales, provide additional allowance/benefits	50% pay no premiums or lump sum mobility payments for moves within the same continent: 36% pay a separate incentive for intercontinental moves	27% of companies do not make incentive payments. 55% of companies which pay an incentive do so with the normal pay cycle
	Between 35% and 43% provide one or more of the following; one-off performance-related bonuses, long-term incentive plans, share based schemes and hardship/location allowances	72% pay a separate hardship allowance if considered applicable: 65% do not cap it: 94% do not phase it out during the assignment 77% permit expatriates to participate in home	44% pay relocation allowance - average paid was one month's salary tax free 60% pay a hardship premium: most include it with the regular pay cycle

Component	ECA	ORC	PW
Benefits and allowances (*continued*)			
	Circa 90% using a home based system pay incentive allowances	country profit-sharing or stock-option plans as per home country employees	Circa one third retain employees in home country bonus arrangements
	83.5% using a home based approach pay a location allowance 11.5% set a 'ceiling'		
Local Accommodation	Circa 60% provide 'free' accommodation with 50% specifying a 'local ceiling value': employees pay excess	80% provide support where host country costs are greater than those at home	Overall 38% provide free housing in all locations
	13% expect an employee contribution	On average, about two-thirds pay costs but deduct a home country 'norm'	Nearly one third deduct a housing 'norm'
		76% discourage home ownership in the host country: on average about 19% provide company-owned or leased houses: this increases to about 27% where housing is not readily available or where it is tax beneficial	
Utilities Payment		40% pay actual utilities cost, without limitations	32% of comapies meet utilities with a further 10% meeting costs up to a set limit
Relocation: Temporary Accommodation Shipping and Storage Insurance			Hotel expenses are generally paid: 59% reimburse meals
			61% of companies cover these costs on arrival in the host

continued overleaf

Table 5.2 *(continued)*

Component ECA	ORC	PW
Relocation *(continued)*		country with 30% meeting costs up to a set limit and 5% considering doing so on a case by case basis
Shipping and Storage Policies	Nearly all companies meet the shipping costs of household furnishings: some apply certain restrictions; eg. weight: 90% will permit air freight on a case by case/ restricted basis	Circa 50% pay the full costs of 'approved' items: one third set weight/volumetric limits Majority will pay for the shipment of furniture and household appliances
Medical Entitlement	78% of companies retain expatriates and their families in their home country plan 95% retain life insurance in the home country, where possible	45% of companies use a specific medical plan: circa 31% retain expatriates in the home country plan: and 21% use a host country plan: 36% require contributions
Holidays	A large majority of companies provide annual home leave for single (80%) and married accompanied (81%) expatriates 60% do not require home leave to be taken in the home country: 24% do not pay costs if leave not taken at home 46% of companies provide rest and recreation (R&R) leave: 37% pay all expenses for the	88% provide home leave. For unaccompanied assignments, 45% of companies provide one home leave trip per annum, 24% provide two and 31% provide three visits per annum R&R is usually provided as an additional component for 'difficult' locations. The average period of R&R is three to seven days

Component	ECA	ORC	PW
Holidays (*continued*)		employee and family: 25% pay a *per diem*: 29% pay travel only	
Education	90% provide support for children's education	53% of companies indicate they will pay pre-school costs 91% and 94% will contribute to primary and secondary education costs respectively	99% contribute towards the cost of primary and secondary education for dependent children
Language and Cultural Awareness		7% permit pre-assignment visits to all countries Circa 35% pay the cost of language tuition for employee and spouse/partner	57% always provide a pre-assignment visit 96% provide language training always (or on a case by case basis) reducing to 75% where this includes the spouse or partner and family Only 10% send the expatriate (and spouse) on a cultural awareness course. An additional 21% will do this where the location is culturally 'difficult'
Travel/ Company Car		50% of companies report that senior managers travel business/club class; 37% report that senior managers travel economy class (possibly upgraded depending upon duration of flight). 43% report that other employees travel economy class. Economy class travel increases for home leave trips for all levels of staff	Majority permit all staff to travel business class (only 7% permit first class travel for Senior Managers)

continued overleaf

Table 5.2 *(continued)*

Component	ECA	ORC	PW
Travel/ Company Car *(continued)*	17% of companies provide a car scheme	The majority of companies provide a car/allowance: some always and others depending upon seniority, job need and/or local practice About 66% provide some assistance with purchase for employees who are ineligible for a car	93% either provide or give access to a company car in the host country 19% always provide a car, 13% if eligible prior to the secondment
Tax	76% provide tax equalization; ie, employee does not gain or lose 11% provide tax protection where company reimburses employee for taxes greater than hypothetical home country tax. Employee generally retains compensation where host country tax is less than hypothetical home tax	89% of respondents equalize tax; ie, employee pays no more tax in the host country than in the home country	46% of companies apply tax equalization (most common approach)

Sources: **ECA** - Employment Conditions Abroad Limited, November 1996. The survey results are based on 241 questionnaires, covering a wide cross-section of international companies. Over 45 per cent of participants each employed more than 50 expatriates. **ORC** - Organization Resources Counselors, Inc, August, 1995. This worldwide survey of international assignments policies and practices based its results from 351 organizations and 33,183 expatriates. **PW** - Price Waterhouse, 1995. Results were obtained from 180 companies, across 17 European countries.

Table 5.3 *Model expatriate reward policy*

Core component	Basis for calculation
Annual remuneration	
Base salary	• Host country market rate (gross)
Plus allowance	• Round sum allowance derived from dual approach build-up comparison
Long term benefits	
Pension	• Home country policy to continue
Life assurance and Prolonged Disability Insurance	• Home country policy to continue in first instance; if this not possible, host country policy or global policy to minimum standard of home policy will apply
Accommodation	
For home-owner	• Individual is responsible for meeting accommodation costs if no home country commitments
For non home-owner	• 'Excessive' accommodation costs only to be reimbursed in host country, unless already accounted for in host country salary/package or where accommodation of a reasonable standard is not available
House hunting assistance	• To be provided in accordance with host country policy
Relocation	
Freight	• Actual costs to be reimbursed for the shipping/air freight of personal effects (assumes furnished accommodation in the host country) – including pets and insurance
Temporary accommodation	• Up to 14 nights living expenses (including meals) in appropriate accommodation on arrival for employee, spouse or partner and dependants
Incidental expenditure	• A round sum allowance to be provided according to family size during the secondment and upon return
Familiarization trips	• To be considered on a case by case basis
Storage in home country	• Reimbursed only for renters of unfurnished properties in home country
Education and language training	
Nursery education	• Reimbursed up to 50% of excess cost over home country practice
Primary and Secondary	• Full cost of tuition, books and transport to be reimbursed if adequate non-fee paying schools unavailable in host country • Home boarding school fees and holiday visits

continued overleaf

Table 5.3 *(continued)*

Core component	Basis for calculation
Education and language training (continued)	
Language training	• Tuition provided for secondee to a standard appropriate to the needs of the secondment; language training provided for spouse or partner
Cultural awareness briefing	• To be provided for employee and spouse or partner
Spouse recognition	
Spouse/partner support	• Practical support should be made available in terms of ongoing education, job search etc
Travel	
Airfares	• Normally, economy class airfares for employee and dependants to be provided at the start and end of secondments
Home flights during secondment	• One home leave trip per annum. During final year of secondment, trip should be linked with career development/ repatriation discussions
Car policy	
Car policy	• Host country policy applies
Medical entitlement	
Medical cover	• Minimum cover to home country standards, either through home/host policy or other measures to fill gaps

REWARDS FOR LOCAL NATIONAL AND THIRD COUNTRY NATIONAL STAFF

Given that the significant majority of multinational organizations' employees are citizens of the countries in which they work, it is important that one understands the local practices and employee needs in various countries selected for international business activity. Such employees are rewarded based on local competitive market practices and local legislation, both of which have developed through the years, usually in a way unique to each country. It is not enough to take practices existing in one country and then apply them unaltered in another country (for example applying Anglo-Saxon incentive programmes in the Far East, in the Germanic territories, or

South America). Practitioners supporting internationalizing businesses need to study the local market closely, to identify what is competitive and what reward systems will support the process of attracting, motivating, retaining and developing good employees for sustained high performance.

Consequently, an internationalizing business must make some strategic choices, controlling the extent to which they will operate as a 'local' firm versus that of a 'foreign controlled' business. While it is true that some of the options are mandated by the local, national or international legislative frameworks, many are within control of the company. Often, organizations do not develop strategic global philosophies to provide guidance in making these reward choices. This can result in inconsistent and often inappropriate reward and performance management practice.

In helping to frame questions surrounding the policies and practices to be adopted in determining local rewards, I have found it helpful to draw upon the model shown in Figure 5.8.

Essentially, this model helps us, in building a total compensation framework for a particular territory, to think through the issues of regulation, indicators for the sector and for those appropriate to the particular business. It also prompts us to frame views of what management, both locally and at 'the centre', and any investing partners, anticipate. In addition it enables us to build some understanding around the critical area of employee expectations. The model then encourages us to go on and consider both short, medium and long term goals for reward strategy. It helps us to make decisions surrounding the degree of variable reward and 'gearing' which will be appropriate to the local situation. It then asks us to take some view of the management process for performance improvement and the framework for monitoring, evaluating and gradually evolving the practices themselves over time.

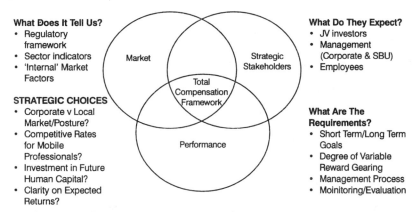

Figure 5.8 *Reward planning and design – convergence factors.*

Table 5.4 *Frequency of salary payments around the world.*

UK	12 months
USA	12 months
Germany	13.3 months/statutory requirement
France	13 months/statutory requirement
Singapore	13 months/statutory requirement
Thailand	13 months/statutory requirement
Philippines	13 months/statutory requirement
Mexico	up to 14 months/statutory requirement
Venezuela	13–14 months/statutory requirement
Malaysia	up to 14 months/statutory requirement
Italy	14 months/statutory requirement
Korea	18 months/statutory requirement
Japan	variable 'bonus' months/trade practice

Finally, the model will remind us to make some strategic choices, comparing the corporate versus local market postures, and to determine what our competitive rates for mobile professionals and other groups of staff are. It will also facilitate choices around the question of whether the organization wishes to invest in future local human capital, offsetting this against the ongoing costs of expatriates. However, it will also begin to force decisions regarding the expected returns from investment – whether this is expatriate or locally focused.

REGULATION AND CUSTOM

It is important to be aware that statutory regulations and local custom and practice influence the frequency with which basic pay is delivered in different parts of the world.

These factors require careful investigation and analysis in specific circumstances, before corporate decisions are taken regarding reward management options for individuals and groups recruited or acquired as part of international business expansion. Different strategies are likely to apply in acquisition situations, compared with greenfield developments, which may offer significant scope to establish company-preferred reward plans and processes counter to local norms.

PERFORMANCE-RELATED REWARD

The concept of *pay for performance* can have different relevance in different territories, for example, as follows:

❑ Japan: progression is based on age and service
❑ France: based on service and performance
❑ Latin America: in early stages of acceptance
❑ Eastern Europe and China: the concept is new

Throughout much of the world, 'automatic' pay progression is the accepted norm: people are rewarded for who they are, or how long they have been there, rather than what they contribute to the organization's performance. Equally, there are instances (eg, Germany, Mexico, Taiwan) where the concept of 'acquired rights' in employment makes it difficult to reverse pay practices.

One must anticipate challenges, therefore, in attempting to export what are deemed to be sound western practices for performance management and reward on a cross-cultural basis and integrate them into the host country and its employment environment. It does not mean it cannot be done. My own recent experience of this has included going into the southern part of Europe; into East Asia; and the Indian subcontinent for example. I am currently attempting to do likewise in a Central/Eastern European environment, as part of a fundamental change programme with the introduction of private capital, and a more commercialized business regime, to an erstwhile state-owned enterprise. The challenge is to balance strategic and cultural imperatives, taking account of the ethnic and collectivist environment in which one is seeking to operate.

It has been suggested that the introduction of performance related pay simply will not work. Of course there are the critics of performance-related pay in Anglo-Saxon businesses, let alone in the developing world. However, having spent time researching what had already been achieved by organizations, both international and local, in introducing some of those practices which provide a greater focus between individual and team performance and their outcomes and rewards, it certainly proved possible to achieve the company's aspirations to do likewise in our own circumstances.

In Southern Europe, for example, we recognized, and accommodated, the cultural norms there; a rather more collectivist environment where at least at a national and political level trade union activity was far more pronounced than tends to be the case nowadays in the Anglo-American *laissez-faire* environments. Account also needed to be taken of the more *feminine* cultural values which form a part of this cultural environment. An added twist to the project was the cocktail of nationalities involved in the management process itself.

The project was a joint venture drawing inputs from the UK, France, Spain and Portugal. We needed to ensure that we spent time understanding what would motivate all these individuals to find a common purpose, and to ensure that, in designing the actual reward scheme relevant for their circumstances, we were able to respect and indeed gain leverage from the cultural environment in which we were seeking to make our performance-related reward arrangement work. We just made sure that we did spend time, and that the local line management spent time, aided by the HR team, in developing the necessary credibility as well as capability to design arrangements, communicate them effectively, and to implement them soundly, which would deliver performance-related reward management reflecting the more collectivist, more structured, traditionally seniority-based setting.

There was an emphasis on team rewards, where individuals could be rewarded by the way in which they were judged to contribute to the operation of team performance as a whole. We spent a lot of time explaining there was nothing that would be threatening from the arrangement, and that great advantage would exist for individuals to work with the regime, within the overall parameters of cost and outcomes required, to tailor it relevant to the business circumstances in which they found themselves.

Expatriate: local tensions

Lifestyle and standard of living comparisons between people working side by side, can represent a major cause for in-company friction. This is enacted through the highly visible effects of reward policy where 'home' market rates plus international terms for expatriate personnel create a sense of inequity among local colleagues undertaking similar activity for the firm. The situation becomes even more compounded where companies are trying to find an opportunity to 'park an employee in oblivion', as one commentator expressed it to me recently. Where there is no value-added the local staff are even more demotivated.

People tend to fully understand where someone, at short notice, is parachuted in to 'put out a fire'. This may involve uprooting their family and managing related domestic upheavals. Where one can be clear on the justification for an expatriate – if one can communicate the differences and achieve local buy-in – differentials are not a problem.

However, where these roles are purely for development purposes – where one sees the more junior individual adding less value than the more experienced local, or where it is a 'parking' situation – uncomfortable issues can arise, which can lead to a reduction in the value-added by the local team overall. The long term dis-benefits are very real risks for the organization concerned to consider and address.

Here is an example of such tensions, experienced in Southern Europe. A few years ago, I heard that a multinational energy company had a group of British and Spanish PhD-qualified physicists working alongside one another, at an installation in Madrid, engaged on research into solar panels for electricity generation. The Spaniards were paid 6m pesetas per month, whereas the expatriates, while receiving the same salary of 6m pesetas, in addition received a ten per cent cost of living allowance, together with housing provided free of charge in one of the most up-market areas of Madrid, close to the plant, and also close to the international schools. So, the British PhDs being deployed on an expatriate basis in Madrid were receiving, all told, 2½ times as much as their local colleagues for exactly the same job and contribution. In addition, company cars were provided to the Brits 'because they were expatriates', but not to the locals. Inevitably, relations were not harmonious.

More imaginative companies now are finding ways to negotiate with individuals being expatriated to accept they must forego certain 'on the ground benefits' during the course of the assignment, on the basis that they will be rewarded financially and in other ways on termination of the assignment, when they are no longer visibly part of a 'ghetto' community.

Regional skills – premium rates

But what about the terms and conditions for employing individuals who are identified as part of a corporation's international cadre from within a particular region, from which they are drawn, and in which they are likely to remain for most or all of their career? Given the intensive competition for scarce skills in a variety of environments – the 'tiger' economies of South East Asia are a particularly fine example – the price that organizations have to pay has increased exponentially over the last decade. I have found, in these cases, that imagination and flexibility have been an essential ingredient.

There was a situation I experienced, where a high level search had been launched to recruit a regional director to run a business development team covering the whole of the Far East sector. The search, which itself had not been without difficulties – finding individuals with the right combination of Asian values and links, with the western sense of urgency – had been an interesting challenge both for me and the search consultants in its own right. Eventually, however, we found the ideal candidate. This was an individual with an impressive background of working both in an Asian and western environment, for a leading multinational US corporation, operating out of Singapore. However, it looked as though the assignment might fail due to our difficulty in balancing the need to recruit an individual at the going market rate with the realities of a domestic business in rationalization mode, where internal relativities would be adversely affected.

In the end, the way round it was to treat this individual as though he was an expatriate living in his own country(!). We found a way to set a salary and incentive regime which would reflect the going-rate for the job applicable across the organization. However, we were able to find other ways in which to provide additional finances – as a halfway house measure, as we began to develop the organization's corporate reward arrangements, to bring them into line with the aspirations of this new internationalizing business – such that the individual was suitably motivated to sign his contract, while ensuring that the organization's corporate needs were not unduly compromised.

I experienced a similar challenge in the course of integrating a top management team in the North American market. This was a group who had been acquired with the business which we had acquired at the same time. Their reward arrangements were to say the least extremely generous and imaginative. However, they were grounded in what had been a very successful start-up business operation.

The organization had been formed as a subsidiary to a business where this activity was something of a side-line. However, the organization was starved of cash at that time, and limited investment funds were available. However, the business team had managed to deploy themselves in a way to create extremely lucrative additional new business and new revenues for the parent corporation. In addition they had grown a business to the extent that it could be packaged up and sold as a going concern at a premium to an interested and willing buyer. All of this meant revenues for the original parent organization which otherwise might not have been available.

The individual executives had ensured that, by virtue of their reward arrangements, which had evidently been negotiated fairly early on in the organization's life, they would have a stake in and hence access to a significant share of the new value which they had created. The challenge here was to convince a European parent board that, as part of their North American investment programme, they had to accept that the top team they had acquired might, at times, receive total reward levels above their own. This was the market context; and talent to grow the business had its price. A long-term talent-linked business investment perspective was needed.

Continental rewards

The increased mobility of labour, particularly across regions of the world, is giving rise to the notion of 'continental' pay and conditions. So, third country nationals are being deployed by international businesses between a variety of countries close to their country of origin, but within a regional geographical setting. These intra-regionally mobile executives are individuals who either do not aspire to or are not appropriate for membership of a truly global executive cadre. However, they increasingly have skills which businesses find appropriate to deploy across their regional operations, and individuals are prepared to comply with this for career development reasons.

A heavy investment emphasis in certain regions of the world in particular, for example, the high growth Asian countries means that supply and demand are pushing up the rates across the region necessary to acquire, retain, and motivate talent. This is providing some interesting comparisons between the developing and mature economies. In a survey by consultants William M. Mercer Inc, it has been estimated that in some growing Asian economies, managers' 1997 salary increases will outpace local inflation rates by a wide margin. This situation contrasts with the experience in the United States, Canada and much of Western Europe, where differentials between managers' salary growth and the consumer price index will be much smaller. The same study projects double digit 1997 salary increases for managers in India, China, Thailand, Indonesia, and Hong Kong.

Another international consultancy, Towers Perrin, recently conducted interviews with personnel directors at 50 multinational companies which are major players in Europe. The parent countries for these organizations were spread between the UK, the US, Japan, and continental European countries. The topic for consideration was the impact on human resource and reward practices of the coming introduction of the single European currency. Writing in *People Management* magazine, Don Cuthbert (1997), reveals that the vast majority had no plans to prepare for a single currency. When forced to think about the issue, the personnel directors tended mainly to expect an optimal currency area, similar to that existing in North America, with general mobility of labour, pan-European employment policies, and harmonization of pay and conditions across member countries. The scenario, he says, will, in reality 'lead to a fundamental transformation of the labour market. It will be much harder for multinationals to hide the fact that they are paying more to employees in one member state than to those in another'. There is currently a wide variation in basic pay according to the different costs of living in each country across Europe. There is also a wide variation in the level of compulsory employer social insurance contributions, which are the highest in France and lowest in the UK. Clearly such differences would be difficult to sustain under the scenario which has been proposed, Cuthbert argues.

Towers Perrin forecast two possible routes towards harmonization of

European pay and benefits. One would be a levelling up of pay across Europe, with salary rates increasing to match those in the highest paying countries. Alternatively, they believe the EU may define convergence criteria and provide bands within which countries must operate. So, employers operating in Europe need to analyse their existing pay systems in all their operations, identify where there is convergence, and look at how they communicate with their employees on these issues. They will then need to devise a strategy based on the EU convergence criteria and implementation timetable. In this way they will be able to identify which practices they need to change as a result of the single currency.

One global corporation's region: country reward management mix

Region-wide, a key European strategic issue for IT company Hewlett Packard currently, is harmonization of the *management process* of reward, and reviewing the fundamental question: is the pay system delivering against intended corporate goals?

Taking the second issue first:

❏ At present, in continental Europe, they have been concerned about a seniority/time serving bias (this is an issue in Germany for example). Reward systems quickly become outdated. When driven by a workers' council/trade union agenda, the outcome is a seniority based pay organization. Hewlett Packard's business agenda is performance biased, so a culture clash results.

❏ The company is also trying to reduce the amount of job evaluation-based pay across the region ('too much of a burden'). They are asking: 'Can we comply with equal pay regulations without traditional (ie, job evaluation) tools: is this the lazy man's way?'

❏ They are applying more and more US-style approaches, as part of a 'catch-up' programme. Neal Wagner, HP's European Compensation Manager told me: 'The European Region now is where the US was some years ago'. Neal says the response has been constructive. 'People are open to the new techniques – our customers want harmony with US/corporate processes, and our people appreciate this flows right through to reward practice'.

The key process aspect of HP's harmonization initiative, is:

❏ 'We're asking how can we run a seamless European organization, rather than one where process gets duplicated country by country; we can no longer afford the "value added" of each country's ideas.

❏ 'So we're looking at job families, levelling and scoping jobs, to put in place simpler processes.

❑ 'At present, for example, if we have an employee based in Italy, but part of the regional team, two people are involved in doing the personnel management role in relation to performance and reward issues. The argument is that it's too complex for a manager outside the country to be taught the techniques and "rules" needed to pay an Italian (ditto for each Euro country). Our regional response now is:
— either find ways to teach the in-line manager, or
— simplify the process.
'We're therefore implementing remote management – it's how we're structured for business so the question is why can't we run personnel processes this way too?'

INTRA-REGION MOBILITY AND DIVERSITY

Sitting in one part of the world, it is very easy for human resource professionals to think of other regions as homogenous in their customs, practices, laws and approaches to rewarding employees. The reality is significantly different, and inappropriate managerial action must be guarded against at every possible step.

Consider the following two major regions as examples.

Europe

Scandinavian countries have a high level of social benefits. The UK provides company cars to a very wide population, despite changes in fiscal practice. In German company pension plans, employees require ten years in-post for vesting purposes. In Hungary, western reward practices seem to be accelerating more quickly than in Poland.

Asia-Pacific

Pay levels are still relatively low in India, Borneo, and the Philippines. Conversely, pay levels tend to be high in Hong Kong and Singapore. In some areas in India and in China, housing is provided as part of the total reward package. In Malaysia, there is a typical 48 hour week, yet Singapore is closer to a 42–44 hours per week. In Japan, housing allowances are provided to staff, and promotions reflect age and service.

In terms of vast geographical territories, such as China, these can act as a region on their own with variation between coastal China, rural China, and major cities such as Beijing.

Other factors which have tended to characterize certain regions include inflation. Latin and South America tend to be dubbed as high inflation countries. In reality, this tends to be concentrated in countries such as Venezuela. Countries such as Chile, for example, have very low levels of inflation.

INTERNATIONAL VALUES AND REWARD POLICY

Let's look in a little more depth at the concept of diversity. Not just in custom and practice, but in terms of fundamental values, or 'world views'. International reward strategies need to be examined in terms of what they deliver for corporate performance. Studies of 'cultural differences' suggest that reward system design and management needs to be tailored to local values, to enhance the performance of overseas operations.

The question of cultural values goes to the heart of the purpose of reward strategies, which is to deliver corporate performance. However, research I am presently undertaking together with my colleagues, Professor Chris Hendry and Paola Bradley, at City University Business School, suggests that cultural difference studies are too generalistic and fail to provide an adequate guide to the design and management of reward systems. It is necessary to incorporate attention to corporate and industry effects, since it is companies, within national legal structures and in managing specific business environments, which design reward systems and have to cope with problems involved in managing them. Therefore, our programme of study is investigating reward systems through the specific lens of particular multinational enterprises (MNEs) in particular cultural contexts.

Increasingly, researchers and practitioners alike are concluding that the exportability of management theories and practices is determined by the comparability of the cultural values between the importing and exporting nation. For example, Mamman *et al.*, (1996) observe: 'Depending on their cultural backgrounds, it would seem that employees will perceive criteria for pay systems differently. Thus organizations operating across borders should take these potential differences into account when rewarding their employees.'

The Strategic Remuneration Research Centre is engaged in a wide ranging programme of research into 21st century reward strategies, with the support of a consortium of blue-chip multinationals. One sponsor recently observed that: 'Reward management and incentivization may need to be targeted for different countries. Having a global bonus scheme is a bit of a "holy grail". The benefits, however, would be convenience, control, national understanding and the ability to move people between regions more easily.'

Cultural dimensions likely to have an impact on performance management and reward systems so far identified by the centre include:

❏ individualism versus collectivism (eg; differences in how bonuses are paid)
❏ acceptance of failure
❏ openness to discuss performance issues ('face' and seniority)
❏ quantum (for example, how much more for incremental effort and the size of differentials)
❏ the appropriate balance between reward and penalties.

TOWARDS A MODEL OF NATIONAL CULTURE AND REWARDS

According to Schiffman and Kanuk (1994): 'A value is a relatively enduring belief that serves as a guide for what is regarded as appropriate behaviour and is widely accepted by members of a society. Values differ from beliefs in that:

1. they are relatively few in number
2. they serve as a guide for culturally appropriate behaviour
3. they are enduring or difficult to change
4. they are not tied to specific objects or situations
5. they are widely accepted by members of a society.'

Values help to determine what we think is right and wrong, what is important and what is desirable. Values will therefore affect how management practices are interpreted by members of a society. When employees from one culture work in an organization operating another culture's management practices, differences between the two cultures may become 'painfully evident' (Gaugler, 1988). One of the attributes of culture is that it can foster a type of ethnocentrism whereby practices or activities that do not conform to an individual's view of conducting business are viewed negatively. There are undoubtedly different 'realities' and views of the world and MNEs are likely to increase their chance of success by understanding the socio-cultural system of the regions in which they operate. They need to be sensitive to different cultural values when designing their performance management systems and reward policy. However, sensitivity of a particular managerial function to cultural or value differences depends on the importance of direct exchange between that function and the cultural environment. Functions such as human resources and marketing, for example, demand more interaction with the local culture than, say, finance (Bradley, 1991).

In a study of matched Chinese and UK companies (Easterby-Smith *et al.*, 1995), there was a marked difference between UK and Chinese companies with regard to reward systems, but consistency within each country, which the researchers directly attributed to 'deep-seated differences between the two countries with regard to attitudes towards rewards'. The likely impact on performance that such practices might have – whether derived from the global parent or adapted to the locality – needs to be considered. More specifically, it is the effect practices have on host country nationals and the cumulative effect on performance of the MNE subsidiary in the host country which needs to be key in decision making. Evidence suggests that, if management practices are inconsistent with deeply held values, this can negatively affect performance. Conversely, management practices which reinforce national cultural values are likely to result in greater self-efficacy and higher performance (Kotter and Heskett, 1992; Earley, 1994). According to Newman and Hollen (1996), the implication for MNE managers is that, to achieve high performance outcomes, it is better to adapt to local cultural conditions.

CULTURAL DUALITIES AND THEIR REWARD IMPLICATIONS

Various writers have attempted to classify the main cultural dimensions appropriate for international comparisons. Geert Hofstede's work based on an extensive study of employees in IBM subsidiaries (1981) has undoubtedly been the most influential, originally yielding four dimensions; ten years later, he added a fifth.

Bento and Ferreira (1992) have produced the most detailed review of the potential impact on rewards of different cultural values. Based on Hofstede's work, they identified the cultural assumptions which would have relevance for compensation plans and organized them into five dualities. These five taken together, they suggest, comprise a 'cultural lens' through which to view different interest groups' underlying assumptions regarding reward systems. The dualities are:

❑ equality versus inequality;
❑ certainty versus uncertainty;
❑ controllability versus uncontrollability;
❑ individualism versus collectivism; and
❑ materialistic versus personalistic foregrounding.

In addition to the dualities comprising their 'cultural lens', there are three other dimensions which are likely to impact on reward systems. These are:

❑ short-term versus long-term orientation

❑ emphasis on people, ideas or action
❑ emphasis on abstractive or associative modes of information processing.

The following tables, extracted from Bento and Ferreira's 1992 work, explore the issues arising from these classifications.

Table 5.5 summarizes the implications for designing and managing rewards deriving from the equality and inequality assumptions.

Table 5.5   *Equality and inequality*

Issue	Equality	Inequality
Planned decision making	Widespread participation by various stakeholders	Centralized decisions by elite group
Link between pay and hierarchy	Loosely related	Closely related
Desired range of diversity in pay	Small differentials	Large differentials
Likelihood of differences in performance	Homogeneous individual performance leading to skewed distribution of outcomes	Normal distribution of potential leading to normal distribution of outcomes
Performance measure	Absolute	Relative
Setting goals and monitoring performance	Facilitated by small power distances	Hindered by large power distances
Contról focus	Inputs	Outputs

Reprinted by permission of *Harvard Business Review.* Ex. 6.2 from *Performance Measurement, Evaluation, and Incentives* by William J. Bruns Jr, 1992, p. 161. Copyright © 1992 by the President and Fellows of Harvard College; all rights reserved.

Table 5.6 highlights the reward design and management issues arising from the certainty/uncertainty duality. Note that the issues identified will differ from table to table because the sets of assumptions will have a bearing on some issues, but not on others. ·

Table 5.6 *Certainty versus uncertainty*

Issue	Certainty	Uncertainty
Primary aim in plan design	Identifying and spelling out behaviours that will lead to desired outcomes	Linking high rewards to desired outcomes and letting participants figure out instrumental behaviour
Security	Plan nurtures feelings about position, rewards and progress	Plan discourages feelings of entitlement to present position and reward levels
Performance measure	Tactical, operational	Strategic
Control focus	Inputs	Outputs

Reprinted by permission of *Harvard Business Review*. Ex. 6.3 from *Performance Measurement, Evaluation, and Incentives* by William J. Bruns Jr, 1992, p. 162. Copyright © 1992 by the President and Fellows of Harvard College; all rights reserved.

Table 5.7 outlines the effect the controllability/uncontrollability duality is likely to have on reward strategy design and implementation.

Table 5.7 *Controllability versus uncontrollability*

Issues	Controllability	Uncontrollability
Expected effect of motivation on results	Large (people can affect results in right direction if motivated)	Limited (desire to achieve results is not enough to achieve them)
Causes of success or failure	Controllable and internal (individual, group or company)	Limited or no control and external (environment)
Performance measure	Absolute	Relative
Control focus	Inputs or outputs	Planned inputs plus adaptive behaviours or outputs adjusted for uncontrollables

Reprinted by permission of *Harvard Business Review*. Ex. 6.4 from *Performance Measurement, Evaluation, and Incentives* by William J. Bruns Jr, 1992, p. 164. Copyright © 1992 by the President and Fellows of Harvard College; all rights reserved.

Table 5.8 suggests the impact of individualism and collectivist values on reward systems and Table 5.9 illustrates the effect of materialistic and personalistic assumptions on reward issues.

Table 5.8 *Individualism versus collectivism*

Issue	Individualism	Collectivism
Organization's responsibility towards employees	Limited (survival of the fittest)	Moral obligation to shield employees from risk
Source of correction for possible unfairness in evaluation or compensation	Market mechanism	Multi-dimensional criteria, recognition of services rendered to collective group
Type of employee the plan seeks to attract and retain	Individuals who are risk-taking, mobile, cosmopolitan, enterprising	People who expect personal security and stability even when making risky decisions on behalf of the organization
Basis for attributing and rewarding attainment of goals	Individual	Group

Reprinted by permission of *Harvard Business Review*. Ex. 6.5 from *Performance Measurement, Evaluation, and Incentives* by William J. Bruns Jr, 1992, p. 165. Copyright © 1992 by the President and Fellows of Harvard College; all rights reserved.

Table 5.9 *Materialistic versus personalistic*

Issue	Materialistic Assumption	Personalistic Assumption
Source of motivation	Monetary incentives, needs for accomplishment	Interpersonal relationships, flexible mix of financial and non-financial rewards
Instrumental behaviours	Competition, striving	Co-operation, mentoring
Mechanisms for encouraging instrumental behaviours	Relative measures of performance, forced rating distributions	
Measure of personal worth	Contribution to attaining specified outcomes for the organization	Stable personal characteristics and skills, roles played in social systems

Reprinted by permission of *Harvard Business Review*. Ex. 6.6 from *Performance Measurement, Evaluation, and Incentives* by William J. Bruns Jr, 1992, p. 167. Copyright © 1992 by the President and Fellows of Harvard College; all rights reserved.

A recent dimension added by Hofstede (1991) is short-term versus long-term time horizon. It marks a dimension concerning attitudes and beliefs about time. On the one hand are western-style concepts; on the other, notions of long-term time orientation adapted from the Confucian idea of virtue versus truth.

Cross-cultural misunderstandings can occur because of differences in the concept of time. In the US for example, time is a commodity to be controlled for financial gain (note the expression 'time is money'). In other cultures this is considered vulgar and offensive (Taoka and Beeman, 1991).

Closely related to this is the cultural view of the future. For example, in the UK there is a major assumption that in business individuals can influence future events. For example, long-term incentive plans are designed with this in mind, with a view to motivating future performance. In other countries, such as in Latin America there is a much more fatalistic view which could affect the success of similar plans (Bradley *et al.*, 1997).

According to research carried out by Bond (1988) respondents with a long-term orientation are more concerned with the future. Reward plans should be evaluated in terms of the future benefit to be gained by a project or activity. For short-termists or past-oriented people, plans need to be evaluated in the context of societal customs and traditions and be firmly based on past experience. This adds an interesting dimension to the debate on whether bonuses should be rewards for past action or incentives for future performance.

Some commentators argue that the North American orientation to short-termism has meant that employees do not view long-term performance pay systems favourably.

Two further dimensions are worthy of mention. An emphasis on people, ideas or action, is based on the work of Bhagat *et al.* (1990). In cultures where people are emphasized, it is the quality of interpersonal relationships which is important. In cultures where ideologies are emphasized, sharing common beliefs is more important than social group membership. In cultures where action is emphasized, it is what is done which is more important than what is said. These factors are likely to have an effect on the appropriateness of reward philosophies. In particular, it will impact on issues of equity and equality, differentials and status.

Charles Hampden-Turner and Fons Trompenaars (1993) have added the dimensions of abstractive or associative modes of information processing. In cultures where associative modes of information processing are emphasized, processing is dependent on the context. In abstractive cultures there is a factual, inductive approach to information processing, independent of context. The approach taken will impact on the nature of truth and reality and the way these are determined. This is likely to have an impact on the applicability of different performance measures linked to rewards and the role of appraisals.

Ultimately, however, there is one central practical problem which limits the value of culturally focused studies in interpreting specific HR practices. That is, how does one reconcile the complex, potentially contradictory effects of culture, which as the previous discussion suggests, is multi-faceted?

BEYOND CULTURE: NATIONAL, INDUSTRY AND CORPORATE EFFECTS

Because of the inherent limitations in any attempt to define and measure culture with any degree of accuracy, my colleagues and I believe it is not enough to look solely to cultural difference studies to guide the design and management of reward systems. Other considerations dictate that it is also necessary to look to national, corporate and industry effects.

The choice of management practices in an MNE will be determined by the resolution of the conflict between 'opposing pressures for internal consistency and for isomorphism with the local institutional environment' (Rosenzweig and Nohria, 1994). On the one hand, seeking internal consistency by developing common compensation and benefits policies would facilitate the movement of employees across borders and preserve internal equity. On the other hand, pressures to conform to local practices may be too great to ignore.

There are a number of national, industry, and organizationally specific factors which will impact on the extent to which different practices can be designed to be 'global or multi-local'. In the case of performance management, this is relatively free of host country regulation, and management concern will be focused on striving for cross-national consistency. In contrast, pay determination of manual operatives is likely to be highly regulated and the interest of subsidiary policy coherence is less important.

The key elements of national business culture infrastructure as summarized in Bradley *et al.* (1997) are:

❑ the extent to which factors of production (location, physical, human and financial resources) differ from country to country
❑ the extent to which their economies differ in terms of their category contributions (eg, manufacture, service and agriculture)
❑ the human/machine balance, productivity and competitiveness levels
❑ the country's welfare state.

The relative effect of national values on reward systems will also depend on organization-specific factors such as:

❏ the degree of centralization or decentralization
❏ role of the line
❏ the composition of the line (expatriates or nationals)
❏ growth patterns
❏ degree of technological sophistication
❏ strength of 'corporate branding' (for example, the strength of corporate image may make it easier for firms like Coca-Cola or McDonald's successfully to adopt global reward strategies, regardless of national culture).

VIEWING REWARDS THROUGH THE MNE LENS

While the work of Hofstede (1981), introduced a new sensitivity to the appreciation of national culture in the context of MNE operations, it has also encouraged a crude stereotyping of cultural values in psychological terms divorced from institutional, legal and economic factors. Both levels of interpretation are necessary. However, both styles of enquiry are equally deficient insofar as they fail to take account of people and firms within specific socio-cultural systems. Generalized descriptions of the macro-environment may be equally weak as a guide to actual company behaviour as cultural simplifications, based on surveys, are to individual behaviour.

This points to the need for practitioners and scholars alike to adopt a different approach to international strategic reward management. The firm is the point of intersection at which cultural values and institutional pressures get worked out (Hendry, 1994). HR practices are a primary lightning conductor for this – none more so than rewards, since they embody enormously diverse and complex assumptions about the relations between people. Rewards also have the added significance that they are the expression of corporate attitudes towards performance. It may not be true for all aspects of HRM, but internationalizing companies seeking to define and develop their reward strategies could benefit from a more issue-based approach. 'This means, as an initial step, identifying the "hot" issues the corporation faces in designing and managing reward systems in different parts of the world, while taking account, also, of the particular stage of development and strategic objectives of the organization concerned' (Bradley *et al.*, 1997).

Such an 'inside-out' view would force attention to be given to:

❏ the corporate culture of the MNE

❏ parent country-of-origin effects contributing to corporate culture and reward policy

❏ developmental issues for the MNE and strategic objectives in informing reward policy in the particular location;

❏ local cultural sensitivities (a more useful word perhaps than 'values')

❏ legal and institutional factors in the host country which directly impact on reward management.

An 'issue-based' approach has the rather practical merit of addressing real concerns of managers in MNEs. It also provides a more rigorous and comprehensive focus for exploration through these five levels of analysis.

Let's have a look at the kinds of problems newly internationalizing firms have faced, in my experience, when wrestling with global/local pressures in different parts of the globe.

1. In Eastern Europe there is a keen anxiety to adopt 'western', particularly North American management techniques. As a result, local management tend to have a prescriptive orientation. In the case in question, they wanted to be told what to do and appeared to be unwilling to develop home-grown solutions. The difficulty for the MNE in this situation was to encourage local subsidiaries to take responsibility for designing rewards and other HR policies and practices. The historical circumstances of an economy and political system undergoing a radical transition mean sensitivity on the part of internationalizing managers is required in understanding the pace at which fundamental change can be achieved in introducing fit-for-purpose reward systems.

2. In the USA, in contrast, local management's attitude in an acquired subsidiary was that they knew best. They had been successful (so they believed). They therefore looked to the new parent simply to provide funding within an overall corporate strategy, and then to 'get out of the way'. This may be not uncommon with acquisitions in developed economies. Where there is a strong culture, however, around an issue like rewards, this can become a significant problem in dealing with an executive team. In this case, a North American culture of high financial rewards was reflected in a 'scorecard' mentality in which the executives were more concerned about their pay and status in relation to their US comparators than they were about the medium- to long-term performance requirements of the new parent MNE.

3. In South-East Asia, the pay, culture and strategic growth objectives took on another construction in that (a) the parent MNE needed to land an exceptional person to spearhead their development, but (b) pay in the home market for that person was restrained by local attitudes towards differentials, and (c) the Anglo-Saxon evaluation of a

'high quality' person was not sensitive to the quieter style of the Asian Manager.

4. The Asian environment presented a different problem in some other cases in China and the Indian subcontinent, where operating a plant meant the internationalizing firm acquiring a role in the community. This could be expressed as: 'you think you employ 1000 people (where the business should only require 200 people), but it effectively supports 10,000 people in the community (through families, etc).' The MNE therefore must factor into the investment strategy the cost of these responsibilities in the community, and has to understand this cultural base and be prepared to manage it. This inevitably touches on rewards.

5. Finally, one can compare this with two instances on opposite sides of the globe, in Southern Europe and Australia, where the employment environment is quite highly regulated; in the one case affecting labour management generally, in the other affecting the ability to deploy expatriates. Achieving reward strategy objectives requires fresh thinking, to accommodate local reality, without losing sight of overall corporate goals.

These examples involve different combinations of the five levels of analysis outlined earlier. The 'hot' topic in each case serves to expose the cultural, institutional, and organizational factors which featured in the particular country or region.

This suggests that, in developing policies to accompany international business development programmes, human resource professionals need to identify the reward issues faced, mindful that the definition of rewards is likely to go beyond simply pay and benefits, and embrace recognition and lifestyles as well. They must systematically investigate the complex factors bearing on these issues in each particular location, and then work with corporate and local colleagues to determine a response, adapting organizational principles to fit the local environment, to deliver desired results over the short, medium and long-term.

DESIGNING REWARDS FOR THE INTERNATIONALIZING BUSINESS UNIT

Finally, it is worth briefly making reference to the reward management challenge one faces working with an organization seeking to internationalize itself, and recognizing the need for a distinct cadre of individuals to spearhead the change. In my case, the business had recognized that its future depended on taking its core capabilities into the global market place. However, its top management had realized equally that, in order to create, develop and close the business opportunities to leverage those core capabilities, an additional type of talent was needed. There were a variety of approaches that could be adopted. We looked at a number of them, and acted on them. First, it was a case of going out and buying certain business assets; with them would come the local talent capable of developing the business on behalf of the new parent organization even further.

Secondly, the opportunity to partner with organizations in different parts of the world where new business opportunities existed, using their local know-how and contacts to develop business opportunities, coupled with our detailed technical contribution – including financing capability – for commercial advantage in alliances and joint venture situations. Thirdly, we actually went out to the market place to buy in talent needed in the short term to 'kick-start' the overall process. Quite clearly there was a price to be paid to secure such individuals with 'ready to run' skill sets. To complete this strategy we also looked to identify global capabilities and potential among the existing employee population, and to enhance these as part of a longer term capabilities development programme (see Chapter 4 for details).

What all of this meant, however, was the need to define a reward arrangement which could meet the requirements to pay the going rate to buy in talent, or to reflect what our partners were doing. It also meant creating the headroom within existing arrangements in order to compensate effectively those individuals that we had invested heavily in developing, who with that new know-how would become targets for other organizations, and who, we needed to ensure therefore had the motivation and incentive to remain with us, in order to provide the required return on the investment we had made in their development. However, with an existing, indigenous workforce in a situation where rationalization and downsizing were the order of the day, there was a real issue at corporate level about the need not to compromise internal relativities.

Therefore, we decided to take a generic look at our particular market place, to provide a rationale for introducing changes to the compensation structure for individuals who formed a part of that international cadre, who would not have commitments as to where their next assignment might be; who would be compared with the relevant international cadre in the external market place; and whose terms could be aspired to by indigenous employees when they had achieved the required technical and *behavioural* attributes to be able to perform in a similar way. We identified an appropriate market place, and surveyed organization structures, and the question of balancing internal and external market equity issues as experienced elsewhere. We also looked for examples of best practice; programmes which had been most successful in motivating employees, and those which had been best received by employees in return for their flexibility and mobility on an international front, in an environment of increasing competitive challenge and the pressures that that brought to bear on individuals' business and domestic lives.

Having gathered and evaluated this intelligence, we then developed proposals which the company's corporate management could sign on to, in the context of an implementation strategy which would be defensible in all corners of the business. We made sure that what would be required of individuals to comply with the requirements to operate on an international contract was fully communicated in a transparent form. We ensured there was a heavy emphasis on incentive arrangements, linking rewards to individual and collective performance, which could be measured and seen by the rest of the business in terms of the new business which was flowing in, as a result of the internationalists' efforts, creating positive opportunities for the business as a whole over the medium to longer term.

We also made sure that individuals from within the existing business, developing in internationalist terms themselves, could be recognized and placed on differential terms once they had qualified, not only in the sense of their technical capability, but in their demonstration of mobility and willingness to enter uncertain career situations, validating the reason for such action. We also introduced programmes in a development centre context whereby individuals who had expressed an interest in joining the international group were able almost to self-assess their capability to cope in that different environment, and hence to de-select themselves if they felt the new challenges were those which, at that particular stage in their working lives, they would not be able to deal with. In short, we created company-wide legitimacy for the 'new deal'.

In this way, there was a greater understanding between all employee groups as to the need for differential rewards, and exactly what the company was gaining in return for rewarding at higher levels in the international group compared with those which were appropriate for those in a less flexible/dynamic environment in the home country. In their case, reward strategy was geared to the important need to face the challenges of a shrinking domestic market place.

SUMMARY AND CHECKLIST

Setting and managing rewards in an internationalizing business context matches, in terms of complexity, the very process of developing international operations itself. Not only does the human resource professional, in support of line management, have to learn to manage this diversity and complexity of practice and expectations, there is a great deal of ambiguity to be managed in addition. Organizations are finding it essential to introduce a sense of balance between standardization of corporate practice – in order to communicate strategic business priorities to employees wherever they may be located, and to provide a sense of 'corporate glue' – while at the same time being responsive to the need for differentiation in terms of local culture, values, and market practice.

Moreover, there is an increasing move in a number of parts of the world to a geocentric approach, where regional trends and practices, accompanying the mobility of international executives and professionals, not only globally but intra-regionally need to be considered and accommodated. Such issues demand an analytical approach, patience to collect and analyse the relevant information to inform strategic options, and then the sensitivity to manage what may be potentially conflicting corporate and local reward policy requirements.

Figure 5.9, published in the *Journal of the American Compensation Association* (Autumn, 1992), seems to me very effectively to summarize the issues organizations are having to face up to in determining their international reward policy. These emerging trends in total remuneration reflect the growing number of globally mobile senior executives; moves towards increased simplicity, and cost and tax effectiveness of expatriate reward management; and the increasing importance of talented 'local nationals', who will make a difference between winning or not within a specific market place. Finally, it includes reference to the new breed of entry level employees who will develop global skills and experience before career and family constraints limit their mobility.

Organizations are recognizing the imperative of more effectively integrating their expatriate and local national remuneration. A look at the future suggests the emergence of truly international total remuneration. The smart organizations are already headed there, for business advantage. These trends suggest an increasing demand on the human resources function and the professionals of which it is comprised. For those capable of rising to the challenge, there is a tremendous opportunity to position themselves at the heart of internationalizing business strategy development and application.

The following questions need to be addressed in planning an international total remuneration strategy. Do the proposed policies and processes.

❑ Reinforce and focus energies on the achievement of business organization purpose?

EMPLOYEE CATEGORY	DEVELOPED COUNTRIES	DEVELOPING COUNTRIES	COMMENTS
Senior management	**Expatriates and Local Nationals** Host-country-driven salaries perquisites, and short-term incentives; home-country and/or globally unified long-term incentives and benefits; emphasis on flexibility and cost/tax effective delivery.	**Expatriates** Traditional expatriate packages with emphasis on cost- and tax-effective delivery and greater flexibility. **Local Nationals** Local-national packages with movement toward globally unified long-term incentives and benefits.	Growing number of globally mobile senior executives. Diminishing importance of headquarters country; multiple locations for division headquarters.
Middle management, professional and technical employees.	**Expatriates** Traditional headquarters, home-country and composite system; growth of regional systems for those who are regionally but not globally mobile. **Local Nationals** Local programs with some movement towards globally homogenised approaches.	**Expatriates** Same as in developed countries but somewhat more generous **Local Nationals** Same as in developed countries.	Employees for whom traditional systems were designed. Trend toward simplicity, mobility facilitation and cost/tax effectiveness.
Global trainees	Host-country compensation with modest supplements to subsidise short-term conditions of assignments.	Similar to traditional expatriate packages but with few financial incentives; a bare-bones approach with minimal allowances.	A new breed: entry-level employees who will develop global skills and experience before career and family constraints limit mobility.

Figure 5.9 *Emerging trends in total international remuneration.*
Reprinted with permission from ACA Journal, Autumn 1996, copyright © ACA

❏ Reflect a complete understanding of the needs and expectations of diverse employee groups across the international business?

❏ Follow a future-effective analysis of 'expatriate' reward priorities; for globally and regionally mobile professionals and executives?

❏ Provide a focus on where the business activity is to be conducted, and the requirement for cohesive teams, reinforced by how an organization's investment in reward is handled, rather than the geo-cultural source of particular individuals?

❏ Sensitively accommodate diverse world views and value sets, while nonetheless supporting an aligned corporate approach to an organization's people, wherever they are located?

❏ Integrate with total HRM strategic goals?

❏ Fully involve all stakeholders in setting and managing international rewards, with the benefit of a partnership between expert human resources professionals, navigating towards fit-for-purpose solutions, and line management and employee populations, ensuring ownership and acceptability at every level?

Chapter 6

Business Development – a Model for HRM Due Diligence

ACQUISITION OR GREENFIELD?

Not all internationalizing business development projects are of the same type. Some are purely acquisitions of existing enterprises (brownfield); others involve the development of the business – including often operational site construction – on a greenfield basis. In a number of cases, international ventures will be at some intermediate phase; for example, the acquisition a part completed manufacturing or process plant. The second major source of variation lies within the location of the business project itself. This may be located in the developed world or the developing world. The developed world would be defined as those countries of North America, Europe, Japan and Australasia where the capitalist system can be deemed to be mature. Developing countries lie in the emerging markets of the Far East; particularly the Chinese, South East Asian and Indian subcontinent regions, the Middle East, and of course those countries emerging from the previously communist European eastern bloc. Business opportunities are also being pursued with varying degrees of enthusiasm in Central and South America, and Africa, particularly the South, now it has emerged from isolation. Cultural, political and background economic factors in different parts of the world will significantly effect the human resource issues which will in turn affect the achievement of strategic business goals.

These two major sources of variation may be characterized independently. This gives rise to the need for a model for reviewing project issues, and conducting pre-investment due diligence, under four principal business development headings (see Figure 6.1). Using the model will enable human resource professionals to position themselves at the centre of strategic debate on both commercial business development and harvesting return on investments, anticipating the 'big ticket' risks, and designing and implementing strategies tailored to the cultural and structural circumstances of international ventures.

A FRAMEWORK FOR INTERPRETING INTERNATIONAL PROJECT HR ISSUES

The model in Figure 6.1 is intended to provide a generic framework to assist in the interpretation of the focus for HR activity in approaching business acquisitions or greenfield developments on an international basis. Table 6.1 builds on this to provide an overview of those issues which will need to be addressed in various international business development activities, from both a line management and human resource professional point of view. In addition, there are a number of tools and information sources which it is suggested will be helpful to have to hand in assessing the viability of the project and the human resource consequences in each case.

Figure 6.1 *Projects issues matrix.*

Table 6.1 *International business projects – generic HR model*

Issues to be Addressed	Line Activity	HR Activity	Tools/ Information
The Project itself Capabilities required for the project	Evaluate the capabilities required for the project		HR Manual HRM database
Country labour and business practices	Establish critical issues and evaluate	Develop proposals for an operating framework	HR Manual and HRM database. Cultural Due Diligence
Organization	Develop and cost staffing proposals in the eventual business units		Organization checklist (Chapter 3)
The Project Team Capabilities required for the project team	Evaluate the capabilities required for the project team		HR Manual
Capabilities in the territory and partners	Evaluate the skills and competences available within the territory and with prospective partners	Provide a format for gathering evaluation intelligence	HR Manual HR people audit and career management plans
Project team structure and staffing	Identify the team structure required and possible membership – in particular, project manager	Review and provide intelligence Operate selection process Identify available people Identify development opportunities	HR Manual HRM database HR people audit Management development process

The four column headings above are used for each project phase. Note the distinction made between activities to be addressed in the project itself and within the project team.

The subsequent series of tables cover the steps for considering the issues which need to be addressed and likely action taken at various stages of developing international business ventures. The seven phases are:

❑ Phase I — concept
❑ Phase II — evaluation
❑ Phase III — offer
❑ Phase IV — negotiation
❑ Phase V — project close
❑ Phase VI — implementation
❑ Phase VII — operation

Among the sources of information, development by the organization of an HR Manual and HRM Database, tailoring to its own circumstances policy and process guidelines such as those available in this book, and intelligence collected in various 'target' territories is invaluable. This strategic supplement to HRM tools and techniques will assist in capturing learning as part of the internationalization experience, assisting subsequent phases and project teams to benefit from an emerging 'corporate memory'. This can become a key aspect of the organization's leading-edge capability for international commercial advantage.

The HR issues considered would be those which affect the risk assessment of the project in very broad terms.

Table 6.2 *Phase I: Concept*

Issues to be Addressed	Line Activity	HR Activity	Tools/ Information
The Project itself Capabilities fit	Strategic Business Unit to consider	Review proposal and provide intelligence	HR aspects of 'Corporate Memory'
Country labour framework	Consider impact of critical items	Review proposal and provide intelligence	HR Manual
Country business practices	Consider impact of critical items	Review proposal and provide intelligence	HR Manual
The Project Team Strategic Business capability	Ensuring availability and adequacy of skills and staff	Provide ongoing and effective recruitment, training, assessment and development	Recruitment process International Development Centres

The evaluation phase is a development of the concept phase. As numbers are now being considered, the factors listed earlier require more detail in their working through.

During this phase the project team begins to take shape, involving HR in support activity.

Table 6.3 *Phase II: Evaluation*

Issues to be Addressed	Line Activity	HR Activity	Tools/ Information
The Project itself			
Capabilities required for the project	Evaluate the capabilities required for the project		HR Manual
Country labour and business practices	Establish critical issues and evaluate	Develop proposals for an operating framework	HR Manual and Cultural Due Diligence methods
Organization	Develop and cost proposals for staffing areas of responsibility in the eventual business(es)	Support development of staffing proposals	Organization Checklist HR Manual
The Project Team			
Capabilities required for the project team	Evaluate the capabilities required for the project team		HR Manual
Capabilities in the territory and partners	Evaluate the skills and competences available with the territory and within prospective partners	Provide a format for the evaluation and evaluation intelligence	HR Manual Corporate Intelligence Career Management Process
Project team structure and staffing	Identify the team structure required and possible membership, in particular, project manager	Review and provide intelligence Operate selection process Identify available people Identify development opportunities	HR Manual Management process

Table 6.4 *Phase III: Offer*

Issues to be Addressed	Line Activity	HR Activity	Tools/ Information
The Project itself Project manning	Develop manning model with costs. Include: • Expatriates • Partners • Local hires	Develop manning model framework. Develop reward arrangements for expatriates and locals Advise on local consultancy support Provide intelligence and advice on capabilities available and local assessment and development.	HR Manual International Assignment policy (Chapter 5) HRM database
Control of labour issues	Develop agreements for controlling labour factors: benefits, pay, training, monitoring procedures etc.	Develop framework for agreements	HR Manual HRM database
Project team support	Arrange all local issues – visas, accommodation etc.	Provide support as required	International Assignment policy
The Project Team Plant project manager	Select	Provide assessment and selection process Identify available people	HR Manual HRM database
Team information	Structure team	Provide assessment and selection process Review structure with line Identify available people	HR Manual HRM database

Issues to be Addressed	Line Activity	HR Activity	Tools/ Information
Team development	Identify need	Carry out needs analysis. Provide cultural and other programmes. Provide briefing packages for 'technical visitors'	HR Manual Capabilities Development Champions Briefing packages National Information Packs HR planning framework Development centres
Individual development	Incorporate development position	Identify opportunities for development	Performance and development Planning programme

Table 6.5 *Phase IV: Negotiation*

Issues to be Addressed	Line Activity	HR Activity	Tools/ Information
The Project itself Project manning revisited	Confirm manning model with costs Include: • Expatriates • Partners • Local hires	Refine manning model Provide intelligence on capabilities available Develop local HR framework Advise on skills development for local recruitment	HR Manual International Assignment policy
Maintenance of the integrity of the HR proposals	Negotiate	Provide support to negotiators Review proposals to ensure that the HR strategy remains consistent	

continued overleaf

Table 6.5   *(continued)*

Issues to be Addressed	Line Activity	HR Activity	Tools/ Information
The Project team Development of team	Identify shortfalls in team skills and competences	Arrange provision of training and support activities	Team performance review HR Manual
Site construction manager	Identify possible candidate	Provide assessment and selection framework, candidate lists and instruments	HR Manual HRM database

Table 6.6   *Phase V: Close*

Issues to be Addressed	Line Activity	HR Activity	Tools/ Information
The Project itself General Manager	Identify possible candidate	Provide assessment and selection process and candidate lists	HR Manual HRM database
(Joint) Venture board	Identify structure	Provide assessment and selection framework, candidate lists and instruments	Management development process
Project manning revisited	Confirm manning model with costs, including expatriates, partners, local hires Confirm arrangements for implementation	Refine/develop resourcing model with the line	HR Manual HRM database

Table 6.7 *Phase VI: Implementation*

Issues to be Addressed	Line Activity	HR Activity	Tools/ Information
The Project itself			
Members of (JV) board	Appoint board members	Advise on candidates and criteria	Executive development policy
Operations and Commercial Group(s)	Manage build up of group(s) Appoint HR specialist	Recruitment processes – HR framework	HR Manual International Assignment policy HRM database
Job Design and Performance Management	Incorporate PM system Implement Performance Planning and goal setting	Monitor implementation and arrange provision of support and training	HR Manual Performance development and Planning system
Environment Health and Safety	Produce EH&S procedures	Provide intelligence on best practice and local requirements	HR Manual
Development of local teams	Ensure business, technical and team development	Provide structures and packages	HR Manual Terms and conditions statements
The Project team			
Maintenance of project team	Adaptation of team to phase requirements	Assessment and selection process for new members and placement of returning members	HR Manual International Assignment policy

Table 6.8 *Phase VII: Operation*

Issues to be Addressed	Line Activity	HR Activity	Tools/ Information
Maintenance of best practice-	Ensure that best practice standards are known and implemented	Provide / ensure linkage to group HRM initiatives to maintain company's international standing	HR Manual Best practice bulletins and updates HR Audits
Development of the line team	Role development, recruitment of new staff, induction and assessment and development of new staff	Incorporate developmental activities / placements	International assignment policy Career Management Policy

MANAGING STRATEGIC INTERNATIONAL INVESTMENTS

We now look specifically at some mechanics in relation to making acquisitions and greenfield developments work, in people management terms. So often, once the deal is done and the commercial people have flown home, existing management teams are left wondering how best to ensure the success of a new international venture. That venture will be successful through the combination of the efforts, commitment and talents of the people involved. Those people will involve both the successful investor, as well as any local people who have been acquired as part of the venture.

It is of great benefit to internationalizing businesses to stop and think seriously and systematically about the way in which they will enable all those concerned with managing business unit investments to meet their strategic goals.

In my experience, it is useful to undertake this series of steps:

❑ Establish guidelines on the company's strategic objectives in asset development and acquisition, which will assist at the time targets are identified.

❑ Review core capabilities to ensure the organization is well organized to handle turnaround situations.

❑ Identify people across the parent organization, who will be those best placed to provide the support to project and team leaders in the valu-ations, development, due-diligence work, and implementation of their projects

❑ Provide focused training and business awareness, to ensure financial and commercial success from implementation.

❑ Provide suitable capabilities development modules to add with corpo-rate training programmes (see Chapter 4).

The tables on the following pages attempt to set out the core HR levers and principles for developing capability in relation to the management of international investments.

HR DUE DILIGENCE FACTORS

In working with business development teams expanding internationally, HR professionals need to add value to the process of interpreting busi-ness opportunities. One of the ways in which this can be done is through collaboration with commercial and finance colleagues in the due diligence process. This needs to apply whether the project is an acquisition of an existing or partly completed operation, or whether it is to engage in the development of a greenfield opportunity.

I have found it helpful to work with a set of checklists, to ensure that a whole series of angles necessary to understanding the likely benefits to be derived from a project, whether or not it fits the organization's strategic business objectives, and also to determine the basis of an investment value for negotiation purposes are highlighted. In this way, the HR professional can add value to the process of interpreting and developing business opportunities, as well as ensuring an effective approach to negotiation and project close.

The following checklist (Table 6.10, starting on page 150) is intended to enable HR due diligence to occur on a vigorous and systematic basis. The object is for the project development team to examine each of the factors identified, seek answers to the questions that follow, and then explore in the context of legal or statutory requirements of likely contrac-tual outcomes, which should feature in achieving a successful negotiation and commercial project close.

Managing International Acquisitions and Business Start-ups

Table 6.9 *Core HR mechanisms*

Components/ Sub-Components	Resourcing				Levers/Principles			
	Organization	Recruitment and Selection	Training and development	Performance Management	Communication	Culture Building	Reward and Recognition
• Defining the core business competencies and gaps to be filled	• Use organization capability analysis to identify gaps in competence	• Consider the extent to which gaps can be filled by recruitment rather than through acquisition	• Develop and apply a methodology for measuring the existing inventory of critical competencies • Ensure adequate resources of business strategy expertise • Use capability analysis to produce rigorous analysis of existing core competencies				
• Formulating and articulating an overall acquisition strategy	• Ensure clear allocation of responsibility for acquisition strategy		• Develop capacity to 'think outside the box'	• Set clear objectives for acquisition activity – not just for results	• Create an acquisition climate internally in advance	• Define any significant cultural gaps to acquisitions	• Ensure reward strategy for acquisitions takes account of the economic

	• Identify stand-by project teams for major acquisitions and temporary cover for their regular roles • Ensure the organization structure is sufficiently flexible to accommodate acquisitions	• Ensure clear and robust criteria for making acquisitions	• Explain this process of acquisition • Establish constraints and rules of confidentiality	model of the business being acquired and does not automatically impose the approach
• Ensuring allocation of sites reflects maximum return to Group	• Operate formal or informal committee to review site allocation between businesses	• Run cross-business workshops on evaluating site potential	• Incorporate breadth of business perspective into competency definitions	• Emphasize value to group shareholders as essential criterion rather than maximizing results for a single business — Publicly recognize instances of being given another business in order to maximize group-wide benefit
• Taking a broad approach to the measurement of	• Ensure that organization structure issues	• Use this capability analysis to	• Include ability to judge potential in competency	• Identify any significant cultural gaps which could

continued overleaf

Table 6.9 (continued)

Components/Sub-Components	Organization	Resourcing Recruitment and Selection	Training and development	Performance Management	Communication	Culture Building	Reward and Recognition
				Levers/Principles			
potential and evaluation of acquisition of opportunities	(such as who reports to whom) do not constrain potential acquisitions		create a methodology for broadly assessing the resources of competence in a potential acquisition	definitions •Ensure objectives encourage breadth of vision •Use number of acquisitions considered as a performance indicator		be filled through acquisition (eg: stronger marketing or execution focus)	
•Encouraging the finding of sites	•Ensure clear allocation of responsibility between Property Division and businesses for site finding			•Set clear objectives for site growth – subject to caveat of maximizing value to shareholders	•Define characteristics of likely sites •Encourage all to spot possible sites		
•Finding acquisition targets and	•Ensure clear allocation of responsibility for	•Plan the recruitment of additional skills		•Set clear objectives for acquisition	•Produce outline communication plans for staff in		•Provide special recognition awards for sites identified by employees which are acquired

	finding acquisition targets	needed to capitalize, or fill gaps in the existing business caused by transfers to the new business		activity not just results	the acquisition and enact them before the acquisition target becomes public
providing support and resources	• Identify project teams for pre-acquisition activity and their temporary replacements			• Ensure acquisition plans incorporate resource requirements • Use number of targets evaluated as a performance indicator	
• Executing acquisitions effectively	• Ensure clear reporting lines to the acquisition team • Determine the organization structure post-acquisition	• Execute plans to fill gaps	• Ensure world class project management skills	• Set clear objectives for effective execution • Incorporate skills in executing acquisitions into competency definitions	• Implement communications plan to acquired and group staff • Establish fast-track briefing systems	• Ensure clear understanding of the relative economic models of the acquired business and the group • Determine differences in reward packages and the basis for deciding on the extent of harmonization

continued overleaf

Table 6.9 (*continued*)

Components/ Sub-Components	Organization	Resourcing Recruitment and Selection	Training and development	Performance Management	Communication	Culture Building	Reward and Recognition
				Levers/Principles			
● Maximizing the total value of acquisition			● Use this capability analysis for assessing the resources of competence in the acquired firm ● Identify transfers of acquired staff to other SBU's where the new perspective or skills may produce additional benefits	● Set demanding targets for extracting value from acquisitions ● Incorporate breadth of business perspective into competency definitions			● Recognize success in maximizing value through variable pay
● Minimizing disruption to the core business and effectively manage the transition phase	● Create transition management team and temporary replacement cover		● Build expertise in managing acquisitions	● Establish clear milestones for transition phase ● Ensure adequate emphasis is placed on managing the core business	● Emphasize importance and value of existing businesses	● Achieve balance between importance of acquisitions and managing existing businesses	● Use variable pay to recognize success in maintaining core business performance

● Locking in the value of acquisition	● Ensure integration of organization structures takes account of views of key staff in acquired firm	● Prepare contingent recruitment plans to cover gaps caused by staff leaving the acquired firm ● Explain selection/Transfer/Promotion criteria to acquired staff to show wider opportunities within the group	● Run workshops, etc, involving acquired firm's staff and group staff	● Include interpersonal sensitivity in competency definitions ● Identify measures to value the acquired firm which cover all aspects of a 'balanced scorecard' ● Track performance against these measures	● Define and communicate the implicit employment contract for acquired firm's staff, emphasizing development support and opportunities which may now apply	● Identify any conflicting cultural aspects and decide how to manage; not automatically seeking to apply the culture	● Identify key staff and develop appropriate contract terms ● Use variable pay to focus managers on monitoring value of acquired business
● Managing joint ventures and alliances effectively	● Ensure organization structures are sufficiently flexible to accommodate joint-ventures and alliances	● Use experience in managing joint-ventures and alliances as a criterion in the recruitment and selection processes	● Involve joint-venture and alliance partners on programmes ● Consider selling core firms training expertise to partners ● Consider partners' training expertise (ie; outsourcing to partners)	● Set clear targets in conjunction with partners as well as goals which are not shared with partners	● Joint review external communications policy and practice	● Seek to learn from and/or influence partners in cultural aspects	● Use variable pay to reward value derived from joint-ventures and alliances ● Seek to learn from and/or influence partners in recognition and reward plans

Table 6.10   *HR due diligence questions*

Issue	Questions	Legal or Statutory Position	Contractual Position
1. Date of Employment	In projects where we take over existing plants, what is the deemed date of engagement of existing staff for employment continuity purposes?		
2. Reward	How are employees paid? • Weekly • Monthly • In cash • At source deductions for tax and national insurance • Employers' contributions (if so, how are they calculated?) Are statutory minimum wages and salaries in force? • What are the current constraints and opportunities? • What overtime arrangements and payments are in place? • What is traditionally included in a reward package? • What is the customary split between salary and benefits? • What is custom and practice with regard to tax efficient compensation?		
3. Holiday entitlement	Is there a minimum annual entitlement? • Will this change with length of service? • Are statutory holidays to be included?		
4. Sickness/injury	Are standard sick pay policies in force? • Are there maximum periods of sick leave before ill health retirement? • Does 'ill health retirement' exist? • If an employee is injured are there standard rates of compensation? • Is public and employers' liability insurance in force? • Is this compulsory? • What dependant liabilities are in force?		

	Issue	Questions	Legal or Statutory Position	Contractual Position
5.	Pensions	Are pensions provided for employees? On what basis? • Does the employer contribute to state pensions? • Does the employer contribute to personal pensions? If so, what are the contribution rates?		
6.	Notice periods	What notice periods are employees entitled to in respect of redundancy/dismissal?		
7.	Trade Unions	What is the position with regard to trade unions? • Do they exist? • Must they be recognized? • Are there employee contributions? • Do they have industrial power (strike capabilities)?		
8.	Redundancy and Severance	In the case of a redundancy situation are there minimum awards? What is an acceptable level of severance? Are there any negotiation provisions with the trade unions? Do consultation periods apply?		
9.	Disciplinary Procedures	Do these exist? • What are the minimum requirements? • What are the penalties in cases of non-compliance? • How is the employment law enforced (do industrial tribunals exist?)		
10.	Equal opportunities/ sex discrimination	Are sex/age discriminations/equal opportunity laws and practices in force? • How do these apply? • What are the implications for retirement ages? • Ratios of disabled to able bodied employees? • Provision for maternity leave? • Provision for paternity leave?		
11	Health and Safety	• Health and safety standards and requirements • Minimum standards for site safety		

continued overleaf

Table 6.10 *(continued)*

Issue	Questions	Legal or Statutory Position	Contractual Position
12. Time off	Are employees allowed to take 'time off' in certain instances? • Illnesses in the family? • Transporting spouse to doctor? • Bereavement? • Searching for another job? • Interviewing for alternative employment?		
13. Hours of Work	• Do minimum and maximum standards apply? • If so what are they? • Do these apply for all staff levels? • What arrangements are in place for part-time working?		
14. Tax and Social Insurance	What are the employer's and employee's levels of contribution?		
15. Flexibility	What are the attitudes of employees to flexible working practices? • Will employees accept further responsibilities? • Are there any precedents within the company, project or country which might affect thinking in this area? Are there any particular barriers to flexibility? • Manual and supervisory demarcations? • Traditional use of 'mates' and similar practices? • Status issues? • Religious issues?		
16. Retirement	When does retirement come into force? • Is this compulsory? • Are exceptions possible? • What is custom and practice?		
17. Temporary Workers	Are special provisions in force for temporary workers? • How are they treated generally? • What are the employer's responsibilities?		

	Issue	Questions	Legal or Statutory Position	Contractual Position
18.	Short-term Visits and Business Trips	Are there any special provisions with regard to foreign workers in the host country? • Ease of obtaining entry-to the country (short-term entry visas) • Medical health insurance • Available facilities • Qualifications • Language What are the experiences of other multinationals?		
19.	Long-term International Assignments	Are there any special provisions with regard to expatriates and long-term assignees in the host country? • Ease of obtaining visas • Attitudes towards expatriates • Acceptable numbers of expatriates • Medical health insurance • Available facilities for spouse and family • Educational facilities for children • Qualifications • Language What are the experiences of other multi-nationals?		
20.	Facilities	Are there requirements for basic facilities on site (eg; Medical facilities for employees)? Are these only operative when minimum numbers of workers are employed?		
21.	Allowances	Are allowances or special customs in force in respect of matters such as: • Travel • Lunch • Alcohol consumption on site • Alcohol allowances provided by the company		
22.	Letters of Appointment	Are there special provisions for appointment? • Must these be by way of letter? • Are special contractual provisions required?		

continued overleaf

Table 6.10 *(continued)*

Issue	Questions	Legal or Statutory Position	Contractual Position
23. Termination	How is employment terminated? • Are trial periods possible? • Is unfair dismissal in force, and if so, what are the penalties?		
24. Qualifications and Training	Are minimum qualifications or training in force for certain posts? • Can individuals be trained to the required standards? • Is there an obligation to train? • Are local training facilities available?		
25. Training (levies)	What local constraints, pressures or opportunities exist?		
26. Manning Levels	• What are the local expectations and accepted standards? • What action needs to be taken in the short-, medium- and long-term?		
27. Tenure	• What are the current constraints and opportunities? • What are the potential implications for profitability and performance?		
28. Patronage	• What opportunities and constraints must be addressed?		
29. Multinational Experiences	• Are employees experienced in the ways and methods of international organizations? • What local experiences (good and bad) may be relevant? • What are the risks in retaining key staff? How buoyant is the local labour market?		
30. Future	Are there any future legislative or other planned changes in the pipeline which might affect decision making in any HRM matters?		

EXPECT FRUSTRATION – BUT SEE IT THROUGH

In my experience, particularly where one is working in countries which are developing, it can be extremely difficult to acquire systematically all of the information which is necessary for a comprehensive HR due-diligence process. In one exercise which I was involved in leading in Southern Europe, where we were acquiring a business from a state-owned corporation, it took many months of constant badgering of the relevant officials – moving from department to department – to ascertain all the factors which would have a major impact on the value, long term, of employing staff and the associated costs of that activity within the operation to be acquired. Failure to ascertain the relevant information can lead to major cost issues later on. In one case, an issue regarding the long term pension fund and associated healthcare benefits had not been fully clarified, based upon available information. Deals were done with the local staff to compensate them for buying-out traditional 'custom and practice' with regard to employment benefits, only to find a number of months later that there were other 'hidden' benefits which had never become clear in the course of the due-diligence process.

This is where it is essential to have local assistance, individuals who understand the problems of acquiring information within their territory, know who to ask and how best to ask in a way to elicit a positive response; and who will keep up the pressure until all the answers have been received to the relevant questions. In order though, to have the confidence that this process will be vigorously conducted, it is useful to have data collection instruments in the form of comprehensive checklists such as that given above, customized to the specific requirement of the organization, the country and the project in question.

CASE STUDY EXAMPLE – HR FORAY INTO PAKISTAN

At this point I believe it will be useful to provide a case study in the form of a 'travel-log', based on my own experience a few years go, in relation to one particular international development project in an emerging market. The market was Pakistan. The object of my visit was to ensure that my client company would fully understand the commercial, cultural and people background for engaging and developing our staff for a major greenfield infrastructure investment project. I also wanted to be sure that I fully appreciated the local circumstances into which the expatriate senior management team would be deployed. My due diligence report begins with initial impressions on arriving in Karachi – the commercial capital of Pakistan – and then covers the series of discussions I had with a variety of people in different institutions and businesses throughout Pakistan; from the desert South, through the interior, and into the North. I am reproducing it in full to give an indication of the kinds of issues that one faces, the kinds of questions that one can usefully pose, and to summarize at the end the kind of lessons which one can learn from such an investment of time.

Initial impressions

From the first moment you knew you were somewhere different. As soon as you left the airport, you got into the 'mad cap' race that was the main road into Karachi, with the myriad of different colours, the sights, sounds and smells! Initial impressions included brightly painted coloured, buses and lorries, all sorts of different shades: as my guide said, these were 'statements of personal expression'. Talking about personal expression, two-wheeled vehicle traffic has to be seen to be believed. I observed a whole family, literally a family, on a motor bike. A father, a mother, two or three children, usually a baby as well all riding along in this hair-raising traffic. And of course the buses are also sights to be observed with people hanging on at every corner, climbing on the top as well as being jam-packed inside. There is no doubt about it, rules there may be, but rules are not to be obeyed on the roads in Karachi. People overtake on the left, on the right, seem to go across roundabouts, not having any interest in apparent rights of way and so on. At least to begin with, a local driver is an essential part of the equipment for the Western inpatriate.

During the first afternoon, our guide took us on a trip of the Bazaars where all sorts of different merchandise are available. We saw pottery, rugs, clothes; you name it they were selling it. There is an incredibly rich diversity of life. Their value and standards – particularly in relation to matters of health, hygiene and regulations – are totally different to those which Westerners are used to. However, there is an incredible creativity amongst the Pakistani people and Karachi is a microcosm of that.

Visit to Pak–German Institute

We set off the first morning after our arrival, on a journey of about one and half hours, to the Pak-German Institute. This is an industrial training centre, sponsored by the German Government, in the Hub Chowki area of Baluchistan Province. The journey again through incredible traffic was something to be believed. Everywhere we went, honking and blasting through the traffic, there were donkey carts, horse-drawn carts, camels, pedestrians, buses, huge lorries in convoys, all fighting for their place. The villages that one travels to on first sight are like something out of the 'wild west', refuse piled high on the road side. All sorts of equipment and machinery stacked just where it falls. Produce also lining the streets! Everywhere, vast quantities of people. The journey itself is a revelation; almost at every turn, particularly once Karachi is behind you, there are large bumps in the road and other hazards which need to be circumnavigated. All of this does not seem to deter people driving, however. They still go along at a hair-raising pace overtaking at every opportunity, even when vehicles seem to be hurtling towards you in the opposite direction, so that you narrowly squeeze through, avoiding what seems to be the inevitable impact.

On arrival at the Institute itself, we were greeted by the Principal and the 'Chairman', a German gentleman who had been there for several years to set the place running. They took us around and certainly, in terms of the facility and equipment, the place was very impressive. The only thing which seemed to be lacking was the students. There were a few people engaged in classroom and workshop activities in the various parts of the Institute, and according to the Principal all employers on the Hub Chowki Industrial Estate were participating in having students attend the Institute. However, the numbers were certainly sparse. Apparently, the problem had arisen because the Baluchistan Government had insisted that only those individuals who had come from the immediate area could be trained at the Institute. In the event that we were to use the facility at all, it would be necessary to reach some understanding with the local administration, that even if we brought people in from elsewhere the facilities could be used and any resultant qualifications properly recognized. The Institute's authorities were certainly very open about the type of arrangements that could be entered into; seminars, specialist courses, as well as any other customized training programmes that we might wish to see installed.

Meeting with banking and legal representatives

In the afternoon, I went to meet the lawyer who was handling my company's business in Karachi. We had a very useful debate on the pros and cons of various types of contracts and the differences between contracts applied to management and staff employees. We discussed non-pay benefits, and one of the interesting things was that pensions were normally administered through the company directly; there was no question of contracting out pension administration in Pakistan at this time. It seems what many companies do is to limit pension benefits to senior and key staff, with a lump sum gratuity paid on termination of employment for all other staff, from which they can purchase an annuity to provide for retirement.

At dinner at our guide's on the first evening we met two representatives of Citibank, our bankers in Karachi. The two seemed very well informed and well-educated individuals who were taking a keen interest in the project.

Visit to Karachi Engineering University

The university is situated about twenty minutes drive outside Karachi. We met with the Chairman of the electrical section and his senior colleagues. We had a tour of the facilities, and although they looked rather old and well used, certainly there seemed to be an adequate amount of equipment, including a new batch of Unysis computing equipment. There was certainly a great deal of enthusiasm amongst the faculty staff for the kind of opportunities which may arise from new infrastructure investment in Pakistan. It was interesting to note that the proportion of males to females was probably 70/30, which was unexpected, particularly in an engineering institution in this country.

The following morning I started the day with a meeting with a firm called Shaikhs. This group are engaged in a number of projects in and around Pakistan supplying staff on major engineering activities. For example, they were involved in a number of desalination plants. In relation to manpower, on the ground, their offer was to get involved with the recruitment of relevant staff, both in Pakistan and, for example, from the Gulf. They would be quite happy to work in partnership with a UK based recruitment firm in this respect. The question arose, however, as to where their exact intentions lay. Did they intend to employ these staff, who would be gaining experience and would develop in our business operation, and who they might wish to sell-on, or simply facilitate the recruitment of them, and for them to be transferred on to the multinational employer's books? The situation remained fluid.

Meeting with Engro representatives

This was an extremely useful meeting to set the basis for further detailed discussions. The information covering the development of this agricultural chemicals company, which was previously owned by the global oil company, Exxon, and had been subject to a management buy out, was provided in the Annual Report and Accounts. In addition, I took away copies of staff agreements reached on a two-yearly basis, following discussions with recognized trade unions. There was a willingness to share information and experience.

In relation to that last point, the representatives of Engro said that on a greenfield site, if it were possible to go it alone, without union collective bargaining, there would be benefits. Their philosophy is to pay workers extremely well. In consequence they do tend to attract and retain the best qualified people. Overall, the bottom line figure on compensation packages was the key, it was said. Packages were made up of various elements but the summation of those was the figure that people tended to focus on at the initial stage. Whilst a 'clean cash' policy was one that the Engro representatives would gladly pursue, they said that unfortunately people would always make comparisons with others and, even if they were doing better *overall*, would tend to seek to include additional items on a comparison basis if they did not appear in their existing package.

Turning to long-term benefits, it was suggested that (as noted at the lawyer's) rather than pay pensions for non-management staff, a gratuity (a cash lump sum at the end of service based upon years of service) was the best approach. This avoided the need for any pensions scheme management. Finally, we talked about the tax efficiency of sophisticated packages, which really only apply to management staff. In relation to what was meaningful to employees the maximum salary in cash per month seemed to be the most attractive, despite the comments made earlier on, about external comparisons. We also talked about health insurance and it was noted that it was best simply to settle claims on a case by case basis for regular health care, with an insurance that costs, on average, one hundred rupees per month (therefore pretty inexpensive), to cover major hospitalization cases and so on. We also had a discussion on the employment of women. I commented on the fact that there were quite a large number of women now studying at the Engineering University. It was pointed out that the difficulty came once Muslim women were married and therefore had interests outside their professional occupation. I was told that, except at management levels, in Pakistan, there were very few women employed in large scale industry.

Visit to Fauji Fertilizer Township

There is no doubt about it. The Fauji Plant is a very good example of what can be achieved by a significant investment in township development. The individuals running the Fauji Plant – which is owned in part by the military – all appear to be retired from the Army. There is very much the 'officer class' mentality amongst the management. This is reflected in the management practices which I observed, the whole site being organized very much along military lines. It does make for a very efficient operation, and all facilities that one could reasonably expect seem to be there in abundance. The difficulty is that the place is inevitably institutionalized. There is a rigid distinction in the standards of accommodation provided to different grades of staff, including a separation of social facilities for management and staff. The number of individuals in the township is strictly limited, with a requirement that anyone due to spend more than twenty-four hours at the plant has to be registered with the security and administration authorities. This prevents the question of any extended families being supported there. Accommodation is provided exclusively for the employee (male), his spouse and any dependant children. Two schools are provided for those children. Once an individual leaves employment, either at retirement or beforehand, they are required, on that same day, to vacate their property and handover the keys, to the township authorities.

We had a discussion with the on-site Personnel Manager, who pointed out that they were very, very careful in selecting individuals to join their company. This was the only way, he said, to ensure top quality staff in Pakistan. For management grades they selected only those individuals who had been to universities overseas which were clearly recognized as among the premier division. In addition, they would only accept individuals with a First Class degree. Below that level, for the technician grades and below, only those individuals who had passed the matriculation in senior schooling were considered for employment. There was a very extensive battery of tests and assessments individuals went through before employment. It was certainly anticipated that, once recruited, the individuals would be there, more or less, occupying a career for life, gradually moving up through the grades as appropriate. We touched only briefly on aspects of compensation, and they were somewhat reluctant to release any material from the site without gaining permission from their head office.

Appraisal-related base pay increases seemed to be the norm, with annual assessments giving rises from six per cent for full standard performers up to a maximum increase for excellent performance of around ten per cent. This is, of course, on top of the annual 'cost of living' increase, which is normally around ten per cent. This visit was extremely useful in showing the kinds of facilities that can be made available, but pointing out the need for absolute discipline and rigour in assessing individuals and controlling families if they are to be run efficiently. In relative terms, for average Pakistanis, the facilities are, no doubt, excellent. Therefore it is important, when debating whether to use such a facility, to consider the operation in the local context rather than with a Western perception, given the feeling of institutionalization which was very obvious. There was a strong suggestion (inevitably) by the Fauji team that, given the power of the military in Pakistan, there is tremendous benefit in having clear links with the military or their retired personnel. This ensured a disciplined approach and procedures which will be recognized as being efficient!

Meeting with a seasoned expatriate

We had an extremely interesting meeting in Lahore with a seasoned long-serving British expatriate. He had been working as an adviser to the WAPDA, the Water and Power Development Authority for Pakistan. The major comment that our contact made was the total lack of any discipline in the way in which individuals work in public sector Pakistani industry. It all seems to come back to the fact that 'no one is ever in a life-threatening situation', he believes. 'The sun shines, there is always food around, no one is going to starve; therefore, there is very little incentive for most people to do other than go through the motions of life.'

Our ex-pat pointed out that, amongst the management grades, given the lack of any merit based progression, the majority of people occupying senior positions in the public sector authorities are 'somewhat incompetent'. They rarely seem to undertake any meaningful activity. Days seem to comprise of 'arriving, relatively late, spending time meeting with their male friends and drinking tea. There is a lengthy break in the day for a prayer meeting and then people return, chat a little more, and then tend to leave the premises. On Thursday afternoon, that people bother to come back from lunch prior to the Friday holiday, is unusual', our observer remarked.

In talking about the balance between expatriates and locals, our contact mentioned that there could be some real benefit in using supervisor level individuals from Western investing companies, not to act as foremen – 'because if left to their own devices, and we have people to do the 'doing' jobs, the locals will sit back and allow them to "do" ' – but instead to act as coaches and instructors to aid the Pakistanis in developing the necessary skills to supervise operations themselves.

Back to the notion of an apparent lack of discipline, as I have experienced in other workplaces, such as the lawyer's office and later when I went to Packages Limited; the workload of the managers within Pakistani industry seems to be in a constant state of disarray, to Western eyes. Their perpetual interruptions – people walk in and out of offices without any real acknowledgement or invitation and carry on conversations – mean that any sense of concluding a piece of business in a timely fashion is non-existent. Even when we were present, there were a number of people who came in and held conversations and our host turned his attention temporarily, but nonetheless exclusively, to them. Pakistanis seem incapable of saying 'no' was our contact's judgement. It also seems, from a religious perspective there is no question of people doing things purely for their own sake. There is no real entertainment here; religious doctrine has removed the normal entertainments as experienced in the West or even in the non-Muslim East (for example dancing seems to have been banned and is considered to be decadent). Consequently, as one manager answered when I posed the question: 'What do you do for your recreation', the answer was: 'Office and home'. This question of not knowing how to say 'no' seems to apply even the most professional and westernized of Pakistanis. Our contact said the way he had found it possible to have any serious discussions uninterrupted with senior local colleagues, was to wait until the end of the normal working day. In contrast to the majority, some professionals are workaholics and in consequence do not seem to mind how many hours they put in at the office. Of course, given that there is not much else to do, then their lives seem quite happily bound-up with their work.

Status of women

From what has been observed and from discussions with locals, and also with our expatriate contacts, the status of women in employment is frankly negligible. For example, although we have seen many females being educated in the Engineering University the reality is that they will be married on an arranged basis shortly after graduating and their life will then revolve around the home. This means in practice that women do not enter into the primary areas of manufacturing industry. It was admitted that there were female doctors and a number of young women get taken on in secretarial and clerical roles in business, although this is mainly in the banking and commercial sector. There are a limited number of managerial positions for women, although these will clearly only be those who are part of the élite. The bottom line seems to be, for all the notion of an equality of opportunity policy, the reality is that this is likely to be unsustainable in practice in much of industry in Pakistan.

It would be almost the same as seeking to include a policy of equality of opportunity for Christians as well as other non-Muslims. One contact told us that if a Muslim wishes to have a Christian placed in a position of disadvantage, it is simply necessary for the Muslim to report to the mullah that the individual has allegedly blasphemed. In this way the individual can be thrown into jail 'never to reappear'. Whilst on the subject of mullahs, one of the concerns expressed by our guide was that, if an overseas investor establishes a major township at the site of their operation, including a mosque, some of the local mullahs may assume significant authority over the workforce; an authority with potential to disrupt production, far greater than that of any trade union involvement!

Maintenance and planning for the future

It was pointed out to us that the very concept of maintenance, to a large extent, in other than exceptional or externally related industries was an alien concept to many Pakistanis. This can be demonstrated by the example of the yellow cabs which were introduced on a highly subsidized basis about five years ago. These vehicles, although brand new at that time, after two years of operation were running around in a very dilapidated state. There is no question of regular servicing to any professional standard or MOT type inspections. Our expatriate contact mentioned that the oil change as part of the service which he regularly and scrupulously observes for his own transport is undertaken by a boy of seven years old. Essentially it seems that many of the people in Pakistan simply never look very far ahead. They make no provision for the future. For many people, particularly those that are not very well educated life is predetermined by God. In terms of the proportion of educated to non-educated it seems that 77 per cent of individuals in Pakistan are regarded as officially illiterate. The definition of literacy is being as able to sign one's name.

In relation to domestic employees, who will traditionally be engaged to service expatriates' homes, one of our expatriate contact's domestic aids lost his wife suddenly. He came to his employer in distress, not simply because of this tragic loss, but simply because he lacked the funds to effect a burial of the body. It seems that only Christians will work for expatriates (ie non-Muslims). The Muslims will not normally take on such employment. However, such engagements carry with them wider, almost feudal responsibilities.

Visit to Packages Limited, Lahore

We were received at the company by its Commercial Manager. Packages Limited seems to be a large organization with overseas connections with Nestlé and also with Tetrapac of Sweden. The company was formed in the 1950s and was publicly floated on the Pakistani Stock Exchange in 1964. It currently employs 3000 people and this plant is its main manufacturing operation in Pakistan based in Lahore. The plant produces 45,000 tonnes of output per annum, comprising tissue paper, cardboard boxes, printed up for a variety of customers including Brooke-Bond, PG,

Lever Brothers, Pakistan Tobacco Company (BAT), and a variety of other well known brands in Pakistan. They appear to have the major market share.

Following our reception and initial chat, we were given a tour of the plant by Mr Jafri, Imports Manager. We started from the raw materials storage facility (wheat, combined in some cases with imported wood pulp which they do not have at present in Pakistan) then going through the pulping process – what they call 'The Kitchen' where they 'cook' the raw materials. We then passed into the actual paper production section where they have four large scale paper production mills operating on a continuous cycle system. This means the plant needs to be manned twenty four hours a day. We were also taken on a tour of their main electricity generating plant, which currently comprises in total about twenty megawatts, which they tend to supplement with about eight further megawatts from WAPDA. To a large extent it is essential that these industries have their own power producing facilities, because of the unstable electricity generation supplies in Pakistan. Mr Jafri pointed out that in the event of a power failure and the machines breaking down they could lose up to four hours production at any one time, whilst the pulping plant was cleaned out and the process properly restarted. Indeed, Packages Limited were in the process of adding to their own power generation facilities in order to avoid the need for any WAPDA inputs.

Walking around the Plant, clearly there were an awful lot of people involved. When we went into the 'finishing' facility, paper cutting and printing and so on, many of the processes seemed to be undertaken by hand. At least in there, the working environment was fairly pleasant. Going back into the actual production facility, turning pulp into paper, although some computerization seems to have been introduced into the control process, to ensure the right supplies of water to materials was being controlled all of the time, health and safety was clearly not a top priority. No one was wearing hard hats, and there were no signs of goggles, even where there was an awful lot of spraying going on. It is a very, very noisy environment, but there were no ear defenders being worn and the absence of guards on equipment operating at tremendously high speeds, again was notable. Given the amount of water being sprayed about (there were large pools all over the floor) there were no signs of any attempt regularly to clean up. Clearly, the health and safety inspectorate, if it exists, is not taking an interest in such manufacturing facilities.

We concluded the visit with a trip to see Mr Mahmood, the Personnel Manager. When asked about Packages Limited personnel philosophy, he said it was all about selecting the right people from the time of their leaving education and then creating careers for life. They were very careful, he said, to select people with the best qualifications at all levels, either management trainees or the technician grades and below, and then to provide them with internally run training, either as apprentices or as management trainees. For the management grades, this can involve periods of time overseas; in particular at the plant in Sweden. There are, in addition now it seems, opportunities for them to link-up with their Nestlé plant in Switzerland.

Continuing the theme of long-term employment, great store seems to be set on providing long-term benefits, with approximately 36 per cent of payroll being spent on those aspects; these include Retirement Gratuity, Provident Fund and Pension. The pension scheme is administered by trustees who are members of the scheme, rather than the management of the plant, although of course management employees are included. The company funds all of these schemes as they go, generally matching contributions of individuals. Contributions to the Provident Scheme are invested in government bonds. The trustees invest the funds on the Stock Exchange and related areas for the Pension Scheme Fund.

Base salaries are set according to a salary survey which is conducted by Packages Limited themselves (which seems to be the common practice in Pakistan), and then any salary increase agreed with the trade unions covers a two year period. Although they have three trade unions at the plant, only one is recognized as the 'Collective Bargaining Agent', which is a government recognized position. Agreements tend to last for two years. In addition to the negotiated increases, merit awards are made on the basis of a performance appraisal. Mr Mahmood said that a very highly performing employee might earn in total a 15 per cent annual salary increase. Our guide had pointed out that this company tended to have salary levels set somewhat behind the norm in terms of the higher paid firms.

Islamabad and government bureaucracy

A meeting with Rhai Khaligue Khan, Joint Secretary at the Ministry of Labour, was extremely useful, from the point of view that we were also introduced to the Government Senior Adviser on labour affairs; who turned out to be someone who had not only worked in the UK in recent years, but also had once been our guide's boss. Naturally, their greetings were colourful. This coincidence of relationships immediately opened up a very useful input to the relevant bureaucracy. In addition the Joint Secretary was a former pupil of our guide's father at the University of Lahore and, once this had also been recognized and extensive greetings and congratulations acknowledged, we had the fullest confirmation that any assistance required in working within the law of Pakistan in relation to labour matters would be provided in abundance. The Joint Secretary was at pains to point out that, of course, without the law there would be anarchy; some people criticize the law, but using it to the employer's benefit certainly was something that he would advocate. In the event that we met any unruly labour relations behaviour, he, on behalf of his Ministry, gave an assurance that he would be able to 'sort matters out' and prevent any disputes from escalating.

Pakistan Tobacco Company Limited

This proved to be one of the most fascinating of the industry visits of the whole trip. Pakistan Tobacco really does stand out as an employer within Pakistan. They tend to pride themselves as probably being the best of employers. On average they claim their employees' salaries are 4000 Rupees per month, which is considered to be well above the norm. They have a very small township at the Akora factory we visited, which is exclusively management residences.

We had a full tour of the plant which was a very interesting continuous process operation, starting from the bales of tobacco, through the separation preparation process and into the final rolling and filter tipping of the cigarettes, before they were neatly packaged, using the packages which we saw the previous day at Packages Limited in Lahore. It seems that Pakistan Tobacco are the major customer of Packages Limited. The interesting differences between Packages Limited and Pakistan Tobacco was the significant interest immediately visible in relation to Health and Safety matters. Everywhere one looked there were signs guiding people in relation to Health and Safety and the whole style of operations seemed to be better geared in that direction. There was also a significant emphasis on quality, with lots of references to it posted around the walls on the factory floor.

After the tour, conducted by the factory Material Manager, we then met Syed Raza, the Employee Relations Manager for the factory. He gave us a run-down of the employment policies which Pakistan Tobacco (a division of BAT) employed in Pakistan. They worked on the basis that in order to get the best out of their workforce they needed to involve them; hence the drive towards quality and sharing of information. They had avoided any significant disputes with the Labour Unions or staff over many years of operation, and were just on the verge of signing a new agreement for a two year period with a settlement that reflected the management demands for productivity improvements, as much as the trade unions demands for salary increases. Pakistan Tobacco operate a system called PACE, which is all about performance and career management. This is a BAT-wide institution which works on the basis that core competencies are identified and senior staff assessed against them. Their development and possible international assignment is then based on a managed career programme.

We then went on to talk about the imaginative ways in which organizations handled labour relations in Pakistan. There was a lot of concern expressed at the way in which the Government intervened in the operation of businesses, either by setting minimum wage levels, or indeed by declaring from time to time, unilaterally, salary increases across the country, which took no account whatsoever of the negotiated bargains reached within individual companies. However, by extending the 'supervisor' concept Pakistan Tobacco had been able to marginalize the impact of trade unions to a large extent. Syed Raza pointed out that, unlike in the UK, as he perceived it, the trade unions in Pakistan were very weak. One of the important additional aspects in having people on more or less personal contracts was that a clause should be included saying (even if there was not already a facility at more than one site) that they could be required to work anywhere in Pakistan. In conclusion, our hosts said, for business success in Pakistan, the key was to start with the smallest number of staff. It was also important, of course, to have total flexibility of working. In addition, before seeking to recruit staff it was essential to have a job specification. In this way, although in the provinces there was often pressure to take on local employees, when an assessment was carried out against the strict requirements of the job, if individuals did not meet the specification, it was possible to say you had tried but sufficient talent was not available for your purposes in the immediate area.

Pakistan Tobacco seem to have been successful in implementing the new productivity based manpower practices. They had achieved a reduction in manning at the factory we visited from 1800 staff down to 1200, quickly without disruption. A further reduction was planned. They had introduced what they call a 'voluntary separation' scheme to facilitate this. People had been given, in addition to lump sum severance payments, counselling, retraining and other assistance, not only for employment outside but self employment and setting up small businesses. Manpower is a very significant issue for Pakistan Tobacco, accounting for approximately 50 per cent of their overall operating costs.

We had a useful discussion about performance related pay at Pakistan Tobacco. Base pay, not bonuses, were related to individual performance. An overall cost of living increase is negotiated with the trade unions; normally around ten per cent but set over a two-year period. In addition, individuals could be considered for a merit increase on a basis of approximately six per cent for full standard performance, eight per cent for good performance and ten per cent for excellent performance. It was therefore possible for a good performer in the top echelon to earn up to a 20 per cent increase in any one year, although of course ten per cent of this would apply for a two-year period. Interestingly, the actual rating system Pakistan Tobacco apply is fairly complicated, on the basis that the below standard performance levels are rated 'E' and 'D'; there is then 'C' for Full Standard, but with shadings minus or plus, according to individual judgements and then 'B' and 'A' for the top ratings.

One final aspect was touched on, namely public relations. Pakistan Tobacco had sought to gain a good reputation in Pakistan on the basis of getting involved with social projects in the various localities in which they operated. There was a lot of kudos to be gained, particularly with photo opportunities at the launch, where providing facilities rather than cash to educational and health institutions was undertaken by employers. This was well appreciated, not only by the local community, but also the wider community in creating the image of a very attractive employer. Many of the practices that BAT were employing in Pakistan clearly were those which they would seek to apply world-wide.

Meeting with Barbar Bashir Nawaz

The final business meeting of the trip was with Barbar Bashir Nawaz, responsible for sales and personnel management with Attock Cement Pakistan Limited. This is a very well-established company, founded in the earlier part of this century by an entrepreneur, and subsequently acquired and consolidated within a broader group of companies.

We focused immediately on the pros and cons of establishing townships as part of a 'greenfield' site development. Barbar's view was that, in the case of those people operating the Fauji Fertiliser plant, this was located in a very remote area in the South of the Punjab. Many opportunities for development are accessible to major cities, for example, Karachi. There are apparently approximately 10,000 people who work within the industrial centre at Hub Chowki where Attock Cement is situated travelling between Karachi and their place of work on a daily basis.

Barbar's view was that there really was no purpose whatsoever in establishing other than a very, very small amount of housing to deal with bachelor accommodation, and priority worker accommodation close to the site. Otherwise, operation of such facilities became a major burden on the companies, and also, of course, a major administrative headache. Information had been obtained by our guide from Lever

Brothers to the extent that for their colony in Pakistan of 150 houses it was costing them of the order of 20 million Rupees per annum to maintain it.

Barbar explained that buses ran daily from Karachi from a number of pick up points to the Attock Cement Works with a return trip later in the day. In addition to the normal end of working day transport, there was an 'overtime' bus for those people required to work an extension of the normal day. This normally ran at 8.00p.m. In addition, there were a number of shift cycle buses operating services for those people working on a full shift basis. Normally people were taken back to the drop off point, not to their homes. However, amongst the senior supervisory level, a transportation allowance was often paid for people making their way from the bus dropping off point to their place of residence. Barbar's view was that in the context of Pakistan the trip from Karachi to the Hub Chowki area was a simple journey. (I have rarely experienced a less comfortable, more hair-raising ride! The M25 is positively heavenly by contrast.) In addition, of course, as the complex grew there would be further road improvements which would make it even simpler. In relation to rotation cover, where needed for plant key maintenance etc., there was a system operated whereby individuals worked on a seven days on/three days off basis. This seemed most satisfactory to many people involved, because it did give them a longer weekend with their families when they returned to the city. Obviously it was necessary to maintain some sort of basic overnight accommodation on a bachelor basis for such people. In addition, there were, what Barbar termed junior staff quarters, for those who simply lived a bachelor lifestyle at the earliest stage in their career.

In relation to the provision of actual housing, whether on a community close to the plant or elsewhere, Barbar Bashir's view was that only top management should be provided with company housing. Otherwise, problems of administration and 'ownership difficulties' could apply in just the same way as if they were in a managed colony. For the majority of staff in the senior positions below top management, a housing allowance was paid. In Pakistan up to 45 per cent of salary may be paid as a housing allowance tax free. It is therefore obviously a highly attractive and tax efficient benefit. In addition, individuals tend to be paid something like ten per cent for a car allowance which is also tax free.

The grades of employees tended to be distinguished on the basis of a management group, an officer group, sub-divided into senior supervisors and junior supervisors, and a fourth group – operatives.

For the operatives group, paid overtime was an entitlement by law, in addition to which there was a workers' retirement fund to which a seven per cent contribution was made by employers and in addition a provident fund of ten per cent. The provident fund tended to be payable for all categories of staff. In relation to other retirement provisions, new companies in Pakistan according to Barbar were *not* introducing formal pensions. This avoided the need for setting up administration and trustee groups and so on, given the lack of insurance based pension schemes available in Pakistan. In the majority of cases, then, simply the retirement gratuity and provident fund are involved.

Medicare was probably the most abused benefit in Pakistan said Barbar. Consequently very, very tight rules needed to be provided, including the issue of photocards for members. This included both employees and their spouses. In the Medicare plan run by Attock Cement, only employees and their spouses were covered. Cover did not extend to children and other dependants. In addition, because all treatment was provided through the Medicare plan, company doctors were employed on the plant, and workers were required under the rules of the Medicare plan to report any illness to their doctors and be seen by those company doctors first, before being referred on to a general practitioner or specialist.

We finally turned to a discussion on the culture of the Baluchistan province, in which Hub Chowki is located. This was still very much a tribal culture, and in the initial stages there was some concern about how a commitment to employ 75 per cent of the workforce from that area could be met by Attock Cement. This was about five years ago. In practice, an amendment to the agreement was made such that 75 per cent of the *unskilled* labour force only was employed locally. Basically, the objective was not simply to teach people about the way in which they undertook specialized jobs, but also how to behave in an industrial context. Essentially drawn from the tribal culture of Baluchistan, the only individuals regarded as being leaders were the tribal chiefs. People had to learn to work under the direction of supervisors and other key people as part of taking employment in an industrial operation. The unskilled labour drawn from the Hub area was initially deployed in generalized unskilled tasks. However, given on-job training it was quickly found that rather than seek to recruit for craft jobs from further afield and having to introduce those individuals to the way in which Attock Cement worked, they had been able to develop individuals into craft positions, growing from within. This obviously had added political benefits taking account of the local employment scene.

Some lessons

There are a wide number of learning points for internationalization HRM due diligence in an emerging territory, arising from the 'foray' described here. Let's highlight three aspects in particular, as a conclusion.

Recruitment of indigenous staff

The quality of education is the key. It seems that one must invest great efforts in getting this right, otherwise significant problems can arise in the future, dealing with an uneducated workforce who, as we have said, are the majority in this country. In addition to this, in order to retain and motivate the high potential people, benefits and facilities are a key attraction. The designation of staff is material if one is to avoid undue trade union influence. An internationalizing employer will obviously have to be prepared to consider the impact of this in relation to Western industrial concepts of flatter organization structures. Creativity obviously is required in order to achieve overall objectives.

Expatriates

The watch word is 'keep these to a minimum'. Only top management should bring their spouses with them given the difficulties of no entertainment and no real life for females in Pakistan. There clearly seems to be no question of young children accompanying their parents, either for medical reasons when they are very young or for educational reasons once they are a little older. The location of these expatriates is also a critical area to be explored. On the one hand an organization will wish to locate key managers in close proximity to the site of its operations. However, given the lack of facilities then a more permanent city residence and access to good transportation may be deemed more realistic, if one is to keep people feeling reasonably comfortable that they have access to more than the most basic of facilities or a highly regimented, colony type environment.

Beware of costs plus

Final comment certainly needs to be made in terms of lessons learnt overall for employing people in Pakistan and similar developing countries. Here there are people in abundance. However, people with real skills are in very short supply. It would be a dangerous assumption to follow the principle that, because there are lots of people, and the norm is to employ tiers and tiers of individuals, that is something that the investing multinational should follow unquestioningly. The danger with doing that, even if the cost to the payroll would be relatively minimal, is that there is a frequent reluctance of anyone to take responsibility directly for anything. By including hordes of individuals and therefore defusing responsibility levels, you can risk, particularly with a complex operation, and capitally intensive equipment, no one taking responsibility for anything.

POST-PROJECT APPRAISAL

In order to ensure that the internationalizing business continues to build on initial successes, through the development of a corporate memory, it is invaluable to conduct post-project appraisals. In this way events of the project can be reviewed by those concerned – those closely associated with the project, and supervizing management – and, before the project team disbands, information on why particular events occurred and the learning points which could be identified extrapolated.

The lessons behind success and failure may be identified through appraisals of selected investments involving in-depth analysis of key facets. The people dimension is critical

An effective feedback mechanism is essential to ensure the lessons are learned. Thus:

❏ involve worldwide staff who have responsibilities for business development and support;
❏ strengthen investment approval procedures, where necessary; and
❏ provide advice and training to all staff involved.

SECRECY SHOULD NOT RESTRICT THE SCOPE AND OBJECTIVITY OF THE APPRAISAL

Concern over secrecy must not be allowed to restrict full use of corporate resources in support of an acquisition or business start-up. The ability to draw on a large number of disciplines and to make use of the investing group's extensive expertise in such business development without compromising secrecy, offers a potential for gaining a tremendous strategic advantage in planning and negotiating.

From the outset business developers should use the expertise of 'Head Office' and supporting service departments such as:

❏ Group Development Co-ordination
❏ Group Planning
❏ Group Technology

These act as independent commentators and ensure the corporate viewpoint is taken into account. The need for a relevant and effective independent corporate voice in promoting objective decision-making should be recognized at all times.

Let us review some of the major aspects for appraisal.

The team leader

Project leaders should be chosen for a proven track record in successful negotiations and a full understanding of the business.

Post project appraisals must ascertain whether the leader fully met these requirements, was successful in developing a strong sense of purpose and commitment among team members. In optimum circumstances, team leaders' personal contribution will be central to the success of the negotiations, and subsequent management of investment returns.

Corporate representative

The corporate focal point must be a full member of the team, capable of providing an objective independent challenge, tempering business euphoria and ensuring corporate advice is sought where necessary, and then heeded. Also, the corporate representative can be the guardian of the 'alternative strategy'; a critical requirement to ensure objectivity at all stages of the acquisition.

In one case audited by a large multinational, a senior corporate representative enabled the necessary bridges to be made with relevant departmental heads in the HQ location, particularly on commercial and legal matters. He was the focal point who was always available to go anywhere at any time and thus ensured absolute consistency of approach. Furthermore, it was found that a corporate official's insistence that there was a realistic alternative strategy to the acquisition enhanced the team's objectivity during negotiations.

In another case, the absence of corporate representation on the acquisition team meant that relations between the project team and the corporate strategy function became strained. Corporate acknowledged the strategic value of a firm regional base, but were unable to convince the developers of their conviction that the case was inadequately researched and that the price being considered was too high.

Market research

Detailed research is essential for a full understanding of the market, its competitive environment, and how the target company makes its profit. Better to do this comprehensively and risk losing the prey than to rush in following an inadequate review. It is dangerous to rely on the vendor's forecasts. One must also plan for a substantial and aggressive competitor reaction. Success in this endeavour needs careful post-project review and strengths and weaknesses honestly evaluated.

Extensive research undertaken locally over a period of 15 months, by one project developer, ensured a successful basis to develop this case.

Technical evaluation

It is critical that this is done in detail and should extend to test runs where possible. A review needs to cover areas where the technical evaluation uncovered critical negotiating aspects as well as capability shortfalls.

Examples exist of a cursory plant visit giving no opportunity to identify technical difficulties with production equipment, with the result that planned production volumes could not be achieved. Alternatively, there is the example whereby experienced technical staff inspect a plant, but are not production engineers. The risk is they will fail to identify critical deficiencies clearly. This can totally unbalance forecast production and commercial outcomes.

A detailed technical evaluation is essential to a full understanding of the capabilities of the assets being acquired. As well as a review of the nature and condition of the facilities and their past performance, this evaluation should incorporate such aspects as management calibre and experience, organization, reporting procedures, technical support, safety and environmental matters.

It is essential that experts with operations or production experience relevant to the proposed acquisition should visit target company facilities to check on the capability of the plant and competence of the labour force, where possible, by carrying out a supervised test run.

Cultural change

The extent of cultural changes which will be imposed must be carefully assessed and fully allowed for in sales forecasts and in the level of management support to be provided. It takes time to change attitudes both within the company and among its customers on issues such as marketing policies and quality control.

It is more difficult to make a reliable assessment of the future performance of an assortment of companies which have not traded as an entity. Plans should also recognize the potential difficulties of integrating a number of previously separate organizations.

The difficulties involved in turning round an ailing company should never be underestimated. Details of what needs to be done will usually be difficult to assess before take-over. The risk that the desired outcome could take several years to achieve and involve significant management resources and capital expenditure must be taken into account in the valuation process before deciding to negotiate such an acquisition. The extent of change to be imposed on the acquired business will affect the timing of implementation

Staff may be attuned to a flexible 'customized' style of operation. They may, therefore, be slow to react to an acquirer's requirements for a business based on a limited range of high quality products capable of challenging those of its major competitors. Questions need to be addressed regarding success and failure in 'change' interventions, offering valuable lessons for repeating and avoiding in future projects.

One-man negotiations

It is highly risky for one person to negotiate. There is no facility to refer back to higher authority should negotiations become tense, and no involvement from a supporting team. Post-project reviews should comment on instances where this seemed unavoidable, and introduce future checks and balances.

Assimilation

It is important to decide well in advance how the acquisition will be incorporated into existing business, associate and corporate structures

Despite economic shortcomings of an acquisition, the merger of various geographically diverse activities throughout a region with the acquirer's existing operations can be thoroughly planned and well executed. It is beneficial to generate a broad vision of the acquired company's future role shared with its management and involve them in developing detailed plans

Were early decisions reached on the method of incorporation into existing business and corporate structures?

It must be recognized at the outset that successful achievement of the perceived benefits will depend on the effectiveness of the post-acquisition organization. Early consideration of how the new company will be incorporated into the existing business or corporate structures is therefore essential. Indeed, organizational factors could influence the choice of target company and all subsequent stages of the acquisition process.

Was a clear strategy developed for dealing with staff matters before the acquisition took place?

Attention to detail in developing and executing a clear strategy for dealing with staff and the industrial relations aspects of an acquisition, will do much to minimize opposition, even in a highly unionized environment.

Severence terms and pension provisions are always likely to be particularly sensitive issues. Where there is a probable delay before an acquisition is confirmed, the acquirer should attempt to satisfy itself that the target company has plans for dealing with this question and informing its staff. Otherwise the risk must be recognized that the company, when it is finally acquired, will have a reduced value because of resignations, damage to morale or potential union hostility.

Post-acquisition flexibility

Changing market conditions and a better knowledge of the company's capabilities will need to be accommodated. Post-project reviews need to assess how this has been achieved and benefits delivered. Such intelligence then will feed-in to new project planning.

Management appointments

Senior management appointments must be consistent with the need for expertise in new business areas. It is arrogant and dangerous to assume that injecting acquiring company management into acquired non-core activity businesses will work.

In a business with which the acquirer is broadly familiar a few key 'corporate' appointments on day one may be enough to ensure that these 'company people' can relate impressions and effect changes in culture where it was necessary to do so.

Planning and acquisition

The initial planning for an acquisition should take place as far as possible before discussions are held with the vendor. Whatever the origins of a proposal and whether a friendly or a hostile take-over is envisaged, the main considerations will be:

❑ How well the proposed acquisition fits the business strategy and how it compares with alternative means of achieving that strategy.
❑ What the organizational needs will be for evaluating and negotiating the acquisition.
❑ What post-acquisition organizational planning will be required to ensure that the perceived benefits can be fully realized.

What learning points emerged as a result of exploring these considerations?

Consulting the right people

Consideration should always be given to establishing a steering committee which will draw together the various interests in order to progress the
acquisition effectively, to ensure a smooth take-over and to form the basis
for subsequent management. Its chairman should be accountable for
achieving this. The steering committee has particular importance when a
number of businesses are involved.

An important role of the steering committee is to ensure that throughout the acquisition process a balanced and consistent view of the target is
developed amongst the contributing parties. This should include:

❏ Establishing that specialist advice (legal/tax/finance) is not developed
in isolation but reflects the total perspective.
❏ Making sure that no fundamental parties are allowed to remain unresolved over the purpose of the acquisition or how it should be run.
Basic disagreements are sometimes overlooked in the gathering
momentum of the acquisition process.

How did the Steering Group react under the pressures of piloting the project to financial close and beyond?

Strategy

An internationalizing business should never let the strategic drive be at
the expense of a full review of risks and criteria for success. While a fit
with an agreed business strategy will usually be essential to a successful
international business development, blind adherence to strategic objectives must never be allowed to become the primary driving force to the
exclusion of a full review of all risks and criteria for success, particularly
when there is competition with other companies for acquisitions in the
same business area. Moreover, failure to have a well-defined strategy in
place will adversely affect all stages of the investment management
process and may delay the implementation of plans to unlock the added
value. What lessons emerge from a succession of projects which can offer
commercial longer term advantage?

Acquisitions in unfamiliar territory

A specific assessment should be made at the outset of the risks, political
or otherwise, of investing in the particular country or countries concerned, taking into account the views of the relevant region.

The 'culture' of a foreign country needs to be taken into account in pre-investment planning. The importance of personal contacts in doing business must be stressed, especially where intentions agreed by word of mouth carry greater weight than written agreements. Peculiarities of the local 'system' should be uncovered and allowed for; eg, delays in approvals, especially for foreign-supplied materials, payments to individuals, and so on.

Overseas business developments increasingly critically depend on the use of local expertise. The role of the overseas associate support group, the degree to which the business headquarters agrees to delegate responsibility should be clearly defined and communicated from the start and agreed with the acquisition team leader. The efficiency or otherwise of this process must be appraised and suitable adjustments made for future initiatives.

What was the state of communications between the local venture and the Corporate Centre?

For an overseas acquisition good communication channels between the business and the local venture are essential to supplement good leadership and clearly delegated roles for team members. A genuinely international approach can evolve with both groups' expertise being brought to bear on the process.

When a business considers an overseas acquisition which is outside the main activity of the local associated company, the local venture's chief executive should be kept fully informed, particularly concerning plans for integration and control after take-over.

Management review?

A management appraisal is an essential part of the valuation of the investment target, in an acquisition, in order to probe the aspirations, attitudes and inter-relationships of the management team, together with abilities, reporting relationships, responsibilities and levels of authority of subordinate managers. This is particularly critical when acquisition of management skills is an important element in justifying the purchase. The risk should be recognized where it is not feasible to undertake this fully.

The acquisition target's earlier success may have been generated by only a small core of managers. Resignations and other wastage can remove key relevant experience, denying the acquirer the ability to expand rapidly in a new business area. New insights gained in management audit need to be captured, assessed and shared.

Essential expertise must not be lost

In the case of technology or trading activities which are outside the experience of the group's existing businesses, it is important to ensure that essential expertise will be retained after take-over. There is a particular risk if the expertise is held by one person or by a small close-knit team.

It is also important during the evaluation stage to try to understand the robustness of existing management information and control systems in the target company to show to what extent information supplied by the company or its shareholder is reliable and soundly based. This also helps to define requirements for reporting and control in advance of the acquisition, taking into account compatibility with existing systems in the business. Key learning in this area is critical to sustained success in rolling out a strategic internationalization programme.

SUMMARY AND CHECKLIST

In the heat of battle, when approaching an international project, it is often very difficult to ensure a complete and comprehensive look at all the issues. This is why aspiring businesses who wish to internationalize are sensible to invest time in developing a comprehensive suite of approaches in order to model the likely implications of approaching particular projects.

These models should sit alongside the other strategic business tools; project management, technical assessment, and commercial financing evaluation. The issues I believe can usefully be grouped by using the model at the generic level for understanding what the human resources issues will be for projects and project teams, at various organization levels, whether they are greenfield or brownfield, and whether they are located in the developing or developed world. In the foregoing text I have provided an overview of the various stages in approaching an international project, understanding the roles and responsibilities – and access to necessary information – by both HR and line management. We have explored the question of managing acquisitions, and the various human resources levers and capabilities essential to that process.

We have then looked at the issues that human resources professionals would find valuable to explore in approaching a possible start-up or acquisition and feeding in to the due-diligence outturn process. We have also had an example of a specific due-diligence activity – what that involved – and what the learning points were.

Finally, we have explored the issues of post-project appraisal, in order to identify learning points and build corporate memory. It is due to the completion of such exercises – as strategic investment in its own right – that major corporations have established themselves as successful global players over the medium- to long-term. It is about not only creating success and the conditions which go with it as a one-off, it is about consistently replicating that success again and again.

The following questions need to be addressed in undertaking business development human resources due-diligence. Does the organization:

❑ Have a systematic frame of reference for interpreting and dealing with issues associated with business acquisitions and greenfield development; located in developing or developed countries?

❑ Have a human resources due-diligence checklist which will ensure comprehensive feedback to facilitate project evaluation and negotiation?

❑ Have a comprehensive understanding of the various HR levers required successfully to manage start-ups and acquisitions in an international setting?

❑ Have a post-project appraisal framework, generally accepted by the organization corporately and within its project teams, which will assist in unlocking the lessons which have been learned by those involved in leading and supporting business development at its various stages and capturing this as part of corporate memory?

Chapter 7

Performance Management in an Internationalizing Business

Novel thinking is required to align the efforts of 'home and away' teams for sustained shareholder value creation. The approach to performance management, and associated 'success' measures, needs to be evolved in partnership with line managers and other professional stakeholders. Any approach must reflect the realities of deploying various groups of people in different multi-cultural, global business situations.

The HR manager as business partner, helping to interpret key business drivers and linking these to objectives which align people capabilities with the goals for strategic business units, as well as corporate critical success factors, has a critical part to play. The 'motivation factor' is a vital component; performance management processes need to be designed and implemented mindful of the messages they communicate both to managers and staff about the priorities and values of the enterprise and its top management. This needs especially careful handling when messages need to be 'translated' across multiple languages, cultures and traditions.

CONTEXT FOR INTERNATIONAL PERFORMANCE MANAGEMENT

In order to discuss, in an action-oriented manner, the process of managing performance for organizational advantage within internationalizing businesses, we need to explore this topic from a number of perspectives.

Therefore, I shall structure this chapter to cover, first, strategic models for performance management; secondly, cross-cultural frameworks for reviewing performance management; and then, thirdly, guidelines for successfully establishing measures of performance to support internationalization.

At the end of the chapter, we shall look for common themes which emerge in relation to performance management in internationalizing businesses. We will seek out the lessons which can be extrapolated from them for successful organization performance enhancement. We shall then look at those instructive points of differentiation between the way in which performance management is perceived and can be enacted in different territories in various regions of the world, as well as the scope to translate organization performance goals on a common basis, but recognizing the need to reflect the diversity of organization environments in which performance is to be managed.

FRAMEWORKS FOR PERFORMANCE MANAGEMENT

Rummler and Brache (1995), have developed a useful diagrammatic process flow for determining the basis for individual performance setting, monitoring, and evaluation and feedback (see Figure 7.1). This is a tool which can be applied in a variety of circumstances to manage the overall process of

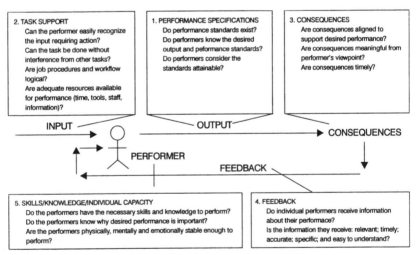

Figure 7.1 *An overall view of content and process in performance management system design.*
Reprinted with permission from Rummler and Brache, *Factors Affecting the Human Performance System.* Copyright © 1995 Jossey-Bass Inc., Publishers. All rights reserved.

performance determination; providing an understanding of the specifications of performance; the support for the task to be undertaken; the consequences of the performance process; feedback in relation to outputs achieved; and the skills, knowledge and individual capacity continuously to learn and improve, based upon the enactment of the performance process.

The difficulty with most approaches to performance management, which is complicated further on an international scale, is that HR interventions often only come in relation to process issues, rather than getting to the heart of the business debate in relation to the objectives for performance management in the context of medium to long term business development.

For that reason, together with my colleagues in the Strategic Remuneration Research Centre, we have developed with our sponsors a new model for performance management, described graphically in the form of a 'ripple pond', to assist human resource practitioners in partnership with line management to get closer to the real issues for performance management, and as a result better to interpret the environment in which they are to be carried out, informing critically the design of particular performance management processes, and then understanding and monitoring outcomes; informing the process of business development itself as well as performance management over the long term. This 'ripple pond' (see Figure 7.2) is

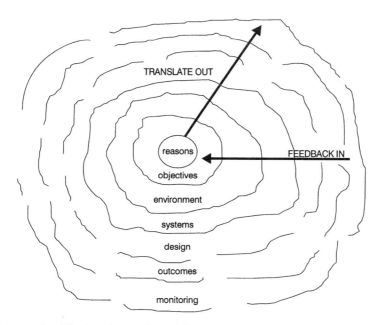

Figure 7.2 *The 'ripple pond' model.*
Source: The Performance Management Diagnostic, © SRRC 1997

indicated to suggest the importance of understanding the position at which the pebble is thrown in the pond, creating a series of ripples for performance, not only going outwards, but also providing an important backwash sensitivity, critical if the dynamic business process of performance management, objective setting, and monitoring, is to be adapted in light of changing competitive and commercial reality.

CHECKLIST FOR PERFORMANCE MANAGEMENT FACTORS

In order to enable a more systematic and structured approach to performance management determination, we have developed a series of questions. When joining in a strategic debate on permanence management issues in internationalizing businesses, it is sensible to work systematically through the list of questions, on the basis that if satisfactory answers cannot be provided at each level, then the organization needs to take several steps back and to question whether it is embarking in a direction that will be counterproductive or some refocusing of the performance objectives in relation to business development are required.

Why is there a strategic focus on performance management now?

Companies are looking more critically than ever before at their performance. They need to do so as part of the challenge all enterprises must meet to survive and prosper, in the face of fierce global competition, and the resulting strains on margins and overall profitability levels. As a result, they are asking whether, for example, reward can be used more strategically, to leverage performance to address this challenge.

I invited our SRRC Performance Management Steering Group members to share their thinking, prompting Mike Redhouse, Director of Employment Policy with Guinness PLC, to observe that, as soon as this question is raised, it begs two further fundamental questions.

The first breaks down into:

❑ does the prospect of reward give incentive to performance, or
❑ is reward simply a way of linking costs with performance?

'Frequently managers at all levels of the enterprise muddle these two issues up', he said. 'There is a distinction between (a) motivating sustained performance improvement as a result of introducing an incentive scheme, and (b) the satisfaction of being able to relate performance to reward, in the sense that it is right to pay people less if they (or their business unit) perform below the expected standard. As we get more sophisticated in operating reward management this confusion demands a more coherent response.'

The second major question is, given this confusion, how do we know what performance to measure? 'It has been an astonishing revelation that our management development colleagues have little more idea now about how to distinguish between good and bad individual performance than they did 20 years ago. We need to get better answers to the question of what we want to measure in business performance which can be identified and assessed systematically,' Mike Redhouse suggested.

Phil Wills, Director of International Compensation and Group Employment Policy, Grand Metropolitan, another Steering Group member, stressed to me his concern that there are a variety of things we understand performance management to be. But there are no HR processes understood to be specifically geared toward improving performance. It is not clear how each of the HR processes link together to meet this aim.

'Most organizations have appraisal systems, incentive programmes (in some cases MBO processes), personal development programmes; we highlight skills development needs as part of the performance appraisal process, for example. But the question remains unanswered as to how these processes knit together – should they? Does the application of all these disparate processes add up to more than the sum of the parts? In this we are frequently close to enlightenment, but then we miss completely again; we keep losing focus all the time.

'In Grand Met, we've recently completed a rewrite of our performance appraisal system, to align with our new organizational values and strategic imperatives, and with our new leadership focus. The objective is to support the new corporate mission, which is to double shareholder value in five years.'

A further perspective is supplied by Martin Day, a senior member of the Group Personnel team at BT, and also a member of the SRRC Steering Group. 'We need to remember that BT has come through privatization and market liberalization. We're now embarked on a major internationalization programme. When we started (in the state sector), people and performance were not considered closely at all; rewards did not change much over time. Then the Company started to feel concerned about competition coming along, and over-reacted, in a way, as far as pay and performance were concerned.

It's like learning to walk; you can read 100 textbooks about the theory, but until you've got your feet on the ground you can't really find out how to.'

Beware a lack of balance

Martin warns against allowing performance management processes to introduce distortions to the way people think they must behave, ultimately resulting in more harm than good. 'The more we looked at the problems with reward, the more we realized performance management was a problem to be addressed systematically. This is not to say we lacked innovation in this regard.

Several years' back, we were at the forefront of developments in introducing a 'corporate scorecard'. This was presented as a dashboard, with the object being to keep all dials out of the red. However, what people tended to do was to fragment responses to performance management. Action was initiated to tackle this or that problem, but ignoring the impact of such action on other factors. We may also have forgotten what was not on the dashboard, but which may have underlying significance.

'So, the result was some confusion about the real management job; some managers tended to be too focused on the task, and were guilty of ignoring management of people. Others were doing the right things – nurturing their people and so on – but feeling guilty that they were apparently not being "commercial" enough.

'Whilst exaggerating to emphasize the point, the shape of what I've said is right in terms of the organizational context. The need was to break out, to give people confidence so they know what good performance looks like; and to be able to monitor it. Also, to discourage people spending time developing measures for measurement sake, overweighting certain aspects, and only developing measures for those things which can be readily measured, rather than what it is important to focus performance on.'

The issue is, therefore, how do we judge the health of the internationalizing business? How to look forward, as well as looking at a snapshot in time; in a non-artificial way; in a way to avoid causing damage; and then to have people share in the rewards engendered by the balanced performance achieved?

What are people's aims for a performance management framework?

Mike Redhouse is quick to point out: 'A big question is how good is business in knowing what it wants to achieve at every level. Do the great corporations themselves know what their long term goal is? It's *the* heart of the business question. When managers are asked to address the question of what the business wishes to achieve, their responses centre around a succession of short term achievements; for example, profit year by year, or contribution year by year. But on a big picture basis the reality is they don't know.'

'The big word is *alignment*', Phil Wills suggests. 'Organizations don't seem to understand whether their HR processes are aligned or whether they are pulling in different directions. In practice, each process operates in a vacuum – we don't even have a catalogue of processes – different functions and different parts of the same function support the operation of individual HR processes. People simply don't talk, so there's no management process actively to co-ordinate and focus each of the elements on overall performance enhancement'.

ORGANIZATIONAL REQUIREMENTS

So it seems we lack a common understanding of what we mean by an integrated approach to performance management. It's unclear from my investigations whether anyone has achieved this in either a domestic or international setting.

It's interesting to ask the question: do people see (people) performance planning and performance management as part of strategic planning and strategy implementation? Most would label it as business management; but who other than people are going to deliver business performance. The action represents the effort to ensure people actually do the right things. Strategic planning just says what *people* are going to do – not what the business is going to do – so there is a missing strategic link.

Financial systems are all about feedback. They tend not to be seen as part of the performance management process; but obviously good feedback is fundamental to successful performance management.

Phil Wills' contention is that the three parties involved in these processes; HR, Finance and Strategic Planning do not collaborate at all in the development of their various processes. There is a need to develop a new sequence and a behavioural pattern to bring these into synch. 'Strategic plans tend to be about numbers and business initiatives, but these do not tend to be qualified by success criteria. One of the things HR professionals can do is to become part and parcel of the international strategic planning process at the earliest stage, highlighting those issues that the incentive plan will either stimulate or not, derived from the strategic planning process itself.'

It is also important to ensure that the right messages are communicated down the line to reinforce the attitudes necessary to achieve the strategic planning objectives. 'One other opportunity is to ensure better integrity of the judgmental process that is required in delivering a strategic plan rather than simply working to an annual budget.'

What are the implications for HR professionals?

'Legitimization and exhortation', says Martin Day. 'Good managers work that way – ie creating the conditions for integrated, balanced performance management – given the freedom to do it. They often don't, because they're being conditioned by organizations and pushed to do the opposite. And performance scorecards and associated reward systems can be part of the problem (as outlined above), from our own experience.

'The real benefit is engaging in this process at the individual level. It's not enough to say to managers: "Here's a process which involves you meeting all your direct reports – this is how you do it." Instead HR professionals can make a strategic contribution by engaging line managers in a debate around how they can get value out of investing an hour a month sitting down with direct reports to review performance.'

'Theory and practice must be fused,' according to Martin Day. 'Good managers know intuitively that every factor of performance you get wrong will show its way through at different points over time. Just as if you try to manipulate a balloon to push in a bulge from one angle, it will quickly reappear at another. But, people need help to believe and experience it.' In large, global corporations, we shelter them from doing so; even if people notice the interplay of factors, we encourage them to disregard it.'

There is a need for greater participation working cross-functionally, and across international business divisions, to enhance the quality of the process in terms of the level of detail required to spell out precisely what objectives are about, which will help in communicating and building understanding. In both the strategic plans and the annual business plans these will be enhanced by the development of clear success criteria. Arguably this is a major role for HR people, if we can go in and grab the attention of line managers, making a business case for devoting the necessary time for this detailed process, and bringing the various parties together working across the business to achieve strategic business goals.

Mike Redhouse adds: 'Astonishingly enough, because managers believe that reward incentivizes, a good way to get managers to engage in a dialogue about what performance should be measured, is to introduce a bonus scheme. Devising even a simple incentive arrangement can act as a catalyst for a strategic debate which provides the opportunity for HR professionals to get to the heart of the business.

'Engaging in this dialogue with a business unit managing director, as a prerequisite for the introduction of a bonus plan, is a powerful interaction. A special role for HR is to be able to turn to the guardians of commercial information, in particular the finance people, and say: "Tell us what to measure; without this we can't introduce an incentive scheme". This provides a very powerful basis for leveraging the debate. The debate then can centre around, for example, whether economic value-added or revenue growth is as good as growing contribution; and is the latter profit contribution anyway? We naively expect our finance colleagues to spend much of their time debating these issues. But the reality is, when you ask them, they don't know. 'For example, if you say: "What's our market share objective for, for example, Venezuela?", they say they don't know, but if the company is going to put money on it they had better do something to find out. So the issue I am wrestling with, at the middle of a complex business debate on a global scale, is the question of what *do* you measure?'

A key role is to improve widespread understanding about the essential 'business management' nature of performance management. Phil Wills again: 'If you asked a cross-section of senior business unit leaders what they understood performance management to be, this would only result in an extremely shallow comment. Performance management is not a term they are exposed to, or think about. They are exposed to HR processes. Performance management is not a designated HR process – there is no piece of paper, which says do performance management – so there is no spur to action

'So managers will do what they've always done if they've joined from other organizations – what's in their blood. Or, they will comply with our HR processes – and there are so many of these; so nobody does any voluntarily, or develops his or her own. I've not come across any organization with a management culture driving the performance management process.'

Martin Day follows on this train of thought, as follows: 'Managers would not necessarily assume this was something coming from HR – more likely from Business Planning – they would see it expressed in financial terms. If they understood it to be from HR, the likelihood is they would think the term related to performance appraisal or development planning, to build skills. They probably would not expect it to refer to the fundamental issue of managing performance day to day. If they did, they might be expected to react by wondering why HR was interfering in *their* affairs.

'The trouble is, things you can say in general sound banal. But these "basics" are the things which are important and which people tend not to do well. There is no pressure for this – the pressure is to follow fads and fashions – this is how we condition managers. A major blockage is something which remains unsaid, but which in fact colours the judgement about performance and development actions by line managers. Most managers don't believe that, if you squeeze them, people are capable of fundamental change or improvement, once they are beyond their mid-30s, and therefore outside the conventional idea of post-educational entry development. So, they don't open doors to release untapped potential; and so the misconception becomes self-reinforcing.'

Where we've got to be, then, is focusing interventions on the basis of integration. We must encourage the organization to look at performance in the round; rather than through partial messages. A fundamental problem is the existence of personnel as a separate discipline. Businesses are organized so as to prompt interventions in the management process by a 'money bunch' of professionals, a 'people bunch', and so on. The truth is, performance is indivisible.

So, do we need to re-brand performance management?

Individual HR processes are beneficial in their own way. Grand Met have recently undertaken an 'endings' initiative, asking the businesses, which HR process they could stop doing, and would the business miss it. No single HR process was identified as not being perceived as contributing to business effectiveness. 'Managers will bitch about doing them', Phil Wills comments, 'but they do not mount a challenge to their existence'.

Again we return to the question: are these processes aligned anyway? Are they pulling in opposite directions? Are they delivering mixed messages? Or can performance management be any one of these you label as such; today, performance appraisal, tomorrow management development. In Grand Met, for example, management development is a synonym for performance management.

Phil Wills believes there is a critical requirement to challenge the role each individual HR process has in raising performance. So, for example, is performance appraisal raising performance levels – individual by individual – and if not, why invest valuable time and effort in doing it? 'Each individual process must, at the individual level – forget the organizational level – demonstrably enhance performance. We need a proven mechanism to track each HR process against the enhancement of each person's performance.'

Measures and rules for setting performance objectives

So, one of the key issues for internationalizing businesses is getting smarter and introducing greater clarity in the way in which performance measures are established, and actual performance is tracked and assessed. Table 7.1 sets out examples under various headings, a variety of performance measures, which may be useful in establishing performance targets for individuals, teams, and strategic business units involved in developing business projects on an international scale.

Table 7.1 *Summary of measures and rules for setting targets*

Corporate financial measures
- extent to which the end result achieves/exceeds company return on investment targets
- meeting project productivity goals in first 12 months of full production
- return on equity
- return on investment
- internal rate of return
- working capital utilization
- cashflow
- net operating income

Measures of employee/team satisfaction and development
- turnover rates by employee category
- numbers of staff ready for promotion
- new skills acquired per year
- levels of project team morale and team spirit (assessed by survey questionnaire)

Other corporate measures
- environmental and safety measures
- ability to adapt to changes in balance between existing capability and market demand
- solutions proposed for managing conflicting objectives; eg commercial goals versus risks of pollution

Time
- meeting agreed schedules
- meeting forecast completion dates
- actual vs. estimated time (at n monthly intervals/key project stages)
- work completed by given dates

Quality
- winning n projects (with minimum y return)

Customer/client satisfaction indices
- meeting defined service standards
- attitude survey results
- customer audits
- rapidity of responses
- number of issues brought to senior management attention

Territory/region specific targets
- new market development targets reached
- winning a project at all costs as a strategic investment
- industrial relations/government relations
- expenses costs to number of projects sold
- evidence of political lobbying power with government and other local organizations
- company image
- management contacts
- ability to spot and prioritize commercial opportunities
- extent to which territory actions are consistent with business plan targets
- quality of territory relationships
- quality of proposed partners; extent to which they meet agreed criteria

Costs
- meeting or beating budgets
- headcount targets against actuals
- outsourcing budget against outturns
- phased expenditure targets
- operating costs per unit of output
- % staff utilization
- % budget deviation
- output per employee
- unit costs

continued overleaf

Table 7.1   *(continued)*

Quality (continued)	Project development/management
• getting *n* projects to bid stage	• output per employee
• getting *n* projects on short list	• % of project staff achieving their
• identifying *n* potential opportunities	objectives
meeting agreed criteria	• areas of duplication of effort
• meeting functional specifications	• relative size of project team
• achieving company and functional	• effective use of management infor-
audit standards	mation systems
• project performs in accordance with	• provision of project data to time and
standard tests	to organizational guidelines
• application of given technology	
• degree of conformance with best	
practice project processes	
• condition of physical assets	

CROSS-CULTURAL ISSUES

Insights into intercultural performance interaction

The history of relations between nations is fraught with the consequences of false assumptions about motivations, intentions, thought patterns and feelings. To do business successfully in the international arena requires us to explore differences in perception, ways of thinking, styles of communication and customary behaviour. Application of performance management principles internationally necessitates careful consideration and application of inter-cultural insights. Figure 7.3 shows that some things about a given culture are immediately 'visible', but that much of a culture is 'invisible' and more difficult to determine.

We need to be able to explain what happens when people who come from contrasting cultures meet, eat, joke, argue, negotiate and co-operate with each other. Awareness should be developed of the feelings people have about each other, their expectations, the effect their interactions have, the manner in which one embarrasses, frustrates, angers or impresses the other.

Such insights help to predict the outcome of encounters between cultures. This will help us to clarify what one must do to become a competent competitor, a trusted colleague or partner. Indications are obtained as to what degree of adaptation may lead to producing the right impact on representatives of the other culture.

In a period of accelerated globalization such as we are experiencing today, understanding the forces that are at work and the cross cultural

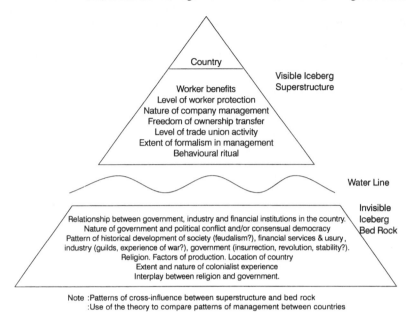

Note : Patterns of cross-influence between superstructure and bed rock
: Use of the theory to compare patterns of management between countries

Figure 7.3   *The iceberg theory of intercultural analysis.*

dynamics that are involved within their interactions, is an essential pre-
requisite for maintaining healthy relationships with people whose performance we aspire successfully to manage, or who interact professionally with
us in any shape or form.

If we take Japan as an example, the distinguishing and unique features
of Japanese culture make harmonious collaboration with nationals of certain other countries a delicate and somewhat complex matter. There are,
however, commonalities of behaviour and outlook between Japanese and
British people; this also applies to some extent to one or two other
European societies. By finding this common ground and developing what
it offers, British and Japanese executives may succeed in creating smooth
relationships, avoiding pseudo-conflicts (which have little intrinsic importance) and establishing a *modus operandi* of durable character.

National culture and communication

What do we mean when we refer to a national culture? Not only a country's music or painting or literature, but rather the whole manner and style
in which the people of a country conduct their lives. A national culture
involves a complete system of customs, habits, rules, values and beliefs,
shared by an overwhelming majority of the country's inhabitants. It gives

them a particular outlook on life, a special mind-set; in short it is their view of the universe.

We can define this form of culture in many ways. One definition is:

The collective programming of the mind which distinguishes the members of one category of people from another.

This programming, which is a type of brainwashing, begins at a very early age; not long, in fact, after we are born. Our first teachers are our parents who start giving us a long list of dos and don'ts which is later continued at playschool, in the community, throughout the educational process and, finally, in our workplace. We are told what is good and what is bad, what is rational and irrational, what is right and what is wrong, what is normal and what is abnormal. Strangely enough, wherever we are born, whatever we do in our own country is normal. Everybody else is abnormal! Collectively we have a set of values which we rarely abandon after the age of puberty.

Therefore, at the centre of each person's being, lies this nucleus of values; his or her core beliefs. When we meet someone from another culture, if we just look at them, we cannot see or be fully aware of these beliefs unless that person moves or speaks. There must be what we might call a *cultural display* before we get any information. For instance, if you walk along a street in a small European continental town, you can learn a lot about the national culture by two or three minutes of observation:

❏ Do they hurry towards their goals or are they relaxed?
❏ How important is time to them?
❏ Do they talk to each other much?
❏ Do they greet each other?
❏ Do they shake hands, bow or touch each other?
❏ How important is dress?
❏ Are they formal or informal?
❏ Do they show their feelings openly?

These cultural displays or events will have an effect on us. They might please us; we might find them strange; they might shock us. In our own culture people's actions meet with approval; we repeat them ourselves; the cultural trait develops; it becomes a national characteristic or tradition. In an alien culture our action meets with resistance; we might defend it; this leads to deadlock and eventual withdrawal. Similar cultures such as Italian and Spanish might show semi-acceptance of each other's characteristics and this would lead to friendly adaptation and essential cultural synergy. For instance, close Latin understanding.

When we think of communication, we naturally try to convey our values to other people. We say or do something which impacts our listener or observer. A kind of cultural ripple is created, where our performance, rituals, admiration for certain heroes or national figures, our use of speech or body language, reveal our values. French, Italians and Americans communicate their national beliefs swiftly and convincingly. Other nationalities, such as the Finns and Japanese, are poor communicators. It is much harder for us to know what they really believe or what they are thinking. Even the British and the Germans communicate their deeper feelings with considerable difficulties. There often occur 'buffer' or 'clouding-over' zones which act as barriers to clear communication. These barriers may be linguistic but more often they are psychological and cultural. Japanese and Latins do not find it easy to communicate, as the latter are much more talkative than the former. One side talks too little, the other too much, both creating distrust in the other. Each side considers its use of speech to be normal. All these factors clearly aid or inhibit performance management in a multinational setting.

When different nationalities, in their explanations or expositions, run up against miscomprehension, they change their style to achieve clarity. But each changes in a different manner. A South American speaks more, a Finn speaks less and with more succinctness. An American provokes, a Japanese becomes more icily polite. A German hammers away at what he believes is the truth, an Englishman tells funny stories to show better what he really means. There is no mutually or universally accepted way of convincing someone that you are right, or even of showing him exactly what you mean. These, albeit stereotypical aspects need to be factored in to the performance management process.

National cultural profiles

When entering into any project, and attempting to deliver performance within a country, it is helpful to analyse the economic and cultural profiles, and to explore scope to empathize with them, by working through the following list of factors:

Economic background

❑ Area
❑ Population
❑ Population per sq km
❑ Life expectancy
❑ GDP
❑ GDP per capita
❑ Principal exports
❑ Principal imports

Cultural characteristics

❑ Religion
❑ Cultural classification
❑ Values
❑ Concepts
— Leadership
— Status
— Space
— Time

Internationalization – The People Dimension

❏ Main trading partners

❏ Cultural factors in communication
— Communication patterns and use of language
— Listening habits
— Behaviour at meetings and negotiations
— Body language

Other

❏ Manners and taboos

❏ How to empathize with them

> *So what are the issues or rules which it pays to take into account when establishing performance measures, processes, and assessments on an international basis?*

Here are ten prompts for success in managing performance in an internationalizing business.

1. *Focus on results and outputs, rather than inputs and process measures.*
   Process measures and compliance procedures are important indicators, but are a means to an end, not ends in themselves. Organizations report that they seem to make progress in measurement when they move away from the traditional emphasis on *inputs* and *efficiency*, focusing instead on *outputs* and, even better outcomes, results and *effectiveness.*

2. *Make sure that measures applied to individuals and projects are linked to long term corporate goals.*
   If an individual's performance assessment (and reward package) is affected by reaching key targets, it is essential that these targets reflect the company's best interests. Sometimes the measures of performance applied to individuals can clash with measures of corporate success or encourage short-term thinking. We have all heard stories of short term decisions which only come to light after the project manager has left. A recent example quoted by a global oil company related to one refinery where the refinery manager discovered that in the mid-1970s a project manager had sanctioned a stainless steel pipe to be painted with zinc:

   'This should never have been done; eventually the zinc molecules permeate the steel and it breaks like china. This will cost us £3 million to fix. My bonus is shot. I've got to go around with the begging bowl now on account of something my father did!'

With regard to projects, the measurement system must promote a culture in which projects which do not meet the company's economic objectives are stopped. The project developer must not have a vested interest in a project moving ahead at all costs.

3. *Use a number of quantitative and qualitative measures in combination.*
Single measures in isolation are inadequate for complex international projects. It is important to combine a number of quantitative measures with qualitative evaluation (observation; reviewing with project team members; formal and informal customer and partner opinion surveys). In one instance uncovered by a management consultant colleague, too great a concern with narrowly defined quality targets at one factory led to a situation in which all the quality targets were met, but the products themselves were substandard. An excessive number of measures can also result in problems; staff can find it hard to know where to focus their efforts.

4. *Involve customers, suppliers and your own staff in developing appropriate measures.*
Measures must be meaningful, credible, and attainable in the eyes of those affected. Gaining input from partners, customers and other third parties provides critical information for assessing performance. It can also strengthen relationships with third parties. Staff need to feel able to influence or control the results; they must also feel the measures are fair. Ideally those who have to implement measures will 'own' them. Saddling staff with irrelevant measures into which they have had no input encourages cheating and creates resistance. But it is also important for management to provide an input on targets and measures. It is not unknown for project staff to set low risk objectives for themselves in order to enhance the chances of reaching a higher bonus.

A management consultant colleague of mine, Tony McNulty, told me about a joint consultant/staff study into New Product Development within Hewlett-Packard, which examined the relative importance of budget and schedule. The findings were conclusive: high technology products which met budget but were six months behind schedule sacrificed 33 per cent of their potential profits over their first five years in the market. On-time projects which were fifty per cent over budget only lost four per cent of overall profit for the company in the same period. Budgets were important, but time to market was critical. Subsequently, an internal HP taskforce developed the 'break even time measure' (BET), defined as 'the length of time from the beginning of a project until the cumulative net profit resulting from the sales of new and affected products equals the cumulative net product investment'. In application, the three underlying factors to BET were:

❑ The length of project time spent in development (cost not revenue).
❑ The speed with which the new product generated sales revenues.
❑ The after-tax cost of capital to the firm.

Staff have developed a software package (*de rigueur* for Hewlett-Packard, of course) to calculate BET; staff specialists also provide advice on implementation.

5. *Carry out pilot introductions of new measures.*
   Developing adequate measures takes time – typically several years. Getting it right first time is rare and a trial period is usually necessary. For instance, it took three years of implementation experience before Hewlett-Packard staff felt comfortable with the BET measure as a way of focusing appropriate attention on speed to market as one of the company's objectives. As a 'rule of thumb', there should be formal reviews of the adequacy of measures at regular intervals, and at least annually.

6. *Be wary of perverse incentives which might encourage the opposite behaviour to that which is intended.*
   Perverse measures are more common than is supposed. When he was with Apple, CEO John Scully liked to boast about the company's very high levels of productivity. Directors in Apple Computers were measured on a productivity ratio of revenue divided by staff employed. But, in fact, this led to a situation in which staff were being laid off on Friday evening, only to be re-hired as costlier independent contractors on the following Monday morning. The measure itself was encouraging costlier outsourcing.
   Another oil industry company recently uncovered a number of quality problems on a refinery project which they traced back to the 'cheese-paring approach' adopted by the project manager twelve years previously. Upon investigation, they discovered that an aggressive bonus scheme had encouraged him to beat his budget, which he achieved by deploying cheaper materials, which proved to have a shorter life. The project manager concerned had long since retired, but the company was now saddled with tackling a number of costly repairs as pipes and other components had to be replaced before time. The short-term bonus arrangement had compromised the company's long-term financial returns.

7. *Don't get so sophisticated that people cannot understand the measures.*
   The IBM aphorism: 'if you cannot measure it, you cannot manage it',

later taken up by the advocates of Total Quality, has encouraged a number of organizations to develop measures of performance. Not all of these measures have proved of value, and there is a growing emphasis on the importance of simplicity. One example of a simple, yet very powerful measure was provided by Exxon. Concerned that Divisional General Managers were reluctant to release their best people to other divisions, Exxon tied 50 per cent of the DGM's bonus to Human Resource Development, defined by a number of crude measures such as a target number of managers in a given year to be promoted out of their division into another division. At a stroke, this encouraged cross-divisional staff movements. In taking steps to develop and then release their best human resources to other parts of Exxon, DGMs could feel confident that not only would they benefit financially, but that a number of high-calibre candidates would be available to their division from elsewhere.

Further problems which are cited when measures become over-sophisticated include concerns that those whose performance is to be assessed may be unable to understand the basis on which the measure is applied; they may receive the information too late to be able to exert an influence on performance; the organization's systems may be unable to provide reliable data (this proved an insurmountable hurdle for British Gas – Construction); a multiplicity of complex measures may result in staff spending too much time collecting data and monitoring their activities, and too little managing the projects themselves.

8. *Provide for auditing and checking.*

An effective audit system needs to be put in place to ensure that the measures applied are achieving their objectives, and also that the information and data provided remains 'honest'. When the Chevrolet Cavalier proved a disaster in its first two years of production owing to poor quality and inadequate performance, an internal GM enquiry was launched. It came to light that the GM President had been tricked into driving a 'doctored' car which had been secretly souped up and filled with special fuel to conceal an anaemic performance. In addition, the test track itself had been redesigned to eliminate sections the car could not easily master.

9. *Get the supporting systems right.*

The success of any performance measurement system rests as much on the strength of its supporting systems as the measures themselves. Systems are needed for gathering a variety of information, such as: monitoring and collecting the data which underpins the quantitative measures; internal information gathering of a more informal nature (inevitably 'conversations in corridors' will form part of this, but measurement against behavioural capabilities can improve this process); external information-gathering (the input of partners, advisers and other third parties as appropriate); project developer/manager views; project comparison data through internal and sometimes external benchmarking.

10. *Use measures in combination with close reporting relationships.*
Complex measures do not replace the need for appropriate management controls and monitoring. As one organization put it: 'If your day to day management control is poor, then no amount of measures will get it right': This is especially important in international projects where geography can reduce the amount of formal and informal contact between the project manager and supervisor.

EDITED SAMPLE PROJECT TEAM EVALUATION FORM

The following checklist may be helpful in systematically reviewing the performance delivered by an International project team.

Performance Factor	Comments

1. Project details
   — size
   — degree of customer satisfaction
   — any significant project details
2. Project description
   — characteristics
   — size/composition of team
   — location
   — project director
   — complexity of the project
   — (technical/management/ relationships/other)
3. Financial management
   — budget realization
   — actual realization
   — rationale for any difference
4. Team member's role
   — role details
   — previous levels of experience
5. Performance factors
   — planning

— problem-solving
— communication
6. Management factors
   — how important was effective project management to the assignment?
   — how effective was the project manager?
7. Development needs
   — what are the training requirements emerging from the project?

Source: A McNulty, unpublished

INTERNAL COMPANY CULTURE

Of course, having created the right process and intercultural environment for performance management, there is still the question of the company's own unique corporate culture. A recent seminar with a group of individuals from a major internationalizing corporation produced a list of ten key action pointers for the ways in which it believed its management could improve the culture and environment for performance management and developing people generally within the organization. Table 7.2 sets out these pointers together with the percentage of votes cast against each of the ten aspects. This is a useful point of reference for any organization in determining the way in which individuals on the receiving end of performance management processes and management action are likely to respond. Frequently, insufficient time is spent understanding the critical employee perspective. Taking time out to research systematically and objectively the way in which individuals are likely to perceive performance actions can pay the organization dividends in terms of the enhanced environment within which performance management practice can be carried out.

SUMMARY AND CHECKLIST

The requirement to deploy the best principles associated with continuous performance improvement naturally comes into play in managing people in an internationalizing context. However, the diversity of circumstances and environments in which the performance management process is enacted adds a further dimension of complexity.

Table 7.2 *Action votes (top ten)*

Action	% Votes
1. Rolling severance: — looking at jobs not people — cost effectiveness — same terms on a continuous basis	18
2. Upward feedback process: — introduce management style checklist	12
3. Performance Linked Pay: — train assessors/assessee. — appraise implementation — reassess scheme in operation	10
4. Set clear Company objectives and cascade to teams.	10
5. Don't use consultants/contractors on core activities.	9.5
6. Train all man managers in good communication techniques.	9.5
7. Consistency/honesty about job security.	9
8. Look at costs *not* people numbers per output metric.	8.5
9. More open and honest communication.	7
10. Training programme to improve leadership skills: — coaching from the very top downwards	6.5
Total	100

The international human resources professional needs to be equipped to pilot management teams through this cross-cultural maze, to ensure the requirement for 'corporate glue' initiatives is capable of translation to meet the requirements of leading individuals and teams – locals and expatriates – in the most effective manner.

The HR professional who can bring flair and creativity to the process, while ensuring ownership for performance management and recognition remains firmly the property of local line management colleagues, can intervene in ways which take HR to the heart of critical, strategic business issues. The key is to ensure such interventions are made at the time key business decisions are being arrived at; the 'why?' of performance management. If this is achieved, subsequent professional contribution in framing performance objectives; designing process and recognition/reward mechanisms; and in monitoring and evaluating outcomes will add greater value to the enterprise over a short- medium- and long-term timeframe.

The following questions need to be addressed in supporting international performance management. Does the organization:

❏ have a well understood and commonly accepted framework across SBUs for identifying core performance issues, and transforming this understanding into prioritized, qualitative and quantitative factors of performance?

❏ ensure all the players in the performance management process; strategists, finance and human resources specialists and line managers integrate their actions to ensure business aligned performance management initiatives?

❏ have facilities for accommodating implicit, as well as explicit, factors of performance which emerge during project and business cycles?

❏ appreciate the inter-cultural dynamics at play, as well as diverse corporate and political influences, in managing individual and team performance in a multinational setting?

❏ adhere to a consistent set of performance management guidelines, to ensure constant and equitable group-wide performance management, while listening to the views of staff at all levels, to ensure guidelines remain fit-for-purpose?

Chapter 8

The HR Professional – an Holistic Navigator

It will be clear at this point, based on the coverage of the book, that supporting business development by internationalizing enterprises is a diverse and demanding challenge. The HR professional needs to explore the people dimension with a wide-angled lens. The best human resources skill sets will need to be deployed, working in partnership with senior colleagues – from other support functions (within and outside the business) – and, critically, line managers from the top level downwards.

I like to see this role HR for professionals, aiding and abetting colleagues in creating, maintaining and harnessing value from internationalization, as one of a navigator. We need to be up front – at times in the co-pilot's chair – but equipped with route maps and soundings to ensure our business driver has all the relevant intelligence and technology to steer an accurate course. The process must, by definition, be integrated and comprehensive – it is no use taking elements of the HR strategy for internationalization in isolated slices – an holistic approach is a prerequisite for success.

WORLD TOUR PICTURE POSTCARDS

In order to bring to life some of the issues that we have been exploring, I thought it would be helpful to tap into the real-life experiences of colleagues of mine operating in various parts of the globe. In some instances these network colleagues are local nationals; in others expatriates. They are all part of a global cadre of executives, working in a variety of business sectors and organization formations. These case-cameos ranging across the whole array of international people management issues, provide a better understanding of what it really means to translate theory into practice when navigating the HR maze in different parts of the globe.

Inevitably, space means I can only provide a relatively small sample of experiences in various parts of the world. However, I have assembled a global:local set of 'picture postcards' (see Figure 8.1), divided into regions as follows:

❑ North America
❑ South America
❑ Northern Europe
❑ Eastern Europe
❑ Southern Europe
❑ Former Soviet Union
❑ China

❑ South-East Asia
❑ Japan
❑ Middle East and Pakistan
❑ India
❑ South Africa
❑ Australia

In each case, practitioners who have a keen understanding of the issues of managing people and performance have shared their views either on a region or country specific basis. I believe from these we can extrapolate some key issues about the reality of managing people in an internationalizing business setting, balancing the need for corporate performance objectives to be met with the reality of local, social and cultural norms.

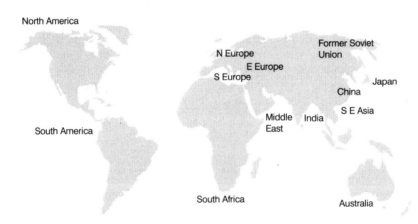

Figure 8.1 *'Picture postcard' regions.*

NORTH AMERICA – PRIMA DONNAS IN THE LONE STAR STATE

First up, a personal offering – reflections on the challenges of making a success of a strategic business acquisition in the USA – headquartered in the 'lone star' state of Texas.

I knew it was going to be interesting from the first day, as I walked into the office the Chief Executive Officer of the newly acquired American subsidiary. 'Well Steve', he said, in a very firm Texan drawl, 'I need to get one thing straight right from the beginning. My executive incentive plan is the cornerstone of the way in which I manage this business'. It was certainly the first really positive illustration I had had about the way in which – certainly in the North American market – compensation was used to drive business delivery. It drove it on the basis of personal self interest; but that personal self interest was closely aligned with that of the organization, and consequently, the desired increase in shareholder value.

Another term was also frequently used by this particular individual, let's call him Hank. That was the notion of what he termed 'immediate gratification'. It seemed to him, that the best way in which he could motivate his team, from top to bottom, was through the knowledge that, as a result of their efforts in business development terms, significant rewards were just around the corner. They were also very keen on the availability of really big prizes, for what they called, using baseball parlance: 'scoring a home run'.

The organization, which had been grown from virtually nothing, in a cash-starved situation, over a period of five years, to one which could be sold for more than a $100m, making a tidy return for the existing parent – a Texan gas pipe-line company – did indeed have an executive compensation strategy at its very core. This had been developed, in the early days of the company's life, with some help from outside strategic compensation consultants. What we soon learned was that, while it was, it was true to say, the very cornerstone of their business management philosophy, the strategy it was directed towards was quite different to that which my organization, having newly acquired the business, had in mind for it.

The challenge, therefore, was to hang on to what was good about the existing regime. I had to go back home and convince the parent board that paying out these hundreds of thousands, possible even a million or more dollars to some of the real high-fliers, was really worthwhile. But also to ensure that, in *not* losing the core elements of the scheme, we fundamentally redesigned its process, in order to focus attention on what the new parent wanted out of the business, over the medium to long term.

We then embarked on what seemed to be months of interminable debate, sometimes with histrionics when we had round-table meetings with Hank and his executives. Sometimes the emotional outbursts took me back to the heady days of industrial relations, dealing with labour union representatives here in the UK; although of course the stakes we're talking about, for a relatively small number of people, were considerably higher in relative terms! But gradually – little by little – with shuttle diplomacy across the Atlantic, we turned things around, and came up with a regime that was going to work for all sides.

The scheme originally had been conceived around the notion of sustained shareholder value creation from the development of new business projects. The idea was to be able to invest dollars in projects that were going to deliver the highest returns. Of course, this is a natural business philosophy and desire. However, the scheme was tailored to the specific circumstances, taking a view of what projected net present value would be over the lifetime of a project; paying back over about 15 years. The executive team were paid out of a pool, which represented a proportion of the NPV, simply calculated.

To ensure that the executives' commitment was more than simply: get the project to financial close and walk away, there was an element where (because plans rolled on year-on-year) there was a kind of 'true-up' mechanism, designed to give comfort to the sponsoring organization. What this meant was that, when the project got to first commercial operation, there was a re-evaluation of whether or not the projected NPV was actually beginning to come through at the levels which had been anticipated. The pool was then adjusted either upwards or downwards, based upon whether or not the original projections were accurate. Clearly, there was an incentive to ensure that projections were about right. At the very least, conservative estimates were provided in order that the individual stood to gain more over the longer term, rather than to experience cut-back, by enhancing NPV above projected levels. So far so good.

The problem was that, in addition to this short to medium-term scheme, there was a long-term incentive plan, which had the potential, and indeed in reality, paid out in millions of dollars overall. The arrangement had been that the team had had a parent which was cash starved, and in need of additional funds, over the fairly short term. The company had therefore been directed towards creating, at minimum cost, a vehicle which was capable of being sold off at a profit.

The newly acquiring company had no such objective for the organization. Quite the contrary, it wanted to ensure that this was a new part of its *globalizing* entity; representing a real business development and operating vehicle in North America. Therefore, what we had to do, was to think about how both short and long-term incentive plans could continue to focus the attention of the individuals, to go ahead and make money for the business, but in a way which was about managing a business to remain with the existing shareholder over the long-term, rather than be parcelled up for selling off.

After many manoeuvrings and debates, we came up with a plan which first re-assessed the basis on which salaries had been set. Given that the existing parent had been cash starved, they were reluctant to set (fixed-cost) salaries at the levels of which the local markets suggested were appropriate. This was made good, in the sense that the potential gains in the variable element over the medium to long-term were above the market norms. We were moving towards a more stable regime; indeed the market was getting tougher, and some of the gains from riding the switch-back were unlikely to be available over the immediate future.

In order, therefore, to hang on to and motivate the talent which had been bought at a significant premium, as part of the acquisition deal, we introduced truly market related salaries; and a short-term bonus plan, which was about ensuring that the individuals kept an eye on and achieved material gain from managing the business which existed at present.

In addition, then, we introduced what was known as the *Project Incentive Plan*. This moved away slightly from the notion simply of projected NPV. My Group CEO was somewhat sceptical of such schemes which took a 'flyer' on what the future might hold. They also have a tendency to get bogged down in debates over key factors in the NPV pool calculations; such as the value of internal cost of capital! We therefore came down on a plan which actually provided the executive team with the opportunity to share a proportion of the total investment to get a project launched. In some ways this was risky – there was an incentive to make the maximum spend – but we felt that within our overall financial accounting strategy we had controls, underpinned by the short term incentive bonus plan, to ensure fiscal prudence. The plan was set up on a cycle, whereby an assessment would be made once every six months of the progress which had been achieved. Pay-outs would then be made; meeting Hank's 'immediate gratification' stipulation.

To complement the overall regime, we then had, what we termed the *Long-Term Value Appreciation* plan. This was very much the brain-child of the existing CEO, Hank. Unfortunately, it had a turbulent passage; not helped when it was decided that Hank was not compatible in terms of philosophy and orientation towards the new business, to remain with the organization over the long-term. The replacement CEO had rather different views. However, in concept, it was an innovative approach and worth sharing here.

Hank, talked a really good game about an entrepreneurial spirit which he had created for this business development vehicle. Within the true spirit of entrepreneurialism then, Hank's view was, that all of the top executive team should be prepared to invest their own dollars into a plan to buy, if you like, a real stake in the business. Just like any other stakeholder then, but obviously based on their own efforts to grow that business over a five to seven year period, he felt the executive stakeholders should see a really healthy return.

The notion would be that the company would be valued, at either five or seven years, as though it were about to be offered on the New York Stock Exchange at an initial public offering. That in itself achieved a way of determining organizational performance in a manner that suited both the parent company's and the executives' views on equity and fair treatment. At the end of the period, a view would be taken, discounting the investments which had been made, as well as the initial investment from the overall evaluated worth of the business, at five or seven years. At that stage, individuals would be entitled to a sizable share of the pool of new value which had been created.

Individuals had the opportunity to leave their funds in place, for a further two years at which time, assuming continued healthy upward progress in growth terms, an even more healthy return would be injected into the pool. For the average Executive Vice-President, this would mean the prospect of becoming a dollar millionaire, over a seven year term.

In short, we did re-focus local strategic attention; we did gain the consent of the parent board to implement a highly geared, 'generous' reward regime; and we did see an increasing integration and motivation among the US team to integrate with the corporate business. This was possible, however, only by coming to terms with the real issues, mutual respect of each other's norms and values, and a willingness to put in the time to get a 'win/win' deal.

MANAGING THE 'UNMANAGEABLE' IN SOUTH AMERICA

International Actuary and Management Consultant Lorraine Zuleta, has shared with me the lessons of 16 years living and working in South America.

In Lorraine Zuleta's view the key aspect of managing international business wherever it takes you, is getting the right people on board. This imperative applies, not necessarily to the top management, as she put it, 'back in Blighty'; but the people on the ground. The skill sets required are likely to vary depending upon the ventures. It is important to distinguish between Greenfield start-ups and acquisitions, where mergers and acquisitions skills are likely to be required. Greenfield start-up ventures go wrong in international developments, because corporate people who have been highly successful in their domestic 'institutionalized' environment are deployed never having worked in a start-up situation previously. They simply lack the entrepreneurial skills required. Further, it is important to distinguish between the skill sets required to work in a wholly owned venture and those appropriate to a joint venture. 'A core competence is managing the politics of working in that joint setting.'

Creativity is the key

Lorraine Zuleta's belief is that you can do what you want in translating corporate HR philosophies into local practice anywhere around the world. It just needs people who understand what it takes to use their distinctive skills and to bring about change in a particular environment. This has a big impact on the capability required. 'You can achieve anything even in "unmanageable" South American countries; you just won't do it the same way as you would do applying corporate policy in the "home" environment.'

'One might be able to introduce a New Deal for a highly qualified workforce, but the low paid and low qualified have problems in understanding these concepts, so it's harder to get through to them.' Functional illiteracy rates are high; eg in Brazil and Venezuela they are 15 per cent plus. It is Lorraine Zuleta's opinion that; 'Whilst the developed nations are moving into a new millennium some of the South American countries are only just getting into the 20th century'. Educated people with money will probably have more international exposure than their UK or US equivalents; but they make up an extremely small portion of society. 'And it is in their interest to keep people under the thumb.' In some cases, this is done through the traditional institutional power of the church; Colombia is an example. However, it would be wrong to generalize; the church's power is not as strong in Venezuela, for example.

The creative human resources professional has to think about ways and means of getting around custom and practice, and accommodating local employment law, to deliver the correct messages that the organization wishes to corporately, without losing competitiveness. Nevertheless, 'In a Greenfield context one may be able apply the same reward strategies as one can almost anywhere else in the world.'

South American benefits

There are parallels in the hidden 'liabilities' of acquiring businesses in South America with those experienced by internationalizing investors in relation to certain 'underdeveloped' territories on the other side of the globe. Where one acquires a company, one is likely also to acquire responsibility for the well-being of an entire township that is dependent upon the one or two companies there. *Noblesse oblige!*

In addition, there are what Lorraine Zuleta describes as 'very strange' benefits practices which internationalizing businesses have to accommodate, if they are to get the individuals to comply with their requirements to come on board with both their hearts and minds. For example, medical benefits may need to be applied not just to the employee; but also to brothers, sisters, and parents as well as the other 'normal' dependants. This extended family is likely to be wholly dependant on the one working employee. While one might not normally want to extend such benefits, failure to do so is to put the organization at a competitive disadvantage in attracting the right people.

In addition, the broader social security system, while it may exist in South American countries in name, either does not exist in relation to certain benefits, or is at breaking point where it does. For example, some companies provide a 'funeral bonus' in relation to covering the cost of burying dependants of the employee. 'Because the low paid are so poorly paid, there is a question of how on $150 a month they can bury granny. It's not just a question of being competitive as an employer – it's the expectations of such elements as being part of the reward package – and the aggro from workers which will result in not being traditionally paternalistic.'

In South America, labour laws tend to be modelled on those which apply in southern Europe. Therefore, they tend to be collectivist in nature. For example, one almost always has to pay severance benefits when terminating an employment. 'Severance benefits are acquired rights in some places.'

There are also constraints on what a company may decide to do in relation to employment conditions as a result of government regulation or collective bargaining. A government might decide to designate certain elements of pay as an acquired right. Individuals cannot sign away their acquired rights. Therefore, these external factors may have a material effect on a company's ability to apply its corporate reward policies. There are some attempts to introduce reforms; eg in Venezuela there are changes being made to reform the system of termination indemnities. Individuals currently have the right to receive redundancy payments of up to two months of their final salary per year of accrued service for unjustified dismissal. This makes redundancy programmes prohibitively expensive.

Furthermore, where a government may believe a redundancy programme may create social problems for them, they may step in to exert direct or indirect influence to prevent companies from instituting mass redundancies. Indirect action can range from strong urging (informal pressure) to action via government agencies (eg customs authorities) which can severely disrupt the imported part of a manufacturer's supply chain, and so frustrate business activity.

Beware of generalizations!

In relation to those corporate initiatives that can be taken, an example is job evaluation. But, it may be necessary to weight evaluation factors differently to the norm. In a salary structure one may simply have to permit more grades than is usual, to achieve corporate objectives.

'One of the biggest follies has been to try and roll out job evaluation systems worldwide (which is why some proprietary systems have become so discredited).' When head office is intent on imposing such a policy, everyone locally simply works on how they can beat the system. 'Hay job evaluation, used to be used in the oil industry in Venezuela. One used to overhear conversations between managers along the lines of: What do we want to pay, how many points do we require, how do we write the job description to ensure this delivers the desired evaluation outcome?'

So, there are a number of common issues such as those referred to; there are also some which are country specific.

In South America one needs to be aware that political agendas merge with personal agendas. For example, the current president of one South American country is an ageing individual towards the end of his life, back in office again, having been the architect of labour models during his tenure during the 1970s. 'He has a "bee in his bonnet" about introducing new labour laws. This is simply because he wants something to "make his mark" before he leaves office/life.'

Deployment of expatriates

A major problem Lorraine Zuleta has identified is where companies send expatriate staff to work alongside local nationals. This is particularly pronounced at the middle managerial level. At country manager level – where there are already major differentials between senior and more junior staff – the problems of expatriate deployment tend not to be so pronounced. 'In Latin America, salaries (short term cash) for top people are not widely different from those which apply among executives internationally. For example, a CEO in Brazil or Argentina will receive short term cash rewards which are comparable or even higher than those which apply in the US. The big differentiator for the CEO from the US is, of course, the long term incentive plans which they participate in, providing massive differential benefits.'

'Among the lower levels of employee in Latin American countries, the lowest employee is likely to earn from 150th to 170th of the CEO rate; the difference is mountainous. Social differences are huge. There is movement from the educated middle classes into the highest echelons but very little from the lower to the middle classes.'

However, in relation to brand or product line managers, for example, major issues can arise. For example, one might deploy a fairly junior manager from the corporate centre in a 'career development' role to a South American country, where they will be paid significantly more than the local who is undertaking exactly the same role. This has a major demotivating influence on the local nationals who cannot see any credibility whatsoever in this company action. Not only is this manifested in terms of salaries – it makes a major impact in terms of the visible differences of living standards and associated lifestyle.

Another of my sources in the region quoted an example of Kraft, Venezuela. A project manager was sent for training purposes from the US, and was paid more than the local general manager. While, in terms of social hierarchy there is no delimitation between individuals in South American countries (for example, the president of a company will happily talk to shop floor personnel both inside and outside the workplace), when it come to rewards there is a huge disparity. For example, a brand manager who is an experienced individual, could easily be paid around US $700 per month salary; approximately US $8,500 per annum. (A professional straight out of university in South America would be likely to attract a monthly salary of US $500.) A similar individual – who may be less experienced – on deployment from the US could easily be paid US $40,000 per annum together with housing and associated allowances. One could therefore see within the Kraft company example, that a brand manager for Kraft cheeses could easily be working alongside a brand manager for Kraft coffees with a massive differential; while doing exactly the same role.

One of the big people issues therefore is avoiding making a destructive impact locally – this can be even more pronounced following a merger or take-over where insensitive management practices can highly demotivate locals or engender a feeling of mistrust and fuel demands supported by staff representatives for excessive compensation which can unbalance the whole local reward scenario.

What price incentives?

Many companies in South America do have incentive programmes. However, in Lorraine's experience, while they were not categorized as team-based incentives, in effect, they *were* team-based. But, this was because managers in these countries are largely unwilling to discriminate between one subordinate manager and another (eg a marketing manager versus a finance manager), unless it is formula driven. Therefore, they tend to go for 'across the board' payments. In relation to sales force incentives, such programmes have always applied. Incentives also traditionally apply among management grades. 'There is no issue of discriminating when pay-outs are formula driven (sales volume, etc.) but, where more judgemental issues apply, there is no real performance-based differentiation between rewards to individual managers.'

While the locals may not differentiate, the Anglo-Saxon expatriates will, however. This can lead to in-fighting between members of a country top team around this clash of cultures and performance orientation. So, for incentive schemes to work at all in these circumstances, they must be very well designed, communicated and implemented. 'Again, this means you can achieve anything you want; but it calls for time investment, determination, and innovation.'

In countries where high inflation applies (say 60–80 per cent in Venezuela) there is also the problem of what represents hard currency. Does one work on the basis of salary paid at the time incentives are paid out or readjusted back to the real value of the payment at the time is was earned? 'When management bonuses are paid, individuals tend to whip them out of the country and into "hard" international currency as soon as possible', Lorraine Zuleta observes.

Environmental issues

There are structural differences in labour markets depending upon where individuals are deployed from and to. Even where a major restructuring following an acquisition in a South American country leads to a flattening of organizational hierarchies, internationalizing businesses will have to accept that, even where they have dismantled the organization, they are likely to have more levels than would normally be regarded as appropriate in the US or the UK, or Western Europe in general.

While organizations import their own working practices, and invest in technology to create efficiency, it has to be understood that any interactions between the organization and other local organizations – in particular governments – who do not have the same streamlining, cannot work in the same way and hence will somewhat negate the company's own efficiencies.

For this reason, therefore, in countries like Peru everyone has a messenger whose role it is to queue in banks to cash a cheque and to deliver letters, because the banking system is so slow and bureaucratic and the postal system doesn't work. 'Therefore, organizations have to be inventive in finding ways to get around the bureaucracy simply because public systems don't work.'

Assume nothing

Therefore, in relation to those aspects which, in an Anglo-Saxon environment one would take for granted, it is important to find novel ways of addressing them. Also, not to be blinded by the idea that wage costs at the individual level are so small that having all these extra people doesn't matter. Rather than simply comparing direct wage costs, Lorraine Zuleta's view is that one has to look at *transactional* costs. People work at their own pace in such territories and in consequence take longer than would normally be assumed appropriate in an Anglo-Saxon environment. Hence the overall costs of securing a transaction may be at least the same if not higher than that appropriate to, say, average Western employees. In taking on too many individuals therefore, one needs to be well aware of the potential for costs spiralling. Also, of course, the need to manage large groups of people who may be poorly educated and easily demotivated can consume vast amounts of managerial time and effort.

In other areas where there may be problems in getting around the system is where bureaucracy applies. For example, any kind of control; exchange control being a prime case, where bureaucracy and corruption can apply. Typically these are the things that throw out imaginative company plans for going into a developing territory, such as a South American country, and turning a situation around. It is possible to instil a culture to get things moving, Lorraine Zuleta says, but it involves a very long timeframe; managers with the temperament and skill to communicate core company values; and a willingness (and sympathetic 'home' management) to operate in a manner which may appear counter-cultural to the western corporation. Lorraine Zuleta's bottom line message is: 'don't assume anything!'.

SOUTH AMERICA – SOME KEY POINTERS

1. Right fit people
   — especially in middle manager roles
   — capabilities in local context to realize technical potential
   — compensation arrangements which are justifiable in terms of contribution (expatriate vs. locals); mitigating the 'pissing people off' factor, as Lorraine Zuleta puts it.
2. Need for imagination regarding
   — township responsibilities
   — extended family benefits

— replacement for state deficiencies
— competitive employer status issue
3. Evaluation of labour costs not in simple employment contract terms, but transactional costs terms; shoring up for bureaucracy/delays (messenger roles).
4. Control/bureaucracy – ways to manage around this hurdle which, unchecked:
   (a) encourages corruption, and
   (b) can frustrate most efficient business plans in practice, once they are obliged to interact with other agencies; especially government/suppliers.
5. Acceptance that western-style organization frameworks will not apply with any degree of precision.
6. A greater sense of purpose and urgency can be instilled; but patience and tenacity is called for plus a material communications investment.

NORTHERN EUROPE – THREE PEN PICTURES

Let's turn to three countries which form part of the North European business-scape. Their differences signal the diversity of this economically converging region. We will then look briefly at Southern Europe, through Portuguese eyes. Yet further distinctive features emerge, colouring the people management landscape in which the internationalizing organization must seek success.

Germany – a social economy

The German tradition of people orientation, realizing and recognizing the human potential (*Personalführung/PF*), and regarding training (*Personalentwicklung/PE*) as an investment is central to stable long-term strategy development, decision making and implementation. Our guide is Volker Rennert, communications and learning expert.

In Germany deregulation of markets, and the labour market in particular, has been less dramatic than in other parts of the developed world, and can only take place within the legal framework and democratic control of the social market economy. There is a trend, however, to more liberalization. German captains of industry can see the benefit of more privatization of 'state owned' institutions, as well as the painful restriction through high labour costs, which makes *Standort Deutschland* (Germany as a place for investment) less attractive.

An emphasis on continuity and security

The German financial system is bank-centred and credit-based and has a weakly developed stock market. A major feature of the German banking system is its relationship with industry. The attitude of German banks towards supporting long-term investment allows German organizational management to pursue long-term strategies; thereby encouraging techno-logical development, and strategic investment in machinery and people.

The German industrial relations system, is recognized as providing job and social security, high wages and legal rights for employees. The system clearly has the advantage of the highly regulated legal framework in which the involved parties know their rights, obligations and responsibilities and has ensured relative industrial peace over the past half-century.

Legal framework

Participation and concerted action are part of the legislative framework in Germany. The *Mitbestimmungsgesetz* (code of co-determination) as well as the *Betriebsverfassungsgesetz* (corporate constitutional law) provide a mandate for regular meetings, participation and joint decision-making in company affairs. Integration of trade unions into corporate structure has become a fact of business life. As a result of close trade union involve-ment in corporate decision-making processes, employers and trade unions refer to themselves collectively as *Sozialpartner* (social partners).

'Social market economy' has expressed the rules for the German gov-ernment's interventionist politics and has set the legal framework in which all industrial forces have to operate. Under these circumstances 'market liberalism' has been constantly balanced with the prime principle of social justice through joint economic growth and 'common wealth'.

The national homogeneity of training content, the range of the skills taught and the certification of skill by outside bodies – the Chambers – make for a high degree of functional flexibility and assure skilled workers of a strong position in both external and internal labour markets.

The Labour Law (*Arbeitsrecht*) in Germany guarantees rights and responsibilities of each party in a labour dispute and sets the ground rules. These are known to everyone; the balance of power is more or less equal, and 'concerted action' towards increasing wealth of the people is the over-ruling principle of collaborative industrial relations.

Representation – workplace democracy

Employee representation can be seen on two levels. There is collective bargaining and co-determination with the involvement of trade unions, industry or sector related, on the one hand, and on the other hand, outside the influence of trade unions, workplace representation through works councils or other company-specific activities.

Workplace representation as indirect and co-determination as a form of direct participation is rooted in three laws, established after 1945, and strengthened over time: the Act on Co-determination in the iron, steel and mining industry (1951), the Works Constitution Acts (1951/1972/1989), and the Co-determination Act (1979). In order to change laws, the procedural aspects of two-third majority voting hinders fundamental changes on the basis of political conviction of one party.

German labour market deregulation in the form of the Employment Promotion Acts (1985/1994) increased the flexibility of the labour market but only marginally weakened labour, and was in conjunction with 're-regulation', for example, in the area of part-time work.

The Works Constitution Act of 1972 (*Betriebsverfassungsgesetz*) for the first time included works councils as a form of employee representation regardless of trade union associations. The size of the *Betriebsrat* (works council) is determined by the number of employees of an enterprise unit which they are representing, whereby minorities are represented in the council by proportional numeric strength. Not represented on the works councils are the managerial and executive staff as they are viewed to decide on personnel recruitment and dismissal. They are, in many German companies, organized in speakers committees (*Sprecherausschüsse*) which are not incorporated in the legal framework.

Legal rights of the works council reach from supervision of the implementation of all labour laws and regulations, information and consultation on matters that affect employees, and, most far-reaching, rights of co-determination regarding general and individual personnel matters.

As changes occur at organizational and workplace level, trade unions have formally no involvement as works councils are responsible. Therefore, employee representatives can express their own stance directly to management. However, influential union impact continues to be felt through works councils members who are mostly members of a union.

The concentration by works councils on workplace and organization issues, gives the management flexibility, whereas employees are ensured full representation rights regardless of trade union membership.

Now, let's look at some examples from Volker Rennert's practical experience.

Case cameo I – the works council

What British and American companies need to understand, Volker

Rennert suggests, if they want to move into the German market, is that works councils are part of the comprehensive legal framework for participation, and a jargon word which was brought into the debate by the end of the 1970s which is called concerted action. This is something which can be considered at the discretion of the employers rather than a legally binding relationship.

'Let's look at a particular case in point. About three years ago, a UK diversified services group; a major publicly quoted company moved into the German market, and for their sales force they employed around 700 people. The operation in Germany was headed by an English general manager located in Munich. The sales force was spread throughout the country, but the majority was in southern Germany. After about two years of operation the sales force and the workforce went down to 350 and that gave rise to some demotivation and frustration.' Volker Rennert received a telephone call from their Group HR Director one day. She was confused about 'a very polite letter' which was sent to them by the head of the Company's German Works Council. 'This letter of one page was phrased in excellent English, with no mistakes, and it was directed to the European Managing Director; who happened to be of American nationality and operated from Wokingham, UK. The letter was carefully phrased, and mainly said the workforce was completely frustrated. It developed from demotivation to frustration in terms of the relationship with the employer and the work situation in Germany. The letter went on "we therefore kindly invite you to our next Works Council meeting which will take place at (date and time given)". It was three weeks in advance of the legal obligation in terms of long notice and so on. The European Managing Director was invited to that meeting, very friendly and kind. He sent a brief one-line note stating that he was too busy to attend these things, and that they should sort themselves out and let him know what their position was.'

The group company immediately faced a huge legal suit, because it is written in the German Works Council law that senior company representatives will, on request, attend the Council's meetings. 'The Works Council called the Managing Director, as the responsible manager, to a meeting that these directors need to attend in order to overhear the process of decision making and so that the Works Council is able to ask responsible managers for their opinion. This is an obligation and a duty and obviously the American Managing Director was not aware of it and didn't bother.'

This highlights how important it is that people who move into the German market should be aware of, and must gain a good knowledge of the Works Council and participation scenario and law. Failure attracts material penalties!

Case cameo II – recruitment

Recruiting and employing people in Germany has a distinctive character. Volker Rennert offers a few examples:

'First, it needs to be understood that in Germany an employee who has been employed by the same company for 14 or more years cannot be sacked. The rationale behind this is that the employer has "exploited" the service of the employee when they were young and cannot just get rid of them when they become older. The other argument about this is that the employer after 14 years never can say that the employee hasn't performed, because every court in Germany will say "wait a minute, if he can't perform you should have seen that before and, after 14 years, that is rather late". That is part of the understanding we need to have.

'Secondly, there are factors which illustrate why there are misconceptions about the current status of unemployment in Germany. People invest a lot of time in education, as everybody knows, which means that the average age of young women who move from university to employment is around 25–26 years and with men, because of the obligation to do army service or social service as an equivalent, two years older; so between 26 and 28. After they have invested that time into education they feel, and this is a common German feeling, that they deserve a job at a certain standard. Standard means job responsibility as well as financial reward.'

Here Volker Rennert offers another case study where one British company who wanted to move into the German market said 'OK, what we do is we recruit graduates because that means we get cheap, young and intelligent labour'. However, nobody in Germany will be prepared to work under the graduate recruitment conditions employers are used to in the UK, for example. 'They will ask for a certain amount of salary. If the salary is not provided they will go on the dole. On the dole, again is not directly comparable with the British situation. If a German employee, because of the market situation, goes, or has to go on the dole and become unemployed for 1½ years, the state is obliged to pay them the salary they would have earned in the relevant job they are educated for. After 1½ years that becomes reduced because obviously this is where, even the Germans think, people who can't find employment need to re-educate themselves and need to invest their own time and money into the process! If people are not prepared to do that, obviously the unemployment money will go down. So again, we have a completely different scenario.'

Thinking behind this all is very much long term. Employees want to stay, as well as employers in Germany want to have their employees stay with them. 'The only people who fluctuate and move from company to company are the very top people. And even they do that at a much slower pace than in Britain and America. The average here is five to eight years, whereas I presume in Britain, for example, we can talk about two years. With all jobs, I would say, which are down from second level; middle management; supervisor level; foreman level; and worker's level the traditional thinking in Germany is that you stay, if you can, for a lifetime with one employer.'

That obviously links into investing in their education; into investing in their training; into the social liability of the employer in terms of paying monies into saving accounts; into insurance; into company pension funds; into the Social Pension Fund which is centrally located in Berlin and is responsible for the pensions of all employees in Germany.

Again this highlights why the demand for a salary and benefits package is fairly high by new recruits and that people want to have a reward, in terms of a financial reward, when they are aged 26 to 28, because they immediately start a family, want to build (as opposed to buy) their houses and stay in the area they have chosen to stay in.

'Employers even have to pay into employees' savings accounts. This is a specific case which was introduced in the middle to late 1970s. There is a law which says when an employee is prepared to pay a regular amount of money into a savings account especially, for example, for building or buying houses and so on, that under specific regulations the employer has to put an additional 35 per cent of this overall sum into the pot. This only applies, as I said, if the employee wants to save that money from his/her salary. As soon as the employee decides to do that on a yearly basis, obviously paid in on a monthly basis, the employer is obliged to pay 35 per cent of that sum, additionally to salary. This law is called "the 624 Dmark law", and as the name says the employee can decide whether they want to put in 624 Dmark per year or they can double that rate to 1248 Dmark, or they can treble that rate. Mainly it is a question of just putting the original sum in or doubling it. Whatever they decide the employer has to put in the 35 per cent.'

The objective is a political one. To guarantee, in the long term, the wealth of the whole population and to ensure that that of the national economy is rising. Obviously nearly every employee does it because it is combined with tax relief, and therefore, it forces the employer to do the same and to support this initiative. Prospective employers, therefore, need to orient their thinking into line with this ethos, while accommodating corporate aspirations, as part of German investment strategy.

HIERARCHY AND BUREAUCRACY ARE A WAY OF LIFE FOR THE GAULS

Surprisingly little has been written about the distinctive management style of French business. This is despite the growing influence of French companies in other countries (witness the award of two UK franchises to Générale Des Eaux).

Jean-Louis Barsoux, a researcher at INSEAD, the French business school, has written recently that being a manager in a French company brings a social as well as a professional status. Those at the top normally acquire their position after graduating from one of the country's *Grandes Ecoles*; a broadly meritocratic system which produces intelligent, numerate and often cultured individuals.

From the beginning of their careers such individuals work between both public and private sectors. This not only builds experience; it also builds strong relationships and friendships which serve individuals and preserve their power in future. There is an even bigger distinction between those classified as managers or 'cadres' in a company. This group have specific legal rights and entitlements. They compare with other employees whose prospects are rather more restricted and who stand little chance of becoming cadres and reaching the upper echelons and who may become demotivated and resentful.

In business, the French work on the assumption that the best individuals in business are those in charge. The corollary is that everyone beneath has their rightful place in the hierarchy.

A distinctive approach to business has served the French and their national economy very well in the past. For example, it was well adapted to the rapid reconstruction of France after the Second World War; in particular to companies specializing in the industrial and technological centres which its education system nurtures. This distinctive style can be curious, even frustrating, for a foreigner thrown in as part of a cross-cultural joint venture team or operating in a French subsidiary from the outside.

Giving preference to brain-power, theoretical reasoning and technical ability, gives rise to the difficulty that this can exclude other managerial qualities; such as motivating staff and responding to business uncertainty. There is an old French joke about a sceptical civil servant who, presented with an idea, says: 'that's fine in practice, but it will never work in theory'. A problem then with the French organizational system is that its bureaucracy may take refuge in dogmatic interpretation of rules, procedures and written instructions, rather than attempting to be innovative and flexible to changing circumstances. Quite clearly in the frighteningly global market place such an approach is unlikely to provide long lasting success for those businesses required constantly to reinvent themselves. Furthermore, a company which is based on a rigid hierarchy drawing on educational qualifications risks squandering late developers who did not go to the right university.

In his book *French Resistance*, Michael Johnson (1997) says that while there are a handful of very successful international French companies, what is not seen is the long tail of depressed companies, which are not reaching their full potential and are increasingly doomed in his view. Growing numbers of French companies are being exposed to different rules and organization cultures; through take-overs and mergers, expansion into foreign markets, or EU regulations. This means more individuals than ever have been educated or worked in other countries. Given the growing importance of the service sector in France as in any other major developed country, where the ability to be innovative and flexible in response to changing market conditions becomes more and more necessary, rigid closed bureaucratic structures are not the pre-conditions for success.

Another key area of difference is the total separation between business and private life in France. Michael Johnson tells the story of an American manager appointed to head his groups' French subsidiary who invited all his colleagues to a Sunday house-warming party. He was delighted that everyone showed up, and returned his friendly smiles. What he did not see was the agony of his guests – who felt obliged to attend – desperately trying to avoid their superiors and inferiors in the corporate hierarchy, with whom they would never exchange a word at the office. Nor did he see their embarrassment at having their private lives exposed and their spouses put on show.

VALUE-BASED MANAGEMENT IN NORDIC COUNTRIES

Traditionally, Nordic owners and managers have led separate lives. However, Dr. Jyrki Veranen, partner at SIAR Bossard Management Consultants, has identified a new relationship between owners and managers, which is now emerging.

The market is seeing a new type of demanding owner. Traditionally, Nordic management has seen owners as a 'necessary evil'. Owners were a source of money that enabled management to pursue its plans for growth. This was exemplified in the late 1980s by the Finnish banks UBF and Kansallis. (In 1995 the merger of these banks created Merita Bank.) The banks focused on getting more money from their owners through share issues instead of boosting profitability. Today's international owners – particularly pension funds such as CALPERS – are more interested in what they can earn instead of how much they can give the company.

The vertical value chain

The horizontal value chain is familiar to most. You produce a product that then spends some time in the warehouse – as little as possible –

before it is marketed and sold. Each stage should bring added value to the product. In contrast, the vertical value chain consists of the owners, ownership structure, governance system, board, management, and reward and control system. Each link in this value chain should also bring some added value to the company.

Owners should be able to give a company more than just capital. The ownership structure should be such that the interests of the owner have a voice; ownership should not be too fragmented, nor should there be too much rivalry between owners or too much cross-ownership.

Dr Veranen argues that the governing of the company should be based on a model that allows the owners to control and support the management. The management handles daily operations and implements the board's views. Last but not least, reward and control systems should be designed so that they help the management strive for the right goal: value creation for owners. 'Most Nordic companies have focused on growth, market share, accounting profit or other issues that are secondary to owners, whose primary concern is increasing value and return on their investment', he says.

Owner : management roles in the post-regulated economy

Risk taking is the basic function of owners. In a regulated economy there were very few risks. But all that has changed. Today you cannot count on government support through regulation. Foreign ownership is also a fact, so the company must create value. This is the fundamental change that has occurred during the past decade.

All this means that the vertical value chain must be competitive in order for the company to be competitive. As the vertical value chain gains in importance, the management must perform in a more owner-oriented manner.

An owner-oriented approach means that the company is seen as an investment. In the regulated economic system, owners had little need to demand returns since the system protected them from the consequences of dumb investments. Devaluations, inflation, closed domestic markets, export subsidy systems, regulated foreign ownership, and the inability to export capital all contributed to the situation. 'You had to be really terrible at what you did to go bankrupt.'

Today a company's main function is to create wealth for its owners. This means that traditional goals, such as gaining more market share, might not be primary or relevant concerns. They are pursued only if they will create added value. For example, if a company operates in an industry with no growth and if the company has no decisive competitive advantage, then investment and market share growth will only make the owners poorer. Growth then becomes nothing but an ego boost for management.

Instead of constant expansion, the management should closely monitor how much capital is tied up in the company and how fast it is turning over. This means that the Nordic tradition of always having state-of-the-art factories is obsolete. All investments must add value. You cannot tie capital into factories unless it is justified by a positive economic return.

Owner-oriented leadership is becoming more common; owners are now a valued asset; and companies must compete for the best ones. Investor relations is consuming more and more of management's time. But, given a lengthy history of management-led operations in the Nordic countries, internationalizing investors may have to take time early on to educate their new managers in the 'new rules' as Jyrki Veranen has described them above.

What is the impact on how Nordic owners own?

There are dangers if ownership becomes overly fragmented. A company with thousands of small owners and no big ones is prone to management dominance. Active and competent big owners add something to the vertical value chain. With a fragmented ownership structure, no one has a dominant financial interest to pursue.

The role of the board has changed as well. Today it is up to the board to determine the company's acceptable level of risk. In the closed economy, boards took incredibly big risks in international acquisitions. The attitude in Finland was to take on IBM in computers, Philips in televisions, and so on. 'Where were the boards when the risk evaluations were done?' asks Dr Veranen.

The board, functioning as a representative of the owners, must evaluate the overall amount of risk and that associated with specific areas of the business. For example, says Dr Veranen, 'if I owned a lot of shares in a car company I would make sure the board would have someone who could competently evaluate product development risks; because the risk factor is incredible. One badly managed R&D project can destroy a car company'. So, setting the ground rules along shareholder value creation lines is an important early intervention by new parent company investors; aligning managers' interacts with those of the group. A sensible commitment of energy here will pay, literally, dividends over time.

Where does the board's role end and management's job begin?

The difference between operational and strategic management is defined in terms of risk. It is not the size of the issue but the risks involved. It can be difficult, however, to define what is strategic and what is operational. Even a minute change in the label of a leading brand is worth board evaluation. This does not mean that management should not be party to strategic planning. However, the demarcation line between board and management should be clearly drawn.

Today, management is asking for support from the board, so the board must have something to give. Managers consider it a major loss when boards listen to the president's presentation and then neglect to ask a single question. Challenging the management's position with penetrating questions is a way of helping management.

Institutional investors such as pension funds have caused all this change. They own such large chunks of some companies that selling is not an option; the market would not tolerate such a sudden massive influx of shares. As a result they have adopted the old adage 'If you cannot sell you have to care'. Gradually, Nordic companies are beginning to learn what that means, and global investors to appreciate the value of such coaching and guidance.

JOINT VENTURE START-UPS AND TRANSFORMATIONS IN CENTRAL AND EASTERN EUROPE

Imagine yourself in the great hall of the Privatization Ministry somewhere in Eastern Europe. As a senior executive of a respected Western firm, it's a moment to savour. In a few minutes, you and the Minister of Privatization will sign the Joint Venture Agreement. After the rollercoaster process of research, negotiations, false starts, and last minute surprises these past months, you finally have your first manufacturing capacity and distribution channel in Central and Eastern Europe (CEE). Champagne, press conference, and on to the next opportunity!

Yes, actually signing a strategic alliance, joint venture or acquisition in Central or Eastern Europe is a moment to celebrate, but it is only the first step on the tortuous route to creating a world-class company that performs with the best-in-class in your existing businesses. Building a company that can satisfy customers, outperform competitors, and create shareholder value is a transformation process more complex than a 'fix it, turn-around' acquisition back home. Figure 8.2 shows the phases of transformation necessary for creating a world-class company following such an acquisition or joint venture.

For a good start-up, it is essential for the partners to agree on goals, define their respective leadership roles, and set some ground rules about how things will run. This important foundation step is often overlooked in the initial flurry of start-up activities.

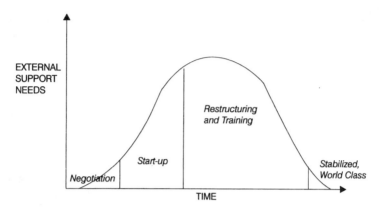

Figure 8.2 *Transformation phases – acquisitions and joint ventures in Central and Eastern Europe.*

Joint venture partners in Central and Eastern Europe are often in constant disagreement about what to do. 'They have long executive committee meetings which get stuck in trivial details, and ignore unresolved critical issues like budget targets, staff reductions, and technology transfer.' Why? Joint venture partners often assume they have the same goals when, in fact, they want very different things. Partners from different cultures frequently have very different views about what to achieve in the initial years of operation.

Frank Sharp, the Geneva-based representative of an international executive search firm, was asked to evaluate such a situation with German and North American investors in a CEE state enterprise privatization. 'The Germans pushed for technical improvements as the top priority. The Americans went for profitability. And, the local government partner insisted on infrastructure development (growth). The partners were not aligned on the fundamental goals for the start-up year. Without alignment at the top, the middle managers didn't know what was expected, so they just continued to do what they did before. Without partner alignment on goals, roles, and rules of the game, it is impossible to mobilize for transformation,' he says.

Unlocking repressed capability

CEE experience with JV start-ups and transformations, informs predictions about what will be deficient, or altogether missing in new partner companies that only yesterday were state enterprises. After decades of centrally planned economies and associated deterioration, newly acquired managers have some catching up to do. While technical university education is strong, the business tools needed to lead and control a company to North American or Western European standards are usually missing. Western investors will need to help their new partners to fill in basic know-how gaps in marketing, selling, competitiveness, profitability, budgeting, cash flow, and management accounting. This means a major executive education investment, integrated with other transformation initiatives.

Even today, managers in the state-owned enterprises are focused on production quotas and maintaining jobs. They have not been rewarded for satisfying customers, reducing costs, launching new products, or generating cash. You have a mentality-shift to achieve, as well as the know-how gaps to close.

But closing know-how gaps is the obvious tip of the iceberg. The JV manager must really start several parallel change processes (see Figure 8.3) to shift mind-sets, restructure critical core processes, and establish core competence in missing disciplines like purchasing, finance, sales, marketing; and human resource management itself.

Fixing the structure, getting the right leaders in the critical positions, and launching restructuring projects are all needed to get the transformation moving.

'Spending time on the basic company structure is a fundamental start-up activity. There are usually too many layers, and very little accountability. Focus on organizing around processes, starting with the customer and working backwards,' Frank Sharp counsels.

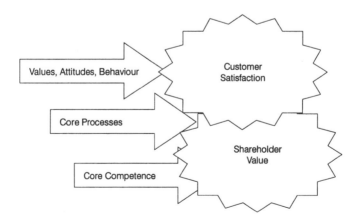

Figure 8.3 *Joint venture transformation – parallel change processes needed.*
Source: Frank V Sharp, 1996

Who will be the leaders of your new CEE company? A US company commissioned Frank to undertake an independent review of their four CEE ventures. The results are instructive in a wider context. The first – a late 1980s pioneer – was still struggling with weak orders and financial losses, while the newer ones showed good progress. In the weak company, five expatriate managers from the US parent were still running the JV company seven years after start-up. The successful ventures had local managers in charge, supported by specialist coaches from the US.

Many western companies send in expatriate management teams to get things started. This generally slows down the learning process of the local managers who are not empowered to take initiatives on their own, and never experience accountability for results. A second generation of high-cost 'expats' often comes in when the first batch goes home, and a self-fulfilling prophecy is perpetuated.

The use of specialist coaches to support local managers is frequently more successful. Late career old hands are good choices for these tasks. 'As "empty nesters", they are easier to relocate', Frank Sharp says, and they often see such assignments as adventures rather than career detours. The coaches are the key to weaving your values and your know-how into the fabric of the joint venture.

Key appointments must be made quickly. People are afraid to act when they do not know who is in charge. The kind of people you put in charge signals your values and expectations to the whole organization. Criticism and blame after the fact were the norm in the old days. The people who were in charge are often stuck in the past and unable to embrace your vision for the future. The strategic task is to sift through the organization, and find the people with the personality to lead, willingness to risk, and ambition to achieve.

Significant incentive compensation opportunities help the new management team to focus on three or four top priority goals: get the orders, fix the factory, and generate cash are good examples. Frank Sharp concludes: 'They will quickly master the tools needed to drive these results if they are not distracted by the laundry list of 25 top priorities.'

However, from my own experience in CEE countries caution is needed in simply importing Anglo-Saxon systems, and expecting them to replicate the behaviours stimulated in the domestic context for which they were originally designed. On an assignment of mine in Poland recently, the senior management were anxious to apply throughout their state-owned, privatizing company a performance pay programme lock, stock and barrel, which a visiting team of American executives had shared with them. While, as it stood, the scheme was perfectly sound – in a US setting – after some discussion, my Polish clients were persuaded to develop a pilot performance and incentive programme, tailored to 'the Polish way' of organization and management.

This allowed scope for early learning among supervisors about decision taking and communication on individual subordinates' performance, which had been an alien concept under state socialism; where outcomes emerged via the systems' invisible hand. Gently easing-in a more transparent, direct and decisive process for getting the best out of people at work (and rewarding them accordingly) enabled the build-up of confidence on all sides. Team leaders had the opportunity to find their way without creating adverse employee relations consequences. And team members could see the investment by the organization in developing competent appraisers, which helped to build their own faith in the integrity of the performance management system.

Achievement-linked team learning

Restructuring projects are a good way to learn and achieve in parallel. Cross-functional teams are a new way to work in CEE countries with a strong 'silo tradition' of protecting one's turf. Learning to set hard targets, commit to schedules, measure results, report progress, and follow up are new habits to establish.

Factory first-pass yield and cycle time is a typical restructuring project. Budgeting and financial reporting is another. Establishing a supply management purchasing capability a third.

Seven to ten restructuring projects to re-engineer or establish the highest impact processes is as much as an organization can launch and maintain. A steering committee that sets targets, conducts periodic progress reviews, and requires accountability is needed to lead and control the process (see Figure 8.4). Restructuring projects are also a natural way to introduce cross-functional teams as a new way to work, eventually displacing functional bureaucracies with customer-driven processes.

Up to 10 projects – 80/20 rule
Restructuring Manager – a full time role
Steering committees
   *targets   *measurable*
   *schedules   *aggressive*
Cross-functional teams
   *get people involved
   *learning by letting
Communicate often
Recognize and reward achievement

Figure 8.4 *Restructuring projects.*
Source: Frank V. Sharp, 1996

'The routes from signing ceremony to success in Central and Eastern Europe are no longer unmapped', Frank concludes. The critical leadership and people management issues are predictable, and the learning points are somewhat portable across industries and national borders. New players in the region can speed up their own transformation to world class performance by studying the route taken by the early investors.

PEOPLE ARE OUR TREASURY

Let's take a specific country example to embellish Frank Sharpe's overall commentary about some of the issues facing the developing countries in Eastern Europe. I have recently been helping two quite distinct organizations in Poland; the one a major state-owned utility; the other one of the Big Six accounting firms, struggling to establish its place in this important market.

The state-owned utility has all the aspects of 'smoke-stack' industries, with their restrictive practices, union domination, and a lack of skill sets at all levels to manage in the dynamic and transforming economy. For this reason, the top management have been brought back, in the main, from major international commercial organizations where individuals escaping the 'communist yoke' developed their education and built their business careers. These then are individuals who are intolerant of the ways in which the traditional manager operated in the state-dominated regime. However, the issues here are not simply about transforming a particular business; they are about transforming an economy and its people. So there are major disconnects which currently exist between the main boards of directors of such enterprises – experienced and dynamic individuals – and the tiers below them (including many very senior managers) who are unused to operating in the new circumstances, but are having very quickly to adapt in order to satisfy the demands being placed on them.

A main board member, with accountability for human resource strategy, in one of the largest state-owned utilities in Poland adopted an insightful approach when he described his attitude towards his workforce; 'people are our treasury', he said. He instigated a series of actions which would help to transform the business in terms of its culture and to introduce know-how based upon the world's best managerial practice.

To a large extent the changes have been driven via the change in the organization. There has been a slowing up of the process of full privatization among some of these state utilities in Poland. Given the impediments to change – generally political and industrial relations driven – the approach has been to split the utility by hiving off various non-core parts, and the abundance of people. Therefore, a kind of back-door privatization; divisionalizing the businesses with services literally outsourced, although with guaranteed activity, at least initially, to provide service to its parent company and employing the same personnel; has been instigated.

There has also been scope, given the long-serving nature of the current workforce, to reduce some staffing by the deployment of early retirement policies. The length of service and age profile of the workforce has made this a similarly straightforward option as it did in many equivalent industries in the western world.

A very different context in which these changes are being enacted, however, is what is being described as capitalism of the 'Wild East'. Everything appears to be negotiable; currency drives all transactions, and conventional norms do not apply outside the protected sectors.

Nevertheless, within the big state-run corporation trade unions remain a powerful force, and are perceived by management at all levels as something of a threat. To a large extent the most senior managers are simply ignoring this and allowing their functionaries to engage in interminable debate; which means that the imperative for change has not being forthcoming. As noted above, other means are being found by re-organizing and outsourcing to diminish over the long term the constraints the old industrial system imposed.

However, some of the problems that the directors below the main board are storing up for themselves are that, rather than looking at the real needs of the business and implementing policies that will help them change, they are looking for 'off the shelf solutions' which they can use to batter trade union resistance on the basis that 'these things have been tried and tested for many years around the world and therefore cannot be argued with'. Talking with the personnel director of my state utility Janus Pietras recently, his view was that for example a grading system should be introduced as though it were 'imposed from heaven', rather than having to engage in 'months of negotiation' over a more bespoke system which would be tailored to the real needs of the business and its requirement for cultural development. Therefore, at the functional level, industrial relations hang-overs and managing around them, rather than the needs of the business, are the drivers of the personnel policies.

However, there are some signs of hope; perhaps the providers of proprietary solutions will be able to draw on their experience in implementing such approaches elsewhere, to avoid some of the problems that 'boxed-in' approaches have tended to create where they have been applied in other parts of the world. Similarly, there seems to be broad acceptance emerging that, at least among the senior levels, things have to change; Janus told me that he had 'got broad agreement from the trade unions to introduce more personalized contracts of employment and related terms for senior managers'.

Under the heading of recognizing that people make the difference, we have developed a series of programmes to transform this state-utility's infrastructure, developing a team of senior individuals drawn from all parts of the organization (a multi-disciplinary grouping) to act as the champions for change, leading the steps which pave the way towards privatization. The object has been comprehensively to transfer know-how and to cascade this in the context of what will work at all levels of the organization.

However, part of the difficulty in making these changes actually come about is that 'senior people are so busy'. Janus Pietras is struggling all the time to get the attention of his top managers in relation to owning and creating the necessary sense of importance and urgency for delivering the people strategy. These individuals, who are not used to working with the impediment of the Eastern European managerial environment, are simply bypassing steps and concentrating on the macro-commercial issues. The difficulty is that, in order to have sustained change come into place, then investment, not only of funds but of management attention will be required to create a culture and environment where these things are seen as essential for success. But at the moment Janus is struggling to get the board members to give time, for example, to attend seminars on performance management, and even to appraise the performance and set new standards for ongoing development and activity of their senior managers. A US organization has come along to introduce their performance related pay and development scheme, and a series of seminars were arranged up and down the company which have attracted attention and involvement at a variety of levels. However, the big gap has been these 'busy' top managers; and therefore the message they give to the organization is that these things may be important but they are not an overriding requirement for the organization, because top management clearly do not commit to make it so.

There are still it seems some – around a third of the people in these state organizations – who wish the old days of 'certainty' would return; they either can't or won't change. But it is encouraging for the future that the majority know and do welcome the change; as Janus says it is now 'the only remaining certainty'.

The thrusting commercial entity

All of this contrasts with the activities of a new service-based organization with whom I have been co-operating. They are one of the 'Big Six' accounting firms who, from a strategic business perspective, must have a place in this critical new market. Their problems are not about creating change by stripping away traditional tiers of management and labour relations. They are about getting and then keeping the talented people who will make a difference in developing the contacts and contracts over the long term.

Each of the major six international companies has spent the last five years or so vying with one another to gain a foothold in this growth marketplace. As a result the investment has not produced a commercial return at this stage. The leaders of these businesses are coming increasingly under pressure by their parent firms, internationally, to deliver appropriate returns on investment. However, given the extent of competition, profit margins are being slashed in order to keep fees at the lowest possible level – the basis on which these organizations are currently competing – because it is the view that that is the basis on which market share will be captured, to be capitalized on over the longer term.

This has lead management to focus very little on creating a consistent basis for managing and developing, rewarding and recognizing their people. The 'Wild East' mentality continues to apply here. Individuals have been taken on with all sorts of *ad hoc* terms; now leading to major disquiet among all groups of people about the basis on which they are being developed and rewarded. Rampant inflation has meant that salary levels are needing to be adjusted not only once a year, nor even once every six months, but at one stage recently on a monthly basis. Part of the difficulty, of course is that no one really understands what the market rate for these jobs is; the situation is so dynamic and people are rising from such a low level of income that there is no commitment to other than the organization who will act as the highest bidder.

For this reason the project with which I became involved was to try to introduce some common sense and to have a more stable rationale;

❑ For establishing market comparison basis
❑ For establishing internal comparisons and relativities
❑ For understanding the basis on which roles should be set and progressed in the future, and
❑ To produce a performance link in the way in which individuals are rewarded and recognized.

All the usual stresses and strains are present, between expatriate and local professionals. The partner group – largely expatriate – are heavily focused on developing their respective practices, and find difficulty in devoting time to formulating systematic HRM arrangements. However, there has been acknowledgement that until such attention is given the negative impact of an unco-ordinated approach to employment issues will act as a drain on morale and efficiency. Consequently, through a programme of coaching and facilitation, they have resolved to set matters straight. The rationale is clear; such an intervention has a clear bottom line impact.

So, while there are obvious contrasts between these two organizations, in terms of their background, the areas of similarity in terms of addressing the people imperatives are notable. It is essential for senior line managers leading turnround/deregulation initiatives, as well as greenfield start-up investments, to address and take ownership of the strategic people management issues. They must balance corporate, internationalizt perspectives and aspirations with the reality of developing local talent. This requires appropriate focus and sensitivity if cross-cultural agendas are to become suitably intertwined for mutual advantage.

SOUTHERN EUROPEAN TRADITION – AN IBERIAN TALE

'Friendship, is born when solidarity is requested to support decision making in emotional and tense environments.' (Jorge Moreira, Consultor)

Portugal – a little bit of history

In order to understand the depth and complexity of the Portuguese character – and its future-facing potential – we must first glance backwards. The story is told by Jorge Moreira, seasoned HR professional and cross-cultural champion.

This small country was founded in 1143 and by middle 13th century was already the same size as nowadays. 'People remain in the same line of origin', Jorge comments.

By that time we had a solid barrier of Iberian kingdoms in the neighbourhood that isolated Portugal in front of the Atlantic ocean. These kingdoms became a confederation of states that have since acquired the name of Spain. Consequently, the 'unique' Atlantic door of Portugal was at the same time a challenge and a way of life.

So, the Portuguese navigators were everywhere before anybody ('our national pride', says Jorge Moreira). But essentially for commercial reasons. 'Naturally, we became colonialists as per the last century's ideological semantic.'

Portugal's continental platform is poor in natural resources and mainly based on very traditional agriculture, importing more than exporting and this imbalance was compensated for by the acquisition of overseas provinces, such as Angola and Mozambique.

In the 20th century the Portuguese began to emigrate ('workforce exportation' Jorge Moreira calls it), initially to Brazil and progressively to Venezuela, USA and Canada. By the 1960s the emigration flows were extended further: to France, Germany, UK, Holland and Belgium.

In April 1974 there was a revolution in Portugal that finished a dictatorial regime of 48 years. This event, besides many others, impacted very deeply on the labour environment. The 1974 revolution had nationalized all the companies that were considered the structural base of the Portuguese economy:

❑ Banks
❑ Insurance companies
❑ Telecommunications
❑ Transportation
❑ Cement industries
❑ Paper and petrol
❑ Power generation
❑ Agriculture chemicals
❑ Shipyards.

Simultaneously the unions became very active and labour law suffered what Jorge Moreira describes as a 'tremendous progression', creating inflexibilities in practices and expectations which foreign investors today need to address. The price can be high for the unwary. Collective agreements by activity sector or by profession were commonly entered into, and such compacts are not easily discarded.

Twenty three years (one generation) on, all this process is now mature. Most of the aforementioned industries are 're-privatized' or are on the way to it.

The Portuguese people

The earlier description of Portugal's history stressed the scarcity of natural resources and the traditional emigration flows. These dimensions, although only briefly touched upon here, are the basis of the Portuguese people's collective behaviour.

As Jorge Moreira puts it: 'We have history, tradition, national pride; we are easy to lead if we trust in the leader, and if we are respected both personally and technically'.

So, we have the essential characteristics against which to form opinions about multinational investments in Portugal, from the people perspective. It is essential, for those advising and leading business development in Portugal have a view about nationalized companies, their 'diseases', challenges, actions, and HRM traditions, because the re-privatization will attract international buyers.

The nationalized companies

According to Jorge Moreira, the companies that were nationalized after the 1974 revolution suffered from the following 'diseases':

❑ Lack of willingness to accept responsibility at all levels of the enterprise
❑ Disempowerment and demotivation of employees
❑ Centralized decisions
❑ Excessive workforce size
❑ Increased bureaucracy
❑ Non-market/non-customer orientation
❑ Enormous non-quality costs
❑ Political managers (party political implants)

Post privatization challenge

The major factors for attention to achieve business success are:

❑ Strategy
❑ Organization
❑ Technology
❑ Organizational Culture

Basic actions to implement

The managerial focus for action includes:

❑ Leadership and inspiration
❑ Increase in average employee education and know-how levels
❑ Reward policies (individual and group; merit oriented versus seniority)
❑ Performance appraisal for business units, teams and individuals
❑ Multiskilled employees and flexible company work practices
❑ Investing in new technology, training, developing and 'reconverting' the employees to a more focused industrial work ethic
❑ Flattening and simplification of organizational structures
❑ Companies' project development shared by all employees (involvement strategies), but with clear leadership assumed by the top management

Human resources contribution

Jorge Moreira's view is that human resources professionals and their interventions must be related directly to the business needs, and should anticipate changes and trends, both internally and externally to identify the real needs and the skills of the right persons, to facilitate:

- ❑ Integration
- ❑ Flexibility
- ❑ Ownership
- ❑ Clarity of each employee's contribution
- ❑ Optimizing diversity
- ❑ The generation and maintenance of a good 'organizational atmosphere'.

International companies in Portugal

'We reject stereotypes but' . . .'
Multinational companies (in all business sectors) have been operating in Portugal for many years. So, companies like Rank Xerox, IBM, 3M, Johnson & Johnson, Procter & Gamble, Ford, General Motors, General Electric, Solvay, Siemens, BASF, Philips, Beiersdorf and many others, already have a considerable management experience in Portugal. Their employees have developed a stable understanding of these organizations.

'However, some companies are initiating business in Portugal and we believe that it is possible to prevent some inadequate approaches to our people and to our culture. Although hospitality is one of the most important characteristics, we appreciate very much the companies that are aware of and trust local skills that are really available. Portuguese people welcome international management and technical skills if they are effectively better that the local ones. So, it is not enough to be a foreigner to succeed in Portugal,' Jorge Moreira warns.

Company culture and values

US companies which have earlier invested in Portugal exhibited more flexibility on 'trans-nationalization' of culture and values, and Jorge believes that this is the most important learning point for European companies that are currently in international projects or in change processes, as part of opening-up the Portuguese economic infrastructure.

On the other side of the coin, he says, US headquarters have not understood yet that in the Iberian Peninsula there are two independent countries and Spain is now at the beginning of the learning process of international management, following a very 'interiorist' period of about 50 years.

Professional competence, leadership and respect are the key success factors for any expatriate in Portugal.

One case – learning factors

In 1993 a British, Spanish and French consortium made a bid to own 80 per cent of the biggest investment ever carried out in Portugal. The bid involved the acquisition of a state-owned asset. British, French and Spanish cultures are historically difficult to mix, so team-based management was a significant challenge. Furthermore, the acquired asset had been operating successfully with Portuguese people within a very strong sub-culture of a monopoly company.

A statement came from the consortium management: 'We are in Portugal to teach you the best world practices'. When the management noticed the employees' excellent technical knowledge it was too late!

'Employees received this message as a deprecation of their tradition and capability. Had the new management been aware in advance, of the potential to untap (or at least demonstrated such recognition), and assembled the multi-cultural team around this combined capacity focal point, early teething troubles might have been avoided', Jorge Moreira opines.

Jorge Moreira's key success pointers:

☐ Learn Portuguese two/three years before taking up post.
☐ Do not hide in 'country clubs' and try to integrate in to Portuguese groups.
☐ We will help!
☐ Never be arrogant! Be fair even when criticizing Portuguese weaknesses.
☐ Understand that Portugal has a very dependant economy but the Portuguese 'have no tail'.
☐ Lunch is an important meal for the Portuguese!

STRATEGIC PEOPLE ISSUES – FORMER SOVIET UNION

The region of the former Soviet Union (FSU) is easily one of the most interesting, yet difficult emerging markets available for investors and companies intent on establishing a presence in the high growth/high risk areas of the world. Since the demise of communism and the disintegration of the Soviet bloc, companies have been attempting to establish and grow organizations with the appropriate mix of local culture and talent, and head office strategic vision. Consequently, few issues are more important to the success of a venture in this region than a coherent grasp of the strategic people issues. Scott Eversman, Russian-speaking American executive, is assisting international investors in the region in resourcing their operations. His hands-on commentary is instructive.

'First, it is helpful to have a general overview of the region as it is today, what the primary drivers are in determining attitudes toward work, career and success. As emerging markets are typically defined, the FSU is in fact atypical. Not only is it possessed of a highly educated workforce, it already has an industrial base and infrastructure (albeit in need of major investment for upgrade). Moreover, especially among Russians in the respective nations of the FSU, there is a sense of Great Power status which, although bruised, is still a component of their collective self image. One of the interesting questions which fostered debate during the Cold War era was how much of the collective and individual behaviour in the FSU is attributable to the legacy of communism – its assumptions, its frame of reference and the kinds of behaviour it encouraged and discouraged – and how much has a deeper, historical/cultural genesis. The assumption which follows is that those negative (or non-commercial) behaviour patterns which were fostered under communism, are hopefully reversible with time and education. On the other hand, those behaviour patterns which are borne from deeper historical roots are much less malleable to our attempts to modify them.

'Second, in referring to the region as the FSU one is in effect referring to 15 distinct nation states with a shared experience, but different historical perspectives on that experience. Therefore, while operating in Central Asia has similarities to operating in Russia, there are important differences which need to be understood to increase the chances for success. This view applies in full measure to human resource issues and especially the critical stage when the company is entering the market.

'Finally, much progress has been made in the past eight years of the post-Soviet experience. Many individuals have seized the opportunity to create wealth and embark on career building. Especially among the young there is a feeling that these are still the early days of nation building and there is everything to play for as regards the future. However, many in these societies feel disaffected and even worse off now than under the previous communist regime. Therefore, in each of the countries of the region it is essential that international business developers are cognizant of the competing and conflicting mind sets that will inevitably be encountered.'

Strategic concepts on building a company presence

'At the level of strategy the core issues any company must consider when planning and executing the people dimension of both an entry and growth strategy for the region, are: first, what is the best structural organization for the company given its objectives and business plan; second, what are the key "cross cultural" issues which need to be addressed between management and the workforce in order to create the kind of environment conducive to success. The key question therefore is, what combination of people and talents meets the Western company's commercial needs and objectives, but succeeds in obtaining local "buy in" and support?

Likewise, it is essential to have in place only the most qualified and competent leaders and work force for the task at hand. This means carefully choosing the expatriates to head up the operation in-country, as well as recruiting, training and then retaining only the very best local talent available.'

Leadership – a fundamental success issue

'In the context of the FSU the types of organizations which have typically realized the greatest degree of success are those who have put into place the fundamentals for success from the outset. In human resource terms this is largely evidenced in the creating of a clear and concise, yet flexible business plan for the specific country of the region. It is crucial that this strategic plan is based on a current and sober assessment of the country and market involved. It is equally essential that the western leadership understand where the "flash points" will be with respect to staffing and managing the FSU division.

'Primary among these is the organizational structure itself. Depending on whether the venture is a wholly owned operation or some form of joint endeavour with a local partner, authority and reporting relationships need to be as clear as possible and with a distinct "chain of command". The story of western operations in the region is littered with unfortunate episodes where senior decision making authority was split or ill-defined. Many a joint venture has foundered over the past years with considerable acrimony due to the absence of specific leadership and responsibility.

'Of similar importance for the western organization is an understanding of how local people view the venture, ie, what are its objectives? From a Western perspective this may seem blatantly obvious. However, with a tradition of companies also providing a series of social benefits for the local communities in which they are located, local partners and employees will have very different expectations of what the corporate objectives are. In fact, unless explicitly stated otherwise, local nationals will expect that the international investor has every intent to contribute to the collective life of the community in tangible ways, as the quid pro quo for being allowed favourable terms of operation in the area.

'At its foundation the human resource policy of any company intent on operating in the region has consciously to seek the optimum balance between western commercial imperatives and local cultural sensitivities.

This is only achievable over time by attempting "cross cultural pollination" or the integration of shared values into a workable and achievable business plan.'

Expatriate issues

'As the company's first representatives in the region it is crucial to put senior individuals in place who know the cultural context in which they are operating. In this regard, individuals who speak the local language can add considerable value to their company's presence, but only if their skill set includes solid business judgement. If faced with a choice between language skills or solid commercial skills, it is usually the latter which have seen the greatest success rate.

'In exchange it is imperative that the company take as many measures as possible to support and back up those individuals with the assets of the company. This is achieved first and foremost by giving the expatriate manager a clear and concise mandate. Although flexibility is essential to success, it is only within the context of a clearly articulated vision for the region that this flexibility can be applied to real returns. This includes a clear articulation of the specific expectations of the managers themselves. For example, what will be the objective criteria for evaluation; what will be the career growth opportunity and progression? These issues need to be addressed before an expatriate is sent to the region in order to spare both the manager and the employer the disappointment of unrealized objectives.

'Similarly, the expatriate must be given as clear a picture as possible as to what the likely career path and rewards are after the posting. Especially in larger organizations, one of the most often heard criticisms of any foreign assignment is that while away pioneering new frontiers on behalf of the company, the young executive is in fact sacrificing his/her future career development either by being away from the centre of corporate activity, or by being labelled as the "Russia Expert", and hence especially of value to that market only.

'As evidence of the company's commitment to repatriate talented individuals many companies have incorporated in the expatriate's brief a clear mandate to identify and recruit his or her local replacement by the end of assignment. This typically means that upon arrival in the region, the expatriate must set about the task of identifying and recruiting a successor to his/her own position. Given the duration of the expatriate assignment this may take place as much as three years before rotating out of country. The intent in bringing this level of talent into the organization at this stage is to give sufficient time for the acculturation of the individual(s), training and even temporary posting back to corporate head quarters.'

Local issues

'Of all the issues facing organizations in the emerging market region, local human resources will be of paramount importance. First, in the minds of local individuals is the perception that western firms pay more than comparable local companies. By and large this is true with one very interesting exception; the investment banking industry. What must be avoided as regards the compensation issues is the tendency to create a "twin track" mentality. This fosters the "us vs. them" mentality and can, if poorly managed, lead to division and inefficiency. Therefore, to avoid compensation and benefits being a divisive issue, a clearly articulated explanation of how various pay packages are arrived at is essential. Herein skill sets and competencies must be correlated with given pay levels in order to create in the mind of local employees a clear and fair understanding of effort, responsibility and reward. Furthermore, this also is part of the career progression continuum.

What western companies have commonly discovered is that far from being totally cash orientated, local workers tend to see a range of other benefits as equally if not more important. These have to do with training and career development. Experience tells us that in the current environment local workers place enormous value on being able to learn western best practice and having an opportunity to train in the West (quite apart from the excitement of travelling abroad). Likewise, an acknowledged career development path which is merit based, in which all positions in the company's local office appear to be open for competition, tends to foster a greater sense of loyalty and commitment to the company and its future.

'As a corollary, the western company must deliver a training programme which addresses requirements at all levels of the company and continually upgrades the quality of talent in the organization.'

CHINA I – THE SLEEPING GIANT AWAKES

Henry Yung is a management consultant based in the People's Republic of China (PRC). A native Chinese who has lived for most of his life in Hong Kong, Henry has recently returned and is now assisting a wide range of international businesses within the republic. Henry presents us with his toolkit for human resource management.

The context

The importance of Asia Pacific as a manufacturing centre, financial centre and market is well recognized and growing. Following a slumber of more than 30 years the People's Republic of China has awoken and has been following a market economy and will, no doubt, be a major economic power in the decade. Internationalizing businesses are rushing to China next to take advantage of the relatively low labour cost, abundance of industrious, skilled and versatile workers, favourable investment environment and more importantly the enormous market of 1.2 billion people. 'Often such companies have had adverse experiences. The tendency has been to point a finger at the local law, people, government, environment rather taking a realistic look at themselves, their awareness of the local knowledge, custom, culture, management style, laws and operating environment', Henry Yung observes. 'One thing is sure: there will be no pat answers to any of these issues because circumstances vary from company to company, location to location, situation to situation, people to people.'

Major human resources issues and challenges

Recruitment

China has the capability of launching satellites for other countries. But the irony is that there are just too few people whom Western companies wish to recruit and employ. Most are not trained. Others have indifferent experience. Some are managers but with little or no cost concept. Still others have a different attitude. All these may be attributable to different political, social, economic and educational backgrounds of the past. We see the new generation of graduates have values which are closer to the outside world. In general, China produces qualified engineers and technical staff. However, finance/accounting, human resource, public affairs, management information systems, industrial engineering, distribution, sales and marketing, material management and quality management professionals are in extremely short supply. There are a few who have been trained and developed by multinational companies operating in China for a number of years, but basically demand greatly exceeds supply. Qualified locals are available but not in sufficient quantity to meet the needs of the increasing number of foreign companies.

Retention

Next on the list is retention: to keep the people you have trained and the people you want to keep. Again this has to do with the supply and demand equation. When we do all the right things we have a better chance of retaining the people we want to keep. This means doing the right thing at the right time, satisfying the right need at the right time. 'When the need is for training –

provide training. When the need is for responsibility – provide such responsibility. Do not try to throw money at problems. It may look like money problems. Identify the real need and provide for it,' Henry Yung advises.

Regular international expatriates

Any multinational company will require expatriate expertise for a long time to come in almost all fields. However, businesses are finding it is worth while to localize as far and as fast as possible especially for technical and supervisory jobs. Chinese technicians and professionals are bright and quick to learn. They have a very strong technical background. New graduates are conversant in the English language. It makes very good business sense to recruit local Chinese staff, because the cost of expatriates is 50 to 100 times more than their local counterparts. 'Promotions to positions which used to be occupied by expatriates sends out very positive signals to local employees in that your company is keen on developing local talents and provides opportunities for advancement. This shows you are a good employer.'

Rules internationalizing organizations should bear in mind for success in Chinese business development and operations.

- ❏ Patience,
- ❏ Perseverance,
- ❏ Persistence,
- ❏ Flexibility,
- ❏ Relationship Focus.

Expatriates of Chinese parentage

There are expatriates of Chinese parentage. 'One should be very careful here', according to Henry Yung. 'Although we Chinese share the same language and all are influenced by Confucius, the cultural differences are quite significant. In fact, Singaporean Chinese are different from Hong Kong Chinese. Hong Kong Chinese are different from Taiwanese Chinese. Taiwanese Chinese are different from their Singaporean, Hong Kong and PRC brothers but, generally speaking, Taiwanese Chinese are relatively closer to PRC Chinese in their culture and mannerisms.'

Use of PRC returnees

Many employers in conducting their campus recruitment have made a point of including in their recruitment campaign graduates from the PRC. They believe that these graduates speak the language and know the culture and may have extensive contacts. When these graduates are recruited, after a brief period of orientation at the company's headquarters, they are sent to China on assignment. They are well-trained, speak fluent English and will have negotiated a package based on western market forces. When they are back in China, they normally face problems associated with acceptance by local colleagues. Local colleagues will soon find that the returnees do not possess any specialized knowledge or technical competence, yet they receive compensation many times greater than locals. Their local colleagues, who may be graduates from renowned universities in China, may think the returnees might not have been admitted to these universities in China had they remained in China. They will not understand how a couple of years' education overseas can make such a difference.

Local labour

China's labour pool comprises three main groups:

❑ traditional group,
❑ educated and westernized group,
❑ traditional and educated group.

Rules to be kept in mind when hiring Chinese staff

In the words of a general manager of a diagnostic re-agent/manufacturing joint venture in China, three factors are key to the success of any venture in the PRC: 'people, people, and people'. According to his experiences, several rules should be kept in mind when hiring local nationals in the region:

❑ avoid taking too many employees from a single source, because this can heighten the risk of hiring a lot of people with similar habits who may reinforce each other;
❑ practice patience and flexibility in looking for high-quality personnel;
❑ resist pressures to over-hire by Chinese authorities;
❑ find a local trustworthy confidant among the local management staff who has experience in dealing with the bureaucracy.

It is with that latter case in mind that many organizations are finding the benefit of Henry Yung's counsel invaluable.

Compensation

Salary escalation

Salary has escalated very rapidly in China. Listed below is a summary of the increases given by foreign owned companies in the Beijing and

Shanghai areas between 1992 and 1995. The increases included merit and general cost of living increases but exclude promotional increases.

Salary Increase (1992–1995 Beijing and Shanghai)

Year	Increase %
1992	29.43
1993	34.49
1994	30.00
1995	30.00

To measure the rate of increase over this four year period, the following tabulation is instructive.

1991(base)	100.00
1992	129.43
1993	174.07
1994	226.29
1995	294.18

The increases over the four year period amount to 194.18 per cent without promotional increases and may amount to 600 per cent or more for those recent graduates when promotional increases are considered.

Salary taxes

Most employers especially those in state enterprises have been underwriting salary taxes for their employees. 'Unless you make a conscious decision, you may inherit the practice of the salary taxes for the employees you inherit from your joint venture partners,' Henry Yung says.

Chinese partner's objection over paying competitive salaries to attract indigenous staff

Internationalizing businesses may wish to localize certain positions as soon as possible and at the same time build a talent pool. In attracting talent from the local market place, their partner may object to paying a competitive salary to attract such people, however, ignoring the fact that the expatriates will cost 50 to 100 times more than locals, on the grounds of equity.

'Clean' salary approach vs. base salary + numerous allowances

The local salaries normally consist of a low base salary and numerous allowances and subsidies. Some of the allowances and subsidies have outlived their time and significance but still exist. When international businesses decide their own salary practice, for their venture in China, they have a choice.

Benefits

The cost of statutory benefits and other benefits provided, to remain competitive in the PRC, amount to 100 per cent or more of the basic salaries and allowances. In calculating the total staff cost, it is important to include the cost of benefits.

Shifting value systems

Young graduates tend to have early and unrealistic career and salary expectations.

Lack of authoritative and correct information

Henry Yung says: 'If you are going ask ten people about Chinese labour law and employment practice, you tend to get ten different answers. The reasons could be:

❏ frequent revisions to the labour laws;
❏ laws not consistently enforced;
❏ rulings and interpretations issued before laws being revised.'

Areas expatriates should heed

There are a number of areas expatriates should pay particular attention to. There is a need to increase awareness of a culture which may be strange to foreigners and to understand how the cultural factors may impact upon job performance and cause basic misunderstandings. 'Many joint venture companies have failed due to differences in culture, value systems, management style and perceptions. The joint venture partners have been operating from these perspectives without knowing. China is a big country; the culture varies from region to region. Northerners are different from southerners. People in Shanghai and its neighbouring areas are different from the northerners and southerners,' Henry Yung warns.

Culture refers to the total way of life of a particular group of people. It includes everything that a group of people thinks, feels, says, does, and makes. Culture is learned. Therefore, different cultures often interpret the same event differently. One is likely to seriously misinterpret other cultures if one evaluates them solely in terms of one's own values, expectations, beliefs and behaviour. 'People often feel that their own language is superior and that people who speak their language are smarter.

Different governments have different tolerance levels.'

According to Henry Yung, the first factor is not a cultural factor but it is most important. This factor is nationalism.

Nationalism

In recent China–US trade negotiation talks, the US side accused the Chinese of 'privacy' while the Chinese accused the US of 'meddling in PRC internal affairs', in an effort to divert towards nationalism. The recent achievements by the PRC in political, social and economic fields have been enormous by any standards. Naturally, the PRC nationals identify themselves with their country and take pride in such achievements. We should be aware of their national feelings to which they are rightfully entitled.

Foreigners who are guests in the PRC should not do or say anything to offend or unnecessarily arouse national feelings. 'National feelings seem to be quite broad and nebulous in concept; therein lies the danger against which expatriate employees should be constantly on guard', Henry Yung counsels.

Offending national feelings can stem from an endless array of causes. Examples are:

❏ making disparaging remarks about host country's political, social and economic achievements;
❏ using foul or abusive languages to local nationals;
❏ calling some local national colleagues stupid;
❏ messing up a local partner's hierarchy or channels.

As a rule multinational companies because of their size, visibility and leadership position in their own industry should be more cautious and on guard as they can be more vulnerable.

Expatriates should also be aware of different governments and even nationals having different levels of tolerance. You may criticize your own president, however, the other government and nationals may not be that tolerant if someone criticizes their leadership.

'Face'

Everyone that one speaks to agrees that most of the problems in communication and in thinking really depend upon understanding the significance of 'face' for the Chinese. Yet it is very difficult to find out what 'face' really means. Lin Yu Tang, a famous Chinese author, in his book *My Country and My People*, said 'It is impossible to define. Face is abstract and intangible. Yet it is the most delicate standard by which Chinese social intercourse is regulated'.

'Face' is human dignity and the Chinese not only care for their 'face', but also must care for other people's 'face' once they have made contact with them. Chinese are caring and feeling people.

In dealing with one's partner, one should be extra careful about not causing your partner to lose 'face'. The result could be very serious. Undercurrents about disputes between partners may be traced to the origin of causing the partner to lose 'face'.

Direct expressions of discontent or disagreement are alien to the Chinese tradition because they will result in the person you are disagreeing with losing 'face' and the worst way to lose your own 'face' is by causing someone else to lose 'face'. There is also the fear of making a fool of oneself. There is the fear of expressing any opinion that may offend others. Never ask the teacher a question because if you ask a silly one you will lose 'face'. If you ask one the teacher cannot answer, then you both will lose 'face'. This is so deeply ingrained that one often has the greatest difficulty in getting participation in a group learning experience.

If you go to the wedding party of your subordinate you will be deemed to give 'face' to your subordinate. Likewise your subordinate will feel that he has 'face' by having you at the party. This is a very important cultural factor peculiar to the Orientals. Besides Chinese, Japanese and Koreans are also 'face' conscious. Causing your partners to lose 'face' is the surest way of having endless troubles in the future.

Guanxi

In China, one is likely hear to this term 'guanxi' everyday. Guanxi is not peculiar to China. In every human society, guanxi exists. The difference really lies in the extent. Guanxi really means 'relationship' or 'contacts'. We often hear that doing business in China requires guanxi. If you have the right relationship or contact, you can do any business. 'Because Chinese are a feeling people, we seem to put more emphasis on relationships. If you establish and maintain the right guanxi, you can work very effectively with all the Chinese parties you are dealing with. If the relationship is abrasive, you will experience enormous difficulties with constant arguments and quarrels. In serious cases you will be hitting against a stonewall.' Henry Yung suggests the following points to consider in maintaining healthy relationships.

❑ Respect others; let the other party know that you respect them. This is the foundation on which to build mutual respect and healthy relationships.

❑ Let others know your stance; let the other party know where you stand and how you will value their relationship in a healthy way.

❑ Establish and maintain healthy relationships; you may need to entertain others but do not be wasteful. Gift items such as inexpensive watches, calculators and diaries may be presented.

Status

Chinese are very 'face' conscious; naturally therefore they are very status-conscious. In news articles covering any government event, all the names must be arranged in descending order of importance. Chinese managers like to be addressed as 'Factory Manager Wang', 'Chairman Li', Engineer so and so. They observe their hierarchy.

Lack of precision

Chinese are generally not very precise. That leads to problems in quality and timekeeping. Basically, 80 per cent of the population belong to the agricultural sector. This may be one of the reasons for slow pace. If you ask a Chinese subordinate for a report, he will most likely tell you that he will give it to you as soon as possible, or he will do his best, or as soon as he can find time. He is not likely to say by when he will give it to you.

Departmentalism

Chinese tend to be clannish. Whenever a problem is brought up for discussion the first thing the Chinese will do is to look at the problem to make sure it is not their fault. Chinese tend to go out of their way to prove it is not the fault of the department they represent. It will take a long time before they will get down to discussing measures to solve problems.

Bureaucracy

Chinese bureaucracy has been enormous. There are principally too many bureaux. Looking after conditions of service and working conditions there are at least two government bureaux. Looking after the Shanghai ports there are at least three bureaux. Within a bureau there are overlapping duties and responsibilities amongst the departments. It has been partly due to the government who have used huge set-ups to provide employment opportunities, thus resulting in overstaffing and inefficiency of government administrative machinery. Things move very slowly, and rules are enforced inconsistently (not to mention guanxi and abuse of authority).

Abuse of authority

This seems to be the other side of guanxi. We live in a relative world. Or, we may say that someone takes advantage, or jumps a queue at the expense of others behind in the queue. 'On your way to Shanghai international airport, many vehicles bearing police and army license plates will come into the lane your car is using, in the opposite direction. This is but one example', Henry Yung says.

Struggle mentality

The laws governing joint ventures seem to encourage division instead of cohesion among partners. Rather than working towards a common goal partners are polarized: Chinese partner, foreign partner. Instead both should be referred to as one management. If the general manager is appointed by a foreign partner, the deputy general manager will be appointed by the Chinese side apparently to counterbalance the other side.

Energy is often consumed in conflict and other counterproductive effort. The whole orientation is a win-lose rather than a win-win relationship as if there were two classes. In a well managed joint venture, there should be an absence of such mentality, a vision, direction and a clear mandate from the joint venture partners.

Conformism

Chinese have a history that goes back about 4000 years. Although not rigidly inflexible they are deeply conservative and they have stylized rules of behaviour that are ingrained. The highest value in China is to live properly, be polite and obey the rules. Chinese people have a strong desire for conformity and correct behaviour.

Attitude toward authority

In the family there is absolute obedience toward elders. In society there is a greater tendency of permanent acceptance of one's position in the social structure. In government, administration is traditionally carried out through a sophisticated bureaucracy. The attitudes towards authority are dependence, acceptance and submission.

EXPATRIATE QUALITIES FOR CHINESE ASSIGNMENTS

They must be technically competent.

They should be good leaders.

They should be sensitive.

They should be willing to share and teach.

They should set a good example.

They should be considerate.

They should not brag about their income or bring up the topic of money unnecessarily.

In case salary/income is discussed purchasing power policy should be emphasized.

They should be good neighbours.

They should respect the existing hierarchy and channels.

They should never lose their temper.

They should not impose their own personal values on the locals.

They should be patient. They should be modest.

They should know that they are guests in the host country and conduct themselves as such.

They should be flexible on details and yet firm on principles. They should be tasteful.

They should be resourceful and adaptable.

Performance management in the PRC

Chinese personnel expect to be told clearly what a manager wants them to do. Subtle indications about management expectations are simply likely to result in confusion and demotivation.

Appraisal of performance in China is traditionally a highly impersonal process. Feedback to an individual is rarely given, and if received, is likely to be taken highly personally; probably resulting in the individual's resignation if it is adverse. Normal practice is for a self-assessment to be conducted, possibly accompanied by peer assessment; on moral, as well as tangible grounds (for example, is the employee a good colleague?). The result is simply fed up the line for noting and to be filed away.

Chinese staff tend only to have short-term aspirations. They expect rapid progression within the jobs hierarchy, and if this is not forthcoming they are likely to leave the organization. Furthermore, if younger colleagues rise through the ranks more rapidly, an individual will experience loss of 'face', and feel compelled to quit. Equal grounds for resignation will be if the organization fails to bring 'best international practice' to the workplace. In that context, their expectations of international business entrants are demanding.

Internationalizing firms taking on a Chinese workforce must be prepared to

❑ adapt traditional performance management processes and standards
❑ invest significantly in training and 'leading-edge' skills development
❑ exercise patience over the medium term, awaiting a positive showing as a result of the coaching and development support which has been provided to staff.

CHINESE PERCEPTIONS II – A BUSINESS DEVELOPMENT EXECUTIVE'S REFLECTIONS

Andrew Gordon has spent 20 years in business development associated with infrastructure investment by blue-chip companies, initially in the oil and gas sector, and now electricity. For five years, he has been leading a series of major investment projects, formed of European and local investment partners in the People's Republic of China. I asked for his reflections around the people aspects of doing business in the territory.

Working the bureaucracy

'One of the things I learnt early in my career, which I certainly have seen subsequently, very much today dealing in China, is the importance of the planning process; managing bureaucracy in getting things done. There are two dimensions to this which I have seen time and time again. There is the dimension of getting things through the planning bureaucracy, which means that there are certain requirements which a number of bureaucrats are going to have to sign off on. For example in the case of China, a project doesn't only have to go to one specific organization which itself has 12 departments, it has to go to several organizations, each of which has maybe 12 divisions. So that project proposal is going to cross maybe 40 desks in order to get approved by the system. How to achieve that is quite a challenge in itself. I've seen many people handle it very differently but I think the people who have impressed me the most are those who actually end up knowing whose desk it is going to go across and can actually contact those people and can say "please put my project to the top of the pile". So working the bureaucracy and planning in my experience, has been quite an important capability dimension in making these things work.

'The other side of that is the whole issue of policy. Several projects I've been involved in have actually had fundamental policy dimensions to be addressed. For example, during my career in the oil industry, I was involved in the controversial issue of gas into power. There was a policy issue in Europe that gas was not allowed to be burnt in power stations. It was necessary to have business developers capable of operating within a highly contentious political environment, to influence opinion in ways which would have beneficial commercial consequences. It's not enough to be able simply to focus on "the deal". In some of these large debt financed projects internationally, there are almost inevitably policy issues which have to be dealt with because of the complexity and because of the requirements of lending institutions. We have to get some concessions out of policy makers, and that whole dimension is actually very important; having access to people who can influence policy and accommodate those requirements.

'In Europe, for example, we get an EEC directive, a sort of blanket policy. In other countries, such as China, it's done in a different way; it's far more specific either to a particular industry or indeed to a particular project. We've seen that in India in power projects where the state government is prepared to provide guarantees for certain projects, and indeed you see that in China where in some cases certain projects will get some concessions which are needed. The risk of making that too open is that it undermines your general policy, and again that is something business developers have to deal with all the time. So, dealing in projects, where both dimensions are very important in the local context, in the countries which one's involved with, institutional "policy influencing" is a critical competence.

'That for me has been a challenge, to see how to get the local bureaucracy on side and approving the things that you're doing, but at the same time working the policy angle to try and get the things you know you require either as an investor for risk reasons or to make financing possible.'

Recruiting and retaining Chinese locals

'One company I was speaking to recently in China were saying that their staff turnover rate was very low relative to other companies. One of the big problems in a place like China of course is that you train somebody up and then they leave for more money somewhere else. This company has managed to avoid that because of the approach it's taken. The approach is actually very expensive, and very time consuming because the focus is very much on a long-term training programme for individuals. The company has also fitted its practices very much to local aspirations; for example, for an annual promotion. Chinese staff look to have an annual promotion, even if it's only a title change; it doesn't necessarily mean more responsibilities. It is status that is a very important part of their own perception of making progress in their careers. The company has looked at that and they've accommodated that.

'The whole people dimension of international business development I think is sometimes one, in the areas that I've worked, one could perhaps spend more time on, pay more attention to. But generally speaking, we try and do things much more in our own way and it's interesting the people you put on jobs release a whole set of potential previously unknown. Sometimes, certain individuals in their own culture may have stuck out like a sore thumb, but are very effective in different cultures. It's quite remarkable what happens to those individuals because they flourish and they build trust with the local people, and I guess sometimes those people are accused of "going native". But I think there is this tension working in multinational companies, not only in the way people do business. There is the whole contractual framework, but also the way people *behave* and that's not new; but it's one that is a very difficult area to get right. However, it is a dimension of project development which, with benefit of hindsight, I feel I should probably have paid more attention to.'

West and East – cultural contrasts

'I was in Shanghai just a few weeks ago and Henry Kissinger made a speech there that was absolutely fascinating. He said something that I am sure other people had heard before but for me it was the first time I had heard it. He began by saying that he wanted to say a few words to help people understand how Americans behave today, and why they behave in this way. What he said was that, looking back in history, the establishment of the printing press was a revolutionary change because what it did was, to free up people to develop their imagination and so, in effect, develop concepts which have carried on right into this century. What you had, through evolution of the written word, was discipline of thought and a conceptual approach to problem solving. Whereas today, what certainly has happened in the United States is the emergence of a "culture of pictures" where people don't read the same way as they used to. Instead, they watch television.

'Kissinger said what has happened in the US is that people respond much more to "stimulus", without complex mental and social assimilation. So he referred, for example, to the President of Taiwan's visit to the US and he said that, when President Clinton said he was welcome to come and visit the US, that was response to stimulus; it was not a thought-through policy which had come through, shall we say, due process within the system. Whereas, in places like China, they haven't reached that point yet. When a leader makes a statement it has been worked through and discussed by a whole series of channels to reach a definitive consensus. I found that a very interesting statement.

'Certainly it is different here in Europe than it is in other countries. Business is changing obviously, but what I see happening here, certainly in industry over the last ten years, is that one is working with an ever decreasing "pot". Industry has contracted, and working in a business environment which is contracting has posed certain challenges. If I contrast that with what is happening in China, which has been growing at more than nine per cent per annum since 1978, the whole environment is very different. What has changed in the developed world over the last ten years is, one has moved from a situation where industry has had to adjust to deal with a contracting home-base, while at the same time trying to expand internationally. In many cases these things are in conflict because the things you do, the organization you set up, and the human resource policies you develop to contract a business are quite different from the structure, not only the organizational structure but, for example, the reward structure and motivation structure which you require to grow a business. I think it is very difficult to marry these two together.'

Role of women

'It's quite interesting actually, to observe women's roles in international business activity, compared with the West. One of the things I've seen in other countries is that there are women in many key organizational roles; certainly in communist countries. In China it's quite interesting to see that there are women there who are very senior within the bureaucracy because of their capability. In the companies that I've worked with there has been a singular absence of women in business and the question is: "why is that the case?" I really think in the Far East, business development team acceptability is more a question of maturity rather than sex, which is a different issue. They do value the grey haired, experienced hand in business whereas in our contracting businesses, those people have retired early and, to some extent, that could be more of a disadvantage than the involvement of women. It depends on the women concerned. I think if you field an experienced, competent female in international business they will be seen just as a colleague and work as part of that team. I don't think there is any business reason why it shouldn't happen and I think its just a question of natural evolution for it to happen. I am a one hundred per cent supporter of that.'

Future optimistic

'Travelling to the Far East as often as I do, I think I actually have a different perspective from people that are more locally focused, and although many people read here in the newspaper what is going on out there, it is in fact an economic miracle. What is going on in these countries in the Far East is staggering and if you look at the total world picture, there are two billion people who are upgrading their whole living standard every year; year in year out, quite remarkably. So, on a world scale, I think there are still enormous opportunities out there and there are opportunities for everybody as a result of that.

'I think what we are having to come to terms with here, certainly in the UK, is how we cope with that balance shifting where the gap is unquestionably narrowing but the power relationship is shifting and how do we come to terms with that? I mean, there are two options really. One is to become part of it and the other is to cut yourself off from it and you know it is partly about living standards, partly about quality of life. But the excitement of self improvement is very obvious in the enthusiasm for education throughout Southern Asia, and what people will do to become educated. How pleased everybody is, how everybody is in a hurry to go about their business; there is nobody obviously sitting around not doing anything. People are productive and enthusiastic about what they are doing, and I think that colours my view of the future.'

SOUTH EAST ASIA – REGIONAL DIVERSITY

Former US Ambassador to Japan, Michael Mansfield, a long time observer of the Far East, once predicted that 'it is in the Pacific and East Asia where we will see things happening in the next century, because the next century will be the "century of the Pacific".' Many business and government leaders around the world have shared this view, and there is evidence to support it. For the past several decades, many countries in East and South East Asia (including Japan, Singapore, Taiwan, and the Republic of Korea), as well as the territory of Hong Kong, have experienced the fastest economic growth-rate in the world.

Such a regional economic transformation has changed the calculus of global competition. Aspiring international businesses, if they are to compete effectively, must maintain a presence in the region. More importantly, they must know *how* to conduct business there. In essence, they must understand the mindset of East Asian business dealings.

This mindset influences the East Asians' overall approach towards business, including the way they define competition and co-operation. Consequently, it effects the way they formulate and execute business strategies.

259

Rosalie L Tung (1994), has developed an analysis of several ancient works from which East Asians generally draw their business philosophies. These writings are widely disseminated and read in East Asia, but get little or no attention in the West. They include the better known *The Art of War* and *The Book of Five Rings*, as well as *The Three Kingdoms* and *Thirty Six Stratagems*. From a comprehensive analysis of these classics, Rosalie Tung reveals that they share 12 themes or principles as follows:

❑ The importance of strategies
❑ Transforming an adversary's strength into weakness
❑ Engaging in deception to gain a strategic advantage
❑ Understanding contradictions and using them to gain an advantage
❑ Compromising
❑ Striving for total victory
❑ Taking advantage of an adversary's or competitor's misfortune
❑ Flexibility
❑ Gathering intelligence and information
❑ Grasping the inter-dependant relationship of situations
❑ Patience
❑ Avoiding strong emotions

Aspiring internationalizing business managers from the West would do well to consider and learn more about the implications of these twelve themes for the conduct of business. These are important too in devising a strategy for human resource management, both in terms of recruiting, developing and motivating local national staff – an increasingly critical aspect of doing business in the region; and also effectively deploying people on an ex-patriate basis.

Because of the emphasis on strategy, East Asians tend to play mind games; they ferret out the hidden message in any type of communication (written, verbal or silent) and develop a strategy to counteract the perceived message. These mind games may have contributed to the stereotyping of East Asians as 'inscrutable Orientals', or as conniving 'Doctor Fu Man Chus'. In the West 'game playing' usually has a negative connotation. In China and East Asia however, it is considered an asset. Thus, mind games are considered manifestations of intellect. Consequently, Westerners who want to conduct business with East Asians – including employing them to conduct business on their behalf – should try to decipher the hidden messages in their East Asian partners' actions, then find ways to counter the strategies.

It has been agreed frequently, by academics, consultants and business managers, that 'Asia is different', and should deserve a significant modification in business practices, behaviour, and norms, if companies want to build and sustain their competitive advantages in the region.

In their article, 'Competing on the Pacific Rim', Philippe Lasserre and Jocelyn Probert (1994), argue that businesses need to identify and then measure 'strategic logic', by which they mean the premises and models that top management of companies use for the formulation of their strategies. The term includes the definition of purpose (what the objectives of business are), the way one approaches competition, and on what criteria business decisions are made.

Oui Chwee Hoon is a partner in a major international services firm based in Kuala Lumpur, but working with organizations throughout the region. She lists the major strategic themes for a western company seeking to develop business interests in South-East Asia as follows:

❑ Relatively cheaper cost of production in Asian markets.
❑ Expanding demand-driven Asian markets.
❑ Proximity to the market place.
❑ Generally expanding economies in Asia.
❑ Development of a double taxation agreement between the host community and the investing country.
❑ A strong economy, stable political environment and a business-friendly government is critical to the success of a new venture.
❑ Relatively good infrastructure, use of English as a business language; although a strong knowledge or understanding of a relevant local Asian language is also useful.
❑ A good legal system and the growth surrounding local industries providing better local materials and support.
❑ Investment incentives making it attractive for foreign companies to operate.
❑ Government bureaucracy should not be too excessive otherwise it may make it difficult and frustrating for the investor businesses to operate.
❑ In certain countries in the region, labour shortage, high turnover and wage increases are outpacing productivity making such countries less competitive.

Distilling these themes into those issues, internationalists coming to the region should be aware of surrounding the employment of people locally and sending expatriates to live and work in host communities, Oui Chwee Hoon says the terms and conditions (pertaining to employment), under which approval has been granted for each project, are critical. Project approval may dictate where a project is to be located. Investor companies should be aware of the availability, quality and supply of labour in the respective approved location. For example, siting a project in an area for which there is no technically skilled and available workforce (eg, in hi-tech industries) requires a review of the project viability and alternative arrangements to bring in expertise from around the region or from overseas.

'Infrastructure is a major issue', Oui Chwee Hoon says. 'For example, where there is no system of public transport, arrangements would have to be made to bus in labour; where there is no housing in the area, the cost of developing the infrastructure will increase the project cost since basic amenities would have to be supplied by both the private and public sectors. This may pose some difficulty in attracting quality people to work in the area.

'Shortage of top general management talent has resulted in spiralling managerial costs throughout South-East Asian territories. There may be insufficient locals with the requisite skill sets. Expatriates may be required to serve that purpose in the immediate term; immigration and relevant government approvals will have to be sought to grant expatriate work permits. Stifling red tape may prolong the issuance of work permits although, in principle, many governments would approve work permits to expatriates provided it is the intention to train local talent to eventually take over from expatriates. Therefore, job opportunities for expatriates should be related to their importing advanced technical know-how and skill transference. The key is to identify and upgrade local talent as soon as possible.'

Companies are now trying to identify and attract western-educated Asian talent who are living overseas (such as in USA, Australia, UK) to return to Asia. This group of overseas Asians forms a relatively untapped pool of resources.

'Increasing willingness on the part of Asians to move outside their own environment into other neighbouring Asian countries is opening up exciting new talent reservoirs. Intra-Asian professional movement is surely creating a special group of talented, mobile Asian professionals who have every reason to remain in the Asian market place. Many companies appreciate that these people will eventually "Asianise" the top/middle expatriate management cadre and that expatriates from outside the Asian region will be reduced. Foreign companies must now accept that local nationals must be groomed to take over their business over time. However, local Asian groups and foreign companies who are expanding their operations regionally are vying for the same group of professionals. There is increased usage of high quality executive search firms with strong local presence, and with international presence, by companies to identify high quality people in a relatively short period of time.'

However, an increasingly tight employment market makes it difficult to secure the right mix of skills, experience and cultural compatibility. In such markets there is the need to identify executives with international experience and the ability to build market share in emerging economies. Skill transfer is involved. There are many cases where there is a need to fill key positions with only local/nationals. 'Where the supply is limited, there is the protracted problem of negotiating for the temporary filling of these positions with expatriates', Oui Chwee Hoon opines.

Cultural factors

Knowledge and respect for the language and culture in each respective country of operation is useful. For example, although English is the business language in Malaysia and most expatriates enjoy the Malaysian work environment, there is the need for expatriates to be more sensitive to locals and the way of life. In Indonesia and Thailand, a knowledge of Bahasa Indonesia/Thai language and culture would be useful for expatriates living there. 'Business moves in "greenfield" countries such as Vietnam and Cambodia will drive most western business groups mad if they do not understand that there is a system in the seemingly unstructured and lawless environment', Oui Chwee Hoon observes. 'Those who appreciate and are sensitive to local cultural issues will be able to make a happier transition and are generally more effective in building their respective businesses.'

The ability of expatriates to acculturate themselves quickly to the local environment is important. Some take too long to acculturate themselves and may not be effective until then. The key for expatriates is to respect local culture and not be overly critical of the business practices that are unique to the particular environment they operate in. Cultural dynamics are critical and often differentiate whether or not the particular expatriates/employees will be successful in their new roles. Seeking out high quality candidates in those environments or those who can adapt to it could be difficult and time consuming.

Another major area of concern would be the length of stay of expatriates in the host communities. Normally, three to five years plus an opportunity for renewal would be acceptable. If they stay for too short a time, they may not be able to discharge in full their functional responsibilities by the time they leave.

Where have multinationals done well in their South-East Asian employment polices?

Oui Chwee Hoon says that essentially, this has boiled down to identifying high quality expatriates to train and develop advanced technical know-how and to transfer technology. A number of multinationals have done well particularly in hi-tech areas.

However, there have been some foreign companies who have deliberately tried to bring in lower quality technological driven transfers because they wanted to retain their more advanced technological know-how in their home country. 'We understand that such companies would have grown much faster and been more profitable had they adopted a more open approach and shared their new technology', Oui Chwee Hoon concludes.

The collective strength of the foreign business community is necessary to lobby for improved business terms and conditions. For example, where there is a key labour shortage, some governments have allowed for the 'importation of foreign labour'; local laws may have to be interpreted and managed accordingly.

Expatriate work approvals are sometimes too long drawn out. Issue of work permits for spouses is an area of concern, since expatriate spouses are a ready pool of qualified educated people who can possibly satisfy short term skill shortages in many industries.

Relationships

'Doing business' in East Asia involves a complex set of relationships – with competitors, suppliers, customers, employees, partners, officials, and society in general – which can be hard to disentangle. One of the reasons often given for the relatively low level of European and American investment in the Asia Pacific region as a whole – compared say, with that of Japan – is the cultural divide between Asia and Europe/America.

Lasserre and Probert (1994) conducted a survey, of almost 900 general managers and marketing managers of foreign companies operating in the Asia Pacific region. One of the conclusions derived from the survey was that, overall, Singapore and Hong Kong were perceived by the respondents to be the places where the rules of the business game seem the clearest and the most familiar. The position of Korea, which attracted the worst scores on both dimensions, indicates that western managers operating in this country experience enormous difficulties in understanding and dealing with the business environment. The lesson here is that it is even more important to recruit and build relationships with individuals on the ground – capable of crossing the cultural divide themselves – who will facilitate the bridge building between the western investors and the local partners/suppliers, customers and staff.

Compromise

One of the key themes to be understood about the East Asian region and its philosophy is the art of compromise. The philosopher, Confucius preached moderation in all undertakings, advocating a middle-of-the-road attitude. Compromise is deemed often to be necessary to achieving a goal. A significant number of stratagems advocated in the ancient classics call for compromise. For example, 'trade a brick for a piece of jade', or 'sacrifice the plum tree for the peach tree', or even 'snag the enemy by letting him off the hook'. These stratagems involve baiting an opponent with a small gain to get an even bigger prize. Consequently, gift giving, lavish entertainment and bribery are common practices in East Asian societies. Indeed, research has shown a strong correlation of high context cultures, characterized by implicit communication and extensive networks, and the use of questionable payments. An estimated 70 per cent of the world's population belongs to high context cultures, including not only the East Asians, but also Arabs and Mediterraneans. Low context societies include the United States and most of Northern Europe.

There are other implications of this. Compromise requires an ongoing relationship (whether co-operative or competitive); otherwise the parties have nothing to trade-off. This accounts, at least in part, for the East Asians' emphasis on developing on-going relationships. To the American or Northern European this is often perceived as an illogical or inconsistent approach. Some do not understand the penchant among the East Asians to concede major issues and yet remain adamant about trivial matters. This may be explained either by the compromise principle or by the difference between what the Asians (particularly Koreans) and the Americans and North Europeans consider to be major and minor issues. Different cultures place different values on different outcomes.

Developing business and engaging trustworthy individuals as representatives in East Asia, means that westerners must develop an awareness of the East Asian mindset to distinguish between a cunning strategy and a genuine cultural difference.

It is equally important to recognize the significant differences between the East Asian cultures. Even for the most 'global-minded' manager it rapidly becomes very obvious that the sheer variety, strategic difference, and the specific needs of the East Asian competitive climate require a regional perspective to enable companies to gather intelligence, mobilize their forces and focus their energies.

Not all the same

While people from Japan, Korea, China, Hong Kong and Taiwan may derive their business sense from the same philosophers, they sometimes differ significantly in the way they interpret and apply the philosophies. These differences are further compounded by foreign religious influences. For example, there are many Chinese and Japanese Buddhists, as well as Korean Christians. Similarly, overseas travel and study, as well as social and business contact with foreigners, have helped re-shape the East Asian mindset. Consequently, while it is wrong to assume that East Asians are exactly like westerners, it is equally wrong to stereotype them as homogenous.

So, adopting a regional 'structure' is not enough. The essential management challenge in East Asia and the Asia Pacific region as a whole lies in developing attitudes and mindsets, as well as in the enhancing of specific competences.

The building of relationships are not so much the result of organizational structures but rather of internal 'processes'. Experiences of companies like Unilever, Shell, ABB, L'Oreal and Wella, which have developed a presence in the region, suggest that commitment, attitudes, and information sharing are important ingredients of success. These are not developed through formal structures or systems, but because of the way decisions are made, how priorities are set, how investments are approved and implemented. It also matters about the way in which information is gathered and distributed, how people are recruited, trained and promoted; and how control is exercised. Finally, it also matters how strategies are debated and formulated on an inclusive basis. In Rosalie Tung's (1994) view, 'to succeed at global competition, we must try to understand ourselves and our overseas counterparts; not just certain management practices and procedures, but also their motivations, morality, and philosophies on co-operating and competing'.

Transactions versus relationships

The author of *Megatrends*, John Naisbitt has expressed the view that in exploring the challenges for human resource managers from western organizations who need to deal with the very different styles and cultures which exist in their Asian operations, a general admonition that is widely known, and widely talked about, can be summarized by the notion that, in the West, transactions are of paramount importance. Conversely, in the East, Naisbitt says, relationships are of utmost importance. 'I have done business in Asia for nearly 30 years and I almost never have had a contract. There is a lot of trust involved. Of course, the other side of that is if you ever, ever break trust, you are out.'

Naisbitt makes an interesting contrast between the way in which employment regulations apply in the United States and Europe, and the implications for Western multinationals taking their business to East Asia. In an interview in the *ACA Journal* in spring 1997, Naisbitt pointed out that in this regard the United States of America is closer to South East Asia than Europe. The USA is much freer and more open than Europe.

'In HR, for example, with the incredibly restrictive labour practices all over Europe, an employer cannot fire anyone. They have to give people an incredible amount of time off. Employees in France work about 32 hours a week. This evidently cannot be changed. In other words, these are very restrictive labour practices. In this respect, the United States is much less regulated than Europe. In turn, most Asian countries are much less regulated than the United States.'

Naisbitt's suggestion is that, in order to reduce the turnover among managers with key competencies working for multinational firms in Asia, new compensation practices should be developed, with a particular focus on equity and profit sharing. 'In some parts of Asia, there is a tremendous labour shortage in some work areas. In Malaysia, a country of 19 million people, one million foreign workers are there because the labour shortage is so great. The Petronas Towers, the tallest structures in the world, were built not by Malaysian construction workers, but by construction workers from Bangladesh and Indonesia. Most of the engineers were from other countries.

Naisbitt's conclusion is that everybody needs increasingly to think and recruit globally. 'Of course, to some extent this is happening. But the need is becoming more and more dramatic. Even the Japanese are accelerating their recruitment of managers for companies. Although it got shoved down their throats, Mazda now has a western president.' Companies are recognizing that if they want the best engineers, commercial managers, and administrators, that means they have to have not only the best engineers from the United States and/or Europe, but the best engineers in the world, no matter where they come from. As individual economies become globalized, those involved in human resource management have to think globally in all regards. 'With international borders becoming less important, it is essential to find the right managers and be able to move them seamlessly, to develop them and keep them. The shortage of such managers at the moment is one of the critical issues facing human resource professionals, in particular in the rapidly developing tiger economies', he concludes.

JAPAN – A CULTURE OF ENFOLDING RELATIONSHIPS

One of the most important differences in Japanese business culture when compared to the Anglo-American model is the emphasis on the development of long-term relationships through which trust can be built. These long-term relationships exist in the company-supplier, employer-employee, superior-subordinate and strategic alliance context. Japanese negotiators like to involve themselves in many seemingly unnecessary discussions (from a western viewpoint) because they believe them to be worthwhile in helping to establish a framework of personal ties within which all future dealings will occur, (Saha, 1990). Japanese managers often keep themselves informed by using personal contacts, be they in different departments of their firm, suppliers or customers (Hickson and Pugh, 1995). This could be somewhat of a culture shock to the Anglo-American manager, who could feel uncomfortable having to sit through many hours of 'getting to know you' formalities with no mention of the matter for discussion.

Rebecca Taylor has been studying, living and working with Japanese companies in both the UK and in Japan. Through her fluency in the Japanese language, as well as a knowledge of the literature, she has detected some critical features which internationalizing western corporates need to bear in mind. She summarizes these for us here.

Japanese business in general has a long-term time orientation. *'There is an Asian patience ... which shows managerially in comparatively greater weight being given to growth and future security as against short-term profit'*, (Hickson and Pugh, 1995). This is facilitated by the cross-shareholdings that typify Japanese companies and the less important role shareholders occupy.

The Japanese like to avoid uncertainty; Hofstede (1991) places Japan seventh out of 53 countries in his uncertainty avoidance index. This is unlike their Anglo-Saxon counterparts for whom uncertainty and taking risks are part of everyday business. To avoid uncertainty the Japanese tend to pay diligent attention to detail (Hickson & Pugh 1995). 'In my experience of working in a Japanese subsidiary in the UK', Rebecca says, 'this attention to detail by Japanese managers often frustrated their British counterparts, when it concerned a matter of urgency which was felt to need a speedy decision.'

Japan is a high context culture (which means who is writing or speaking, body language and nuance are more important than what is said or written). This contrasts highly with English speaking cultures, where language is low context, meaning that what is said and what is written has more significance than the situation in which it occurs (Hickson and Pugh, 1995). In the USA, particularly, this has resulted in detailed written documentation being of the utmost importance. In Japan however, social ties and personal relationships are more important than documents and contracts. The Japanese approach to contracts emphasizes the relationship being created and contracts tend to be vague and usually contain a 'sincere negotiation clause' or 'harmonious settlement clause' (Saha, 1990). There is also a noticeable reluctance to litigate which of course contrasts highly with the situation in the UK and to a greater extent in the USA.

The high masculinity in the Japanese culture (as measured by Hofstede, 1991) means that in the workplace, women are generally second class citizens, although this is changing, albeit at a slow pace. Women are overwhelmingly seen as the helpers of men and usually relegated to serving tea and typing, not being thought capable of doing more demanding work (Sano, 1987). Japanese women in office work are usually referred to as 'Office Ladies', which is abbreviated to OL. Some companies do now recognize that there are talented women who do not want to be an OL and have acted accordingly (Solo, 1989). However, despite the recent changes in attitudes and the fact that Japan has had equal opportunity legislation since 1986, Japan has smaller numbers of corporate women than other Asian countries without such legislation (Abdoolcarim, 1993). Many foreign companies have taken advantage of Japan's pool of underused talented women. For example IBM offers child care provision and flexitime to appeal to such women who often want to combine work and family but are restricted in doing this (Kuriu, 1991). This has paid off for IBM as they are now rated in the top five best employers for women graduates along with NEC, Fujitsu, NTT and Suntory.

The Japanese are an ancient and very homogenous race. They have a royal family which is over two thousand years old and whose members are said to be direct descendants of the first emperor, the sun god Jimmu, who descended to earth from the heavens. Although the Showa Emperor (Hirohito) renounced his divine status in 1946, many Japanese attach great significance to the Chrysanthemum Throne (Crump, 1991). Although Japan is quite similar to its Asian neighbours in some ways, when the characteristics of its culture are put together using Hofstede's 'measures of culture' they form a unique combination. Hofstede (1991) defines Japan as having medium power distance, high collectivism, high uncertainty avoidance and the highest degree of masculinity.

It is maybe not surprising taking the aforementioned into account that the Japanese have a 'myth of uniqueness', believing that foreigners can never understand the Japanese mentality (Watson, 1996). 'I have experienced this personally on many occasions. Despite the fact that I studied Japanese at degree level, have lived in Japan and worked for two Japanese companies, I often find Japanese people feel it necessary to explain very simple facets of Japanese culture to me', Rebecca Taylor says. 'Many foreigners who study Japanese will also no doubt be familiar with the following situation: I ask a question in perfectly understandable Japanese and the Japanese person I am questioning answers in English. This can be rather frustrating when one is trying to perfect one's knowledge of a language.'

Rebecca Taylor concludes that the reasons seem to be as follows: (a) Japanese wish to practice their English, or (b) they are trying to be friendly and helpful to foreigners by speaking English, or (c) they think foreigners will not be able to understand them if they answer in Japanese. The latter reinforces the Japanese 'myth of uniqueness'. Not only can foreigners not understand Japanese culture, but they also cannot learn the Japanese language. 'However', Rebecca Taylor says 'the upside to this is, when a foreigner does learn the Japanese language very well, they are usually accorded respect from Japanese people for having done so (once they have recovered from the initial shock!).'

When looking to hire Japanese personnel, a company needs to take a long-term view of any prospective employment because according to Bob Smith (1991) a Japanese executive will look for a commitment from prospective employers. Smith also mentions, that Japanese candidates are impressed by companies who have made efforts to adapt products to Japanese markets. A Japanese colleague of Rebecca Taylor's once said: 'If I decided to move, I wouldn't look at salary first; position and possible career development is more important', and Smith confirms this. An executive recruiter in Tokyo tells companies that the search process will take longer than in western markets, typically four to six months and warns them not to be blinded by a candidate's English ability, as other skills and capabilities are much more important.

MAJOR INFRASTRUCTURE DEVELOPMENT IN THE MIDDLE EAST/PAKISTAN

If you are developing and managing infrastructure investments in the Middle East or Pakistan there are a myriad of issues to consider. Richard Moss-Blundell, an active HR practitioner, working out of Abu Dhabi for an international energy company, says he makes no apologies for starting off with an observation that is not specifically confined to the Middle East and/or Pakistan.

Company organization/structure

How is your own company geared towards actually helping you successfully develop the projects in your region from a human resource perspective?

Richard Moss-Blundell says he finds that there is no shortage of technical or financial infrastructure available to call upon, but the support available from a people perspective is often a limiting factor. The provision of effective HR support should naturally be balanced between that which can be most effectively handled at the front line and that best handled at the centre in the overall, long-term interests of the company.

An obvious example of the latter would be a ready supply of suitably skilled international assignees, arising from an effective manpower/succession planning system. From the evidence to date, this critical aspect of a company's international toolkit is often sadly under-developed he comments.

Approaching projects in the region

'You need to do your homework before you get there.' Relying on an expectation that there will be an existing network of support systems, contacts, service providers etc, is flawed logic. For example, remuneration and benefits advisers are very scarce in the Gulf and recruitment agencies tend to offer services in this area.

Also within the Middle East generally, the utilities have tended to be used as a vehicle for employing local nationals on over-inflated salaries that have little relativity to the marketplace, therefore using these figures for analytical or comparative purposes can be misleading.

'You must make great efforts to develop your market intelligence as early as possible; it will enable you to reap dividends later on', Richard Moss-Blundell counsels.

Localization

The practice of 'localization' can produce negative effects. For example, while recruiting across the Middle East, Richard Moss-Blundell felt it was sad to see the number of excellent Third Country Nationals (TCN) who had become very disillusioned that they had received no pay increase or promotion for the past five years, yet had repeatedly seen local nationals with few relevant skills and limited experience, appointed into managerial positions above them, who subsequently displayed precious little interest and delivered inconsequential performance outputs thereafter.

'The "localization" trend is becoming very common throughout the Middle East, and you will be unlikely to prepare any significant project proposal without having to include a section covering your approach towards increasing the involvement of the local workforce and methods for ensuring subsequent skills transfer.

'You must, therefore, consider ways of managing this issue within your overall proposal. For example, do you increase the expatriate numbers to compensate, thereby incurring additional costs and reducing your return?'

This 'localization' concept is of course a perfectly reasonable response from those countries such as Saudi Arabia, where the expatriate work-force of around five million represents around 90 per cent of those employed in the private sector. The policy of Saudization was outlined in the government's sixth five-year development plan for 1995 to 2000. Over this period the government's aim is to create 659,000 jobs for nationals. So far the Labour and Social Affairs Ministry has decreed that about 20 positions are to be reserved for Saudi nationals. Expatriates are no longer granted work permits for these jobs. These include personnel managers and administrators, treasurers, auctioneers, secretaries, cashiers, security workers, and insurance workers.

'However the problem of work ethic (or rather the lack of it) of the local staff was a major factor that drove the majority of TCNs we inter-viewed to seek to leave the country, and one should be aware of this when considering the HR issues that may arise', Richard Moss-Blundell warns

'Mr Fixit'

You need a good local contact in the area, particularly in Pakistan where the ground 'tends to shift very quickly' and you need to be able to carry out a 'sanity check' on say, external advice offered. It is worth paying a good local 'Mr Fixit' over the odds (if you are happy that he has your interests at heart), as he can guide you through the maze very quickly, effi-ciently and with an acceptable level of risk.

'Quick and dirty' vs 'Rolls Royce'

In Richard Moss-Blundell's experience, there is nothing wrong with adopting a 'quick and dirty' approach in the early phases of a project's life, but make sure that when necessary you can bring in the required support (both locally and at the centre). 'Don't adopt a cost cutting approach at critical phases – it will rarely represent "more than a drop in the ocean" against the total project costs. As an example, if asked for an indicative manpower cost, use the high level market intelligence you have for the region in question. Factor-in the external advice when the project is in the offer stage and you need accurate data.'

Get the issues into perspective

When dealing with specific issues, don't fall into the trap of getting bogged down in minute detail over non-critical aspects; the law of diminishing returns quickly comes into play in these markets. Give a little leeway early on to save a lot of valuable time later. This is particularly relevant in acquisition scenarios where you may face shrewd operators across the table who are well able to utilize this tactic as a smokescreen or delaying tactic; focus on the overriding objective.

'Don't run away with the heady idea that you are breaking new ground and furthering the boundaries of the HR profession', Richard Moss-Blundell advises. 'The issues are nearly always the same the world over, albeit with the added dimensions such as culture, communication and complexity. The differences are more ones relating to the breadth rather than depth of HR expertise/experience and your ability to adapt.'

Admit and accept your deficiencies

Don't make a decision to save face. If you don't fully understand an issue admit it (perhaps just to yourself) and defer the decision until you have filled the gap. 'Admitting a weakness in a particular area can be a useful strategy as long as it doesn't become a regular feature', he concludes.

Lest ye forget

❏ The market price for labour is increasing, particularly in Pakistan, with the advent of major internationally financed infrastructure projects, and increasing amounts of 'returnees', who have high levels of skills and experience, and expect bigger rewards delivered in a more sophisticated manner.

❏ Status issues remain a problem. For example, in Pakistan, US Power company, AES applied the title 'engineer' for shift technicians to attract them in. This devalues the engineering profession ultimately and causes other problems; eg, expectations and legal classifications of relatively junior staff.

❏ There is an increasing dilemma for companies over the balance of short-term versus long-term benefits. Pakistanis used to go for the short-term but again they are getting more sophisticated in their outlook (eg, expecting full pension schemes). Staff in the Middle East just generally want more of everything.

❏ You cannot expect your employees to be especially loyal to your company when there is even a remote prospect of an increase to be gained from the next.

❏ The only factor that comes close to countering the material aspects is the undeniable pull of the family; this has been demonstrated frequently as the overriding factor in an individual's decision process; eg, returnees.

❑ There remains a mixture of bureaucracy, 'relationships' (corruption) and frustration at various levels of officialdom; the person on the ground is invaluable here; but always retain ownership of issues and decisions wherever possible.

❑ Recruitment must have an objective element to filter the incredible amount of CVs that appear to be a perfect match for your position. Testing is an invaluable tool, but a smarter trick is to put time and effort into the process of screening and shortlisting up front. Don't fall into the temptation of contracting-out this phase of the process if you can help it; again, take ownership and follow through.

❑ Get to know the universities and educational establishments that are recognized for producing good quality people. Likewise, get yourself familiar with local qualifications and institutions.

❑ The overall availability and quality of external advice in Pakistan is better than in the Middle East; it can also be very good value.

INDIA – A COUNTRY OF CONTRASTS

Kusum Sahdev is a researcher and consultant, who practices in both the UK and across India. Her insights into the realities of finding, developing and keeping people in employment in this vast and complex country – with its combination of potential and problems for the internationalizing business – are both profound and practical.

She says India is a country that can be best described as a country of contrasts in terms of the culture, geography, people's expectations of life and levels of education. 'The first myth is the concept of India as an "holistic entity", because in my experience this would be a case of over-generalization. As one travels and works from the north to the south; from the east to the west, there are distinctive cultural differences, and the reality is that quite often the conflicts that occur both in day to day life as well as in corporate life are due to these differences.' Alongside this are the deeply seated beliefs about the caste system that has positioned people in tight categories. This has major repercussions for managing people especially in the 'heartland' where communal factions are fairly commonplace. Against this backdrop, India is also made up of the 'highly educated elites'. It would not be unusual to come across CEOs from Ivy League universities in the US. 'Last but not least is the Indian political system which is a strange combination of "politicians" from the "heartland" of India and a Civil Service and judiciary that is based along the same lines as the British system!'

So when a multinational company (MNC) is looking to do business in India, it can become an overwhelming experience, as there are no clear, visible and tangible procedures that one could follow to get the results one is looking for.

Panning for gold in the talent pool

The Indian education system is as diverse as the culture. The institutions range from the 'Ivy League' institutions in engineering, science, technology, management and medicine to the very basic institutions that also provide degrees. The educational system is a tiered one very similar to that which applies in the US. Funding can be from central government, state/regional/government and private funds. Therefore, the first issue to take into account is to track the educational background of potential Indian recruits in a rigorous and thorough manner. Incidentally, the Ivy League institutions have been historically very attractive to the American universities, that have lured individuals with the best brains of India over the last 25–30 years by giving them substantial fellowships with guaranteed job offers thereafter. The challenge for the MNC in the future will be to recruit from these institutions, especially in instances where there is a start up operation. 'The issue does not end here, of course', Kusum Sahdev says. 'Defined career paths, personal development opportunities and participation in global scenarios would provide the necessary motivation. The products of these top institutions who have decided to stay on in India often face frustration with their career prospects. The most popular qualification in India at present is a combination of Engineering and MBA!' Kusum Sahdev says there is a mad rush to acquire these 'golden' qualifications which in the perception of the vast majority of the middle class secure good career prospects.

The kind of organization that people join is also quite important, especially from the perspective of self-esteem and position in society. For example, to join a Brewery/Spirit manufacturer would be frowned upon by peers and family members. 'Such organizations in my view would need to work much harder at recruiting people of high calibre,' Kusum Sahdev opines.

The key issue to take into account is that, if the MNC is genuinely looking to draw talent, the recruitment and selection procedures have to be spot on. 'The ability to "separate the wood from the trees" is the best possible advice one could suggest in terms of people issues. In my view, effective selection is absolutely critical for future growth and performance', says Kusum Sahdev.

A commanding position

'Within organizations, again without over-generalizing, the command and control style is pretty common. Concepts such as empowerment, team decision making, calling the bosses by their first names is not that common.' India on the whole is a high power distance society, ie people tolerate inequalities and are comfortable with the differentials. Clear position in society and within organizations is quite important to people. By and large people do not confront their bosses or express disagreement. The tendency is to say "yes"; albeit to change one's mind later. A number of organizations have started development programmes, to introduce more western management styles and capabilities. However,' Kusum Sahdev says, 'as yet there isn't enough data to assess the effectiveness of such initiatives.'

The appointment of leaders of the operation within India is crucial. 'This may sound like a cliché, but it is fundamental to the future success of the operation.' The corporate culture would need to be taken into account so, for example, in a traditional hierarchical organization, if a democratic, empowering boss is positioned with a view to changing things, 'he may be creating a recipe for sleepless nights'. The other issue (and this relates primarily to the British companies), is the colonial manner that some CEOs tend to adopt when positioned in India. There are a minority of Indians who still have the memory of the 'raj' but a majority of young executives are from the post-independence era and do not see a close allegiance with Britain. 'The US is a more natural choice for a number of Indians because of the freedom of opportunities that it provides', according to Kusum Sahdev.

When seeking partners to do business with, the 'fit' has to be assessed rigorously. A very traditional organization with a very 'western' style can pose some challenges. In some instances the positioning of the names, ie who is running the show also determines the eventual success. The responsibilities and roles in the case of JVs are crucial in terms of developing a long term relationship.

Where MNCs have taken the time to assess the situation, lived with the nuances of the culture and have used strategically the support of individuals who are attuned in cross-cultural management, the experiences have been positive. One only needs to have informal discussions about these experiences, to hear contrasting views expressed. Some international CEOs would freely comment on how successful they have been while others would turn round and say 'never again'. From Kusum Sahdev's point of view the reasons for these experiences are 'a combination of the personalities involved (ethnocentric approach), utilization (or lack of) adequate support from country expert, nature of the industry, ability to handle uncertainties, ambiguities and bureaucracy'.

SOUTH AFRICA I – AN EXPAT'S OVERVIEW

'This part of the world offers the expatriate a superb sub-tropical climate with a seductive lifestyle, particularly in Cape Town and Durban. Johannesburg being inland lacks many of the amenities of the coastal locations.' There are some secondary locations such as Port Elizabeth and Pretoria but, says John Smith (who spent a number of years working in the country for the Royal Dutch Shell Company), 'I would not consider these unless I wanted a sabbatical from normal life'.

It is essential that country briefings recognize the significant differences between the centres of population. These include language, climate, people, salaries and lifestyle.

One in three of the white population works for the government in some capacity. That leads to a high level of bureaucracy that manifests itself in the time and forms needed to get an ID card, set up a bank account, and generally establish oneself in society.

'This is the kind of expatriate posting that people say yes to in a kind of knee jerk reaction because of the images we tend to have of sunny skies, barbecues and days at the beach. It is easy to overlook the poverty, crime and social costs of this society', Smith warns.

Money

The Rand is a currency under pressure and therefore can be quite volatile. There are currency restrictions that can create issues about taking capital out of the country.

People

A rich mixture in each region. Managers working with international companies should try to understand the tribal differences in both the white and black tribes.

The Natal coastal region including Durban is the only area where English is the predominant language although it is spoken throughout South Africa. In many areas some knowledge of Afrikaans and a tribal language would be useful.

Education

In the case of the affluent whites and middle class Indians, there is generally a high standard of education at primary and secondary level. The universities are good but there is no state funding for individuals, which puts an economic burden on families.

It is not yet the case for others. This leads to a workforce that is substantially less able and sometimes less willing than the western normative model. This can be extremely frustrating and time consuming for expatriate managers whose experience to-date has been in the efficiency-conscious and technologically driven western economies.

Selection

Typically, there is a fault line where people are selected for their technical ability; insufficient attention is paid to their social skills and business skills. This leads to 'square pegs in hexagonal holes', John Smith says. 'This is further exacerbated by the assumption by internationalizing companies that if the expatriate job holder is satisfied then the family will fall into line. This is a common mistake with a posting such as this. Time spent assessing the whole family unit will be beneficial.'

Housing

Housing is generally of a high standard and situated within designated areas, still dependant on colour. 'Although the law has changed it will be some time before there is real assimilation,' John Smith says.

Senior managers in South Africa would normally have a house with a swimming pool and a servant. 'The latter can be something of a culture shock to Europeans while providing the former can be something of a *cause célèbre* for the expatriate's own company!'

In-country induction is very important to understand how business gets done. It is equally important to ensure the family is helped to settle. 'A common fault is to assume that, because it is sunny, then everything is OK. In my time there we lost a lot of expatriates early because their family did not settle in those vital early few weeks.'

It is quite easy for expatriates to settle into a ghetto style of life where one only meets people from work and a restricted sample at that. 'In my early months there I thought that South Africa was one big "Caledonian Society"', John Smith concludes.

SOUTH AFRICA II – A VIEW FROM WITHIN

The changes in South Africa following the election of a black government have not been without their traumas. These can be particularly difficult for the western expatriate. There are those who are currently describing, for example, Johannesburg as 'a battle zone'. People are having to come to terms with the fact that the affluent community lives in a gated society, in order to protect them from the crime which is rife; particularly among many of the black poor and dispossessed. It is likely to be many years before society settles down, in the wake of the fundamental changes that are currently in progress. For this reason, a number of western companies are deliberately choosing to avoid investment in the region. On the other hand, for many years those involved, for example, in mineral extraction, where the country is particularly rich, have found ways and means to manage around the issue. There may well be many contractions in the period to come, as pressure mounts for transfer of appropriate skills and with it responsibility to local nationals.

Other parts of industry and commerce in South Africa are undergoing the same pressures for change as are those organizations in similar sectors in the western world. Recent discussion with Dr John Verster, General Manager (Human Resources) at the Standard Bank of South Africa reveals that his organization is particularly focused on the twin-aims of improving top management accountability and alignment with shareholder interests, and dealing with the requirement for increasing flexibility among frontline staff (downsizing and rationalization of roles; with increasing pressures on survivors), while maintaining this group focused and committed to delivering high-quality services to the bank's customers. So, in just the same way as this is being debated in the Anglo-Saxon world, the question of the end of the 'psychological contract' is very much to the fore, as well as the need for greater managerial efficiency and focus on those aspects which will deliver value to investors over the medium to long term. This is also manifest in the aspirations – with considerable success already – in opening up the organization's target market, by expanding the bank's interests on an international scale.

Dr Verster says 'Standard Bank are spreading our footprints globally; internationalization is a "now" issue'. The normalization of South Africa following a long period of isolation in the world means that 'we're in a rapid catch-up mode'. Across industry in general, South African business is looking at ways to spread activity. There are opportunities both closer to home in other African countries (although there are limitations in terms of business profitability) and in new spheres; for example, opportunities in the Far East.

With South Africa now more accessible, the country has been inundated with visits from multinational corporations coming to look. 'It's what they call LSD trips; look, see and decide. This has involved both government trade delegations and individual businesses investigations. They seem in the main to be taking stock; waiting and watching to see if what they read in the press about a new business context in South Africa is true,' says John Verster. There are not yet too many who have decided to get going in the country. Most are setting up a representative office, and perhaps securing a preliminary trade license. This does mean, though, there is an influx of foreigners. While in most cases the representative office or new business venture is headed by an expatriate executive, they are looking for local talent in support roles. 'The international companies are "cherry-picking" talent from domestic businesses which is having a major impact on the market for executive employment. The problem is being compounded by international appointments providing individuals with access to pay in hard currency; delivering added benefits over domestic employers given the poor international exchange rage of the South African Rand,' John Verster observes.

Domestic companies are therefore under serious pressure to hold on to their talent. 'There is a very visible normalizing of salaries, lifting them to international levels. This is especially true in scarce skill areas such as corporate finance, IT etc,' John Verster says.

This is setting new norms for South African pay and other key contractual areas. In this dynamic market, pay issues are provoking lively debates in board remuneration committees. This is involving upward salary adjustments of up to 50 per cent of pay in key areas. This action is necessary in response to the aggressive policies being employed by incoming multinationals as part of their recruitment drives. Therefore, not only in key skill areas, but across the board in executive level positions, unprecedented pay rises are being applied, all in double figures; and many in the range 20–30 per cent. 'If one opens a discussion with a Chief Executive in any of South Africa's leading businesses, you are unlikely to get beyond the first two minutes before the debate turns to the issue of scarce talent. It is beginning to redefine the way in which human resource issues are being considered', John Verster says.

In the main, reactive rather than proactive responses are being developed in a desperate attempt to hold on to the best people. In some cases innovative kinds of golden handcuffs are being applied; such as massive offerings of restricted shares and other serious wealth accumulation promises in return for individuals signing contracts to remain with their corporation.

There is a danger that too hasty action even by the internationals will be regretted by them (as well as local business) over the long term, setting unachievable ongoing reward expectations in a market which is not delivering aggressive growth at this stage. John Verster commented that this explained the LSD trips for the majority and their wait and see policy; they were not rushing in.

For the first time, business leaders are considering more seriously the human resources constraints on the strategic possibilities to ensure business survival.

Foreign banks are able to come into South Africa with far higher capital bases than domestic banks, with a double benefit of not needing to put down an expensive retail infrastructure. They are able to focus on high margin business in the most profitable sectors. This is delivering to the foreign banks an unfair advantage: 'We have systemic costs which are in-built'. In addition, local businesses face political constraints on their ability to respond to this challenge. It is not as easy for them to reduce costs by engaging in downsizing programmes as has been the case among international firms in their domestic markets. There is immense local pressure from external institutions to create, not remove jobs; from government, trade unions and the community at large. This means that any decisions regarding the future of the bank's distributed branch network where profitability is only marginal, cannot be taken on economic grounds alone. A decision to close a branch has to be taken within the wider political context.

Yet another challenge is the South African government's affirmative action programme. This initiative is to ensure organizations are taking positive steps to include those previously excluded from employment opportunities at all levels. This is involving South African companies – again unlike international competitors – in massive investment in training and development to assist individuals in making rapid progression, facing up to the difficulties where individuals come from traditionally poor educational backgrounds. In this regard, pressure comes from within the business as well as outside, adding to cost pressures. So not only is it difficult to remove people, there is a counter-force imperative to bring people of coloured and black African backgrounds, through development, and up the hierarchies.

A related issue is the question of the calibre and type of people with the capabilities to meet the new business marketplace demands. As with service industries around the world, there is a demand for a more sales and service oriented approach. But traditionally people are not attitudinally equipped for this. In John Verster's opinion, 'They are not individuals who easily engage in deal making; they are not decision takers'. So the challenge is not only downsizing with the constraints described, but also changing the mix of personnel in response to the need to redefine the strategic value proposition to the customer.

Because of the long period of South Africa's isolation, the country is far behind in relation to having a service-oriented business culture. In summary, all the major groupings in South Africa, regardless of their creed or colour tend to have an authoritarian and bureaucratic preference not aligned to the delivery of customer focused service. Again, there are implications for holding on to staff with scarce skills. If they feel moving to an international firm will provide them with greater scope to break from the traditional employment environment, this becomes an added draw.

A major strategic problem is of course that the top people – the decision takers in making the requisite changes – are themselves part of the problem. 'It's the issue of turkeys not voting for Christmas.' This watershed in South Africa's history means that it is open season for foreign consultants coming into the country and 'talking up a storm' and providing the impetus for getting rid of the guys at the top. This does not necessarily mean the loss of all top management; after all the chief executive will generally be the client. But he will be bringing in foreign 'hatchet men' to take out some or all of his senior henchmen.

There are many parallels here with the situation in the emerging markets of the world. There is a requirement for major change, with top management being part of the problem in the sense that their history creates a climate for the organization which is a hurdle rather than an enabler of change. Some of the lessons being learned therefore in the ex-communist bloc and in the developing Asian markets apply equally in what traditionally has been a more sophisticated 'business island' in South Africa.

Privatization is underway in all the major sectors; transport, telecomms, energy and other utilities. They are all going through the process of privatization and deregulation. Their success is constrained by an added complexity; namely the aggressive Affirmative Action Programme. The new guard installed in these businesses must be black as one of the conditions for privatization. This means at CEO and Chairman of the Board level, and other key portfolios, very young and untested executives are being installed. Many have not had access to education and development opportunities in the past to equip them for running major businesses; and in any case their immaturity as executives means they are not ready to tackle the high pace of change in the ex-state firms.

This gives rise to a key resourcing issue; the question of how one is bringing people in. There are not many black expatriates in the world. So the international market provides a limited supply. There is also the question of the new guard fitting in with the existing team with their expectations of past practice, including reward. This is something of a paradox.

It is also the case that South Africa's economic growth is hardly booming. 'The engine of change is currently sluggish, despite the optimistic projections two years ago, and the economists are currently having to reassess their projections.'

Top management is therefore making mistakes; 'that's an understatement', John Verster says. It means there has not been a sufficient level of appreciation of what it takes to run huge state corporations. 'This has meant significant financial underperformance as well as, frankly, an acceptable performance delivery amongst these institutions.'

The same problems apply throughout the public sector; there has been a huge shake out from government departments of experienced white personnel (at a great expense to the state), only to replace them with individuals who are seriously underperforming as are their departments, because of the lack of seasoned, experienced civil servants. This applies at central, provincial and local government level. For example, individuals holding key finance portfolios lack the basic know-how of putting together and then managing a budget.

This has necessitated innovations by the banking community. All government departments have put banking business out to tender. This was previously controlled centrally, with political control manifest. These are exciting opportunities for the banking community; but the banks are having to intervene to support and train their clients to get them to a level of competence where they can fully appreciate the potential of service available to them.

In order to be a player within this new core market for domestic business development, the banks have recognized the need to make this strategic investment, and to understand the long term vision for the transformation of the South African economy. Part of the ANC leadership election platform in 1994 was the development of a partnership for transforming the economy, involving compromise all round. The introduction of partnership between business, government and labour is a very novel concept in a South African context.

At the organizational level, there is a wave of change in relation to the introduction of empowerment to line management. In the past, decision making was very centralized and authoritarian. Work is now under way to decentralize and to place accountability with line managers for decision making; HRM is a key area where this is in progress. The challenge is of course in getting managers 'to step up to the line', John Verster says. 'Many of them are mouthing enthusiasm but are in reality reluctant to accept the new accountability.' Here again, there are strong parallels in developments in Eastern Europe.

In relation to pay and benefits, there is a great hesitancy among managers to accept responsibility; 'there are different levels of readiness for the new roles generally among different managers'. In translating this new ethos into line accountability the challenge is to develop beyond management to leadership; developing the 'softer' skills as well as the decision making requirements.

A final South African anecdote. Geoff Stapley (Standard Bank's Head of Reward) cautioned me against the complacency the mobile international population may have in their interactions with locals anywhere in the world. A colleague of his went to Florida recently for a conference and met a local US delegate who asked him where he came from. He said he came from Johannesburg and his American colleague replied 'I don't get out of state much; how long did it take you to drive here'!

Therefore, major business enterprises in this mature economy – despite the period of tumultuous change being experienced – are, in parallel with mature organizations in the western developed world in general, focused on a drive for greater efficiency. It is not enough to be simply pushing out the boundaries in an expanding economy such as in the Asian 'tiger' regions. This makes this territory a particularly interesting and paradoxical place to be developing business activity both for local nationals and for those engaging in international development from outside the region.

AUSTRALIA – MANAGING BY EXCEPTION NOT INSPECTION

Another mature economy, isolated from the developed West, this time, by geographical distances rather than by politics, is Australia. The problem for the British investor, in particular, is the assumption that this economy will be familiar. In the same way that there are frequently clashes of culture between the business worlds of the UK and the US, said to be 'divided by a common language', historical ties of empire and preconceptions about attitudes and behaviour can easily mislead the unwary western multinational executive embarking on an assignment 'down under'. If anything, modern Australia is finding itself increasingly allied to its neighbours in the Asia Pacific region; the notion of an 'eastern regional culture' may take on new meaning, as perceived by the average westerner, when viewed in this context!

John Maxwell, a native Australian-turned-internationalist, was National President of the Australian Human Resource Institute, and Secretary-General of the Asia Pacific region of the World Federation of Personnel Management, before taking up the post of Director-General of the Global Remuneration Organization. This pedigree makes John Maxwell particularly well placed to offer a pen-portrait of strategic human resource management issues in Australia, combining native insight with the objectivity of a thoroughly global vantage point.

An intrusive framework

'Government legislation is intrusive in the employer-employee process' John Maxwell says. For example, sending someone to Australia as an expatriate business unit leader or professional requires special visas. These are only good for up to four years. 'After this, draconian levels of taxation hit.' So an internationalizing organization may only put its people from the 'home' business in to set up operations for a pre-determined period. The Australian government's view is, after four years, they should have localized. 'So, to an extent, it is how long you've got that drives what you do in setting up Australian activities.'

Motor vehicles are commonly provided to executives. However, employers incur a fringe benefits tax; if the company provides a vehicle, the organization is responsible to pay the tax on behalf of the employee. 'There is scope to agree a reward package to include fringe benefit tax; but, in the case of more senior staff, the less likely it is the employer will get away with it.' The level of taxation is based on a vehicle's value. John Maxwell says a top executive, whose market-related package implies a Jaguar car should be provided, at a level of tax several thousand dollars higher than, say, a Ford car would attract, will simply counter: 'You want me to drive the vehicle; you can't expect me to bear a tax penalty for doing so!'.

Expatriates would normally be provided with housing, which also attracts fringe benefit tax. This is calculated based on the difference between a normal commercial lease and the rate for someone's package. Garaging for employees' vehicles in the office car park also attracts fringe benefit tax. This is established on the basis of what a commercial car park within a mile radius would charge. Country club memberships are not taxed; but the company is not allowed to off-set costs against corporation tax charges. Only when fringe benefit tax is paid can a corporation tax deduction be made. 'So, without due care in package design, in some cases you end up paying 49 cents in the dollar', John Maxwell warns.

Thus, any internationalizing company going into Australia would do well in advance to secure local tax advice and survey information on pay and benefits. Finally: 'A truly international organization would expect to provide a senior employee with an international mobile telephone, so they can be reached anywhere in world (except US and Japan who don't have GSM access), billed for it in the home territory.' John Maxwell has one paid for out of Australia; so anyone can get him in Singapore, say, by dialling an Australian number!

Expatriates may receive their salary and other remuneration in their home country or other 'off-shore' location. However, the organization will need to pay something in Australia, to meet the individual's expenses. The result is, the employer is required by Australian law to offer 20 days fixed leave and long service leave. 'So, whether you like it or not, you must give employees four weeks' leave, and long service leave of 13 times five days, after ten years accrued service. After five years, vesting between five and ten years must be paid to the employee on termination, in addition to severance pay.'

The organization must make choices determining its style of operation in relation to the legislative framework. If the business operates in more than one state, then its employment conditions will come under federal laws; if in only one state, then state laws only will apply. But if a company joins an industry association, the mere fact of joining may put it into federal jurisdiction. For example, anyone who joins the Association of Metal Manufacturers is caught by federal law as far as employee conditions are concerned. If you only join the local chamber of commerce, state laws only prevail. Federal laws can be markedly different in terms of termination payments and related cost obligations.

A deceptive culture

In Australia, 'the work ethic is different' John Maxwell says. 'There is a strong work ethic; but it often appears to outsiders to be *laissez faire*. But Australians' quality of life is a high priority; they work to live, not vice versa.' This may clash with a multinational organization's culture. 'The expat team leader may bring in a rush job near the end of the working day to be told: 'It's 5 o'clock – we're off to the pub; the job'll still be here tomorrow!'. But if they are persuaded there is a real requirement, the local team will work to get it done. 'Aussies work hard, play hard.'

Australia is now a major trading partner with Asia. The introduction of the Common Market in Europe broke UK:Australia trade barriers. Previously, Australia had remained incredibly loyal. Rural products, the lifeblood of the Australian market, suddenly became nothing. 'When the UK walked away, it made a big difference. Previously also Australians had fairly free access to work in UK, this is no longer so, so the ties are severed. Now the country is much more aligned to its Asian neighbours.'

The culture is also incredibly individualistic; 'they hate pomp' John Maxwell warns. 'You have to manage by respect, not by divine right. Many a UK guy points to a title to command a response; and wonders why he gets a bloody nose'.

Multinational errors to learn from

'The biggest mistakes I've witnessed are when a MNC has sent in the wrong person who couldn't adapt to the Australian culture; where they've tried to exercise tight controls which just won't work. To an Australian, this says "these bastards don't trust me" – even where a company has a standard set of world wide procedures – so loyalty doesn't get built. Hi-tech industries have seen some notable failures. In start-up mode they have brought out "technocrats". They needed to go looking for local hires more swiftly than they would normally expect. Also grave errors have occurred in firing senior people without getting advice; especially US companies. In the US, employment is "at will"; so you can easily fire anyone. They tried to do it here and got caught. The right to sue for wrongful dismissal is enshrined in Australian employment law and, 105 per cent of time, the company loses when they go to court on this. Only if there is well-documented evidence is there much hope of the firm's view prevailing; simply not having good enough results won't guarantee rightful dismissal will be allowed. The use of employment and termination contracts is highly developed.

'An executive will often negotiate his/her contract on the basis that: "If I'm going to join XYZ company and the Chief Executive and I don't relate to one another then the firm can't just dump me".'

'There is a lot of creative talent in Australia', John Maxwell offers. 'Where people have gone in humble; said: "this is the task; how can I help you do it? Where people truly manage by results, then they've succeeded. If it doesn't happen then we'll discuss it. As people are you comfortable we can do that? – yea; then go for it." Then you must ensure they are adequately resourced. Otherwise words and actions are not in synch. To build a loyal and productive workforce, an organization has to take on a high level of trust much earlier than normal. Give trust, earn respect', he says.

'Be prepared to have an open mind; try it and then be surprised when it works. Managers are often surprised when someone they've hired does the job. If they don't do it, it's your fault: you've failed in the selection, and in outlining the relationship. For me it's like the art of education: taking an empty mind and creating an open one. It's about accepting responsibility for failure.'

John Maxwell stresses that the great majority of people in Australia are now better educated than they were traditionally. In the past; you could call in efficiency experts. Now what works better is giving a lead, adequately supporting – and then trusting people's self esteem, to achieve corporate goals.

The best rule for Australia is: 'management by exception rather than by inspection', John Maxwell concludes.

'POSTCARD' PRINCIPLES – A WORKING AGENDA

So, what do our holistic navigators have to teach us from their experience? Here are my thoughts around the key lessons.

❏ Take time and trouble to understand on-the-ground realities in full.

❑ Don't expect to 'move HR mountains' – HR breadth rather than depth is a key capability for the practitioner deployed to support international projects.

❑ Anticipate a lack of loyalty among staff in those areas of the world where business investment is accelerating and where competition for skilled people is fierce.

❑ Get to know the institutions which produce seed corn talent for localized management over the medium- to long-term, as well as the relevant accredited qualifications.

❑ Remember capability may exist among indigenous people – it may simply require sympathetic effort to release it for commercially productive purposes.

❑ Don't assume all parties to a joint venture will have a common agenda – patience and tenacity will assist in finding solutions acceptable to maintain the focus and commitment by all parties to a set of common goals.

❑ Basic western 'know-hows' in business are likely to be absent, but can be quickly learnt, in developing economies – strategic, focused investment will be necessary, though, as well as a large dose of patience.

❑ Leadership and accountability have been discouraged among managers and staff for many decades in developing ex-socialist countries – again, patience and encouragement will be required to implant these capabilities.

❑ Team-learning is a valuable strategy: but ensure objectives are adequately communicated and prioritized – don't expect simultaneous action on complex multi-faceted shopping lists. Such initiatives also demand appropriate organizational infrastructure – to set aims, monitor and correct progress, and to assess and recognize achievement.

❑ Rich, deep historical roots and national pride are exhibited in abundance in many countries which commercially seem 'late developers'. Respect for this – and an individual's technical attributes – is critical in growing the trust and commitment by international inward investors for their new or redevelopment business initiatives.

❑ Never underestimate the capability of a people – they may have the power to surprise you, if only you learn to look properly and ask the right questions. Balance western commercial and technical 'superiority' with a sense of humility – a shared learning exercise will cement relations and yield long-term advantage.

❑ There may be conflicting pressures on the internationalizing business in certain developing regions, on the one hand, to cope with the lack of skilling because of poor access to basic education by some or all the indigenous population; and on the other to transfer increasing skill and responsibility away from expatriate appointees and on to local national employees.

❏ Selecting expatriates for technical know-how may be a major mistake for assignments to territories where the organization and domestic environment can be a major source of tension – leading to deteriorating performance levels – among those not cut out to cope with 'extraneous demands'.

❏ Investors and business developers into the social market economies of North Western Europe need to appreciate the fundamentally different organizational drivers which apply – in sharp contrast to Anglo-Saxon economies.

❏ Ability to manage in a regulated environment, acceptance of bureaucratic joint determination, focused on 'increasing the wealth of people' in general, is a managerial prerequisite.

❏ It is important to distinguish between technical capability (people tend to be highly qualified in social market economies) and the underlying capability to meet the performance imperatives required by shareholder value creation focus.

❏ In economies which were previously highly regulated, managements are still coming to terms with a more competitive context for performance management. The question of value-based leadership and creation of wealth for shareholders, as opposed simply to running a business for the convenience and ego of its top management, is now to the fore. However, acquisitions of traditional businesses – with traditional managers – may involve a re-education process as to the new facts of business life.

❏ Sensitivity is required to the attitudes and values of societies which remain more 'closed' and stratified than Anglo-Saxon nations. Failure to observe this characteristic could lead to embarrassment among superiors and subordinates alike, if invited by their new 'owners' to come on parade in unfamiliar social interactions.

❏ It is important to avoid stereotyping, for example, 'Orientals' – there are deep rooted philosophies which characterize attitudes and behaviours in business. Such philosophies may have a common trend in the themes underlying relationships and value systems across a region. However, beware of adopting a regional perspective to the exclusion of an appreciation of aspects which may vary significantly between countries. This more sophisticated understanding may be of particular relevance when forming teams drawn from a mixture of regional economies in South America and Asia Pacific, for example.

❏ Getting the 'right fit' people is a must
— especially in middle management roles;

— with capabilities which are sufficiently attuned in a local context to realize technical potential; and

— open to compensation arrangements which are justifiable in terms of contribution (expat/locals) – mitigating the 'pissing people off' factor

❏ There is scope for internationalizing businesses to translate their corporate HR philosophy into local practice just about anywhere in the world – they simply have to accept they won't do it in the same way as 'at home'.

❏ Imagination is called for in developing a strategic HR policy response to:

— township responsibilities

— extended family benefits

— offering essential replacements for state deficiencies

❏ Labour costs should be evaluated not in salary and benefits terms, but in terms of local 'transactional costs'.

❏ It is possible to instil a greater sense of purpose and urgency, even in apparently the most 'backward' economies – but patience and tenacity is called for, as well as willingness to make a material commercial investment, both in terms of material incentives, but also (even more critically) in management focus and energy.

❏ Convergence is approaching

— technology and commercialization opportunities (western economies need sources for investment) mean it's inevitable

— sound HRM practice – principles apply world-wide

But

— people have different traditions, which must be respected and harnessed

— people are increasingly aware of their worth – their loyalty can't be taken for granted

Therefore

— successful organizations are:

❏ delivering jobs and development opportunities to the highest levels to local people, while simultaneously

❏ developing the organizational effectiveness frameworks to replicate success through people – but not locked-in to a transient 'talent pool'.

Drawing on the insights which my international colleagues have shared with us, and the principles which I have attempted to distil in the foregoing agenda, I believe we can begin to construct a practical, world view of some of the challenges at the core of human resource management in an internationalizing setting. However, individuals charged with leading such developments would, I believe, do well to remember that the fundamentals of good HRM are truly universal. HR professionals in internationalizing businesses need to develop the capability to apply these fundamentals with due creativity, focusing on results, and with appropriate flexibility.

The HR professional must, then, become a respected guide and coach, navigating professional and managerial colleagues through cultural diversity, and the ambiguities inherent in seeking to lead people for competitive advantage in the different regions of the world. HR leaders must remain focused and consistent. But, they need to carry with them at all times a sense of respect and humility. We have something to learn wherever we go, however deep our corporate pockets, and however well versed our technical skills. We can achieve our corporate aims; but this needs the capability to accommodate and appreciate the potential of all groups of people involved in doing so, in all their glorious diversity. If we can help our organizations to recognize and learn from this, the HR professional can add material benefit to any internationalizing bottom line.

References

Abdoolcarim, Z (1993), How Women are Winning at Work, *Asian Business* (Hong Kong), November (29/11)

ACA Journal, Autumn 1996, Vol. 5 No. 3 ACA (American Compensation Association), 14040 N. Northsight Blvd, Scottsdale, AZ 85260 USA.

Adler, N (1991), *International Dimensions of Organisational Behaviour,* Boston, PWS-Kent

Bento, R and Ferreira, L (1992), Incentive Pay and Organisational Culture, in W Bruns, ed., *Performance Measurement, Evaluation, and Incentives*, Boston Mass, HBS Press

Bhagat, R, Kedia, B, Crawford, S and Kaplan, M, (1990), Cross-cultural Issues in Organisational Psychology: Emergent Trends and Directions for Research in the 1990s, in C Coope, and I Robertson, eds, *International and Organisational Psychology*, London, John Wiley and Sons

Bond, M (1988), *The Cross-cultural Challenge to Social Psychology,* Newbury Park CA, Sage

Bradley, F (1991), *International Marketing Strategy,* Hemel Hempstead, Prentice-Hall

Bradley, P, Hendry C and Perkins, S (1997), Global or Multi-local? *SRRC News* #4

Crump, T (1991), *The Death of an Emperor – Japan at the Crossroads*, Oxford University Press

Cuthbert, D (1997), EMU and the Ostrich Position, *People Management*, June 12

Drucker, P (1995), *Managing in a Time of Great Change*, Butterworth-Heinemann

Earley, P, (1994), Self or Group Cultural Effects of Training on Self-efficacy and Performance, *Advanced Science Quarterly*, **39**, 89–117

Easterby-Smith, M, Malina, D and Yuan, L (1995), How Culture Sensitive is HRM? A Comparative Analysis of Practice in Chinese and UK Companies, *International Journal of Human Resource Management*, **6**, 1, 31–59

Gaugler, E (1988), HR Management: An International Comparison, *Personnel*, **65**, 8, 24–30

Hampden-Turner, C and Trompenaars, F (1993), *The Seven Cultures of Capitalism*, London, Piatkus

Hendry, C. (1994), *Human Resource Strategies for International Growth,* London, Routledge

References

Hickson, DJ and Pugh, DS (1995), *Management Worldwide – The Impact of Societal Cultures on Organisations around the Globe*, Penguin Books

Hofer, CW and Schendal, DE (1978), *Strategy Formulation: Analytical Concepts*, St Paul, West Publishing

Hofstede, G. (1981), *Cultures Consequences: International Differences in Work-Related Values*, Beverly Hills, Cal, Sage

Hofstede, G. (1991), *Cultures and Organisations – Software of the Mind*, Maidenhead, McGraw-Hill

International Labour Office, Geneva (1997), *World Employment 1996/7*

Johnson, M (1997), *French Resistance,* London, Cassell

Kotter, J and Heskett, J. (1992), *Corporate Culture and Performance*, New York, Free Press

Kuriu H (1991), IBM Japan's Market-Driven Personnel Strategy, *Long Range Planning*, **24**, 6, December

Lasserre, P and Probert, J (1994), Competing on the Pacific Rim: High Risks and High Returns, *Long Range Planning*, **27**, 2

Mamman, A, Sulaiman, M and Fadel, A (1996), Attitudes to Pay Systems: an Exploratory Study Within and Across Cultures, *International Journal of Human Resource Management*, **7**, 1, 101–21

Newman, K and Hollen, S (1996), Culture and Congruence: the Fit Between Management Practices and National Culture, *Journal of International Business Studies*, Fourth Quarter, 753–79

Rajan, A (1995), *Winning People Report*, Centre for Research in Employment and Technology in Europe

Rosenzweig, P and Nohria, N (1994), Influences on Human Resource Management Practices in Multinational Corporations, *Journal of International Business Studies*, Second Quarter, 229–51

Rummler, M and Brache (1995), *Human Performance – Managing the White Space in the Organisation Chart,* 2nd ed. Jossey Bass

Sachs, J (1997), The Limits of Convergence, *The Economist*, June 14–20

Saha, A (1990), Basic Human Nature and Management in Japan, *Journal of Managerial Psychology* (UK), **5**, 3

Sano, Y (1987), New Technology and Opportunities for Women, *Keio Business Review* (Japan), 24

Schiffman, L and Kanuk, L (1994), *Consumer Behaviour*, 5th ed., Englewood Cliffs, NJ, Prentice-Hall

Smith, R (1991), In Search of the Japanese Executive, *Personnel* (USA), October

Solo, S (1989), Japan Discovers Women Power, *Fortune*, June 19

Taoka, G and Beeman, D (1991), *International Business: Environments, Institutions and Operations*, New York, HarperCollins

Trompenaars, F (1993), *Riding the Waves of Culture*, London, The Economist Books

Tung, RL (1994), Strategic Management Thought in East Asia, *Organisational Dynamics*, Spring

Watson, W (1996), On the Wrong Road to Malay, *The Times Higher*, April 12

Wm M Mercer Inc (1997), *Global Compensation Planning Report*

Wolf, M (1997), Global Opportunities, *Financial Times*, May 6

Further Reading

Armstrong, M and Murlis, H (1994), *Reward Management: A Handbook of Remuneration Strategy and Practice*, 2nd ed., London, Kogan Page

Barsoux, J-L and Lawrence, P (1997), *Management in France*, London, Cassell

Bigoness, W and Blakely, G (1996), A Cross-National Study of Managerial Values, *Journal of International Business Studies*, Fourth Quarter, 739-753

Bond, M and Hwang, K, (1986), The Social Psychology of Chinese People, in M Bond ed., *The Psychology of the Chinese People*, Hong Kong, Oxford University Press 213–66

Brewster, C, (1995), Towards a 'European' Model of Human Resource Management, *Journal of International Business Studies*, First Quarter, 1–21

Cartwright, S and Cooper, C (1996), *Managing Mergers Acquisitions and Strategic Alliances, Integrating People and Cultures*, Oxford, Butterworth-Heinemann

Child, J (1981), Culture Contingency and Capitalism in the Cross-national Study of Organisations, in L Cummings, and B Staw eds, *Research in Organisational Behavior*, New York, JAI

DiMaggio, P and Powell, W (1983), The Iron Cage Revisited: Institutional Isomorphism and Collective Rationality in Organisational Fields, *American Sociological Review*, **48**, 47–160

Dowling, P and Schuler, R (1990), *International Dimensions of Human Resource Management*, Boston, PWS-Kent

Ferner, A (1997), Country of Origin Effects and HRM in Multinational Companies, *Human Resource Management Journal*, **7**, 1, 19–37

Hansen, P (1994), *Expatriate Games*, Towers Perrin – Connections

Harris, P and Moran, R (1992), *Managing Cultural Differences*, Houston TX, Gulf Publishing

Hollingshead, G and Leat, M (1995), *Human Resource Management: An International and Comparative perspective*, London, Pitman

Iloneimi, E (1997), The New Owner, Making Value Creation Management's Bottom Line, *Nordicum*, 2

Moss-Kanter R (1992), Transcending Business Boundaries: 12,000 World Managers View Change, *Harvard Business Review*, **69**, 3, 151–64

Further Reading

Phatak, A.V. (1992), *International Dimensions of Management*, 3rd ed., Boston, Mass, PWS-Kent

Schein, E (1985), *Organisational Culture and Leadership*, San Francisco, Jossey Bass

Sparrow, P, Schuler, R and Jackson, S (1994), Convergence or Divergence; Human Resource Practices and Policies for Competitive Advantage Worldwide, *International Journal of Human Resource Management*, 5, 2, 267–99

Terpstra, V (1992), *International Dimensions of Marketing*, Boston, Kent

Tilghman, T (1994), Beyond the Balance Sheet: Developing Alternative Approaches to International Compensation, *ACA Journal*, Summer 36–49

Torrington, D (1994), *International Human Resource Management: Think Globally Act Locally*, Hemel Hempstead, Prentice Hall

Zeira, Y, Harari, E and Izraeli, D (1975), Some Structural and Cultural Factors in Ethnocentric Multinational Corporations and Employee Morale, *Journal of Management Studies*, 12, 1, 66–82

Index

Index

best international practice 51
beyond culture: national industry and corporate effects, 123
Bhagat 122
big six accounting firms 232, 235
blocks to thinking internationally 27
Booz Allen & Hamilton 27
Borneo 115
BP 64
Bradley, F 117
Bradley, P *et al* 85, 117, 122, 124
Brazil 211, 213, 237
Britain 276
British 111, 193, 195, 219, 221, 240, 276, 284
British colonial rule 52
British Gas 199
Brooke-Bond 163
brownfield 51, 133
BT 185
business units, designing around people 16
buyer/seller relationship 26
BZW Equity Research 23

cadre of internationalists 77
Calpers 224
Canada 113, 237
capabilities
  definition 65
  development module levels and target populations 80
  development programme 77
  for international business 69
  development training 80
  identification and development 59
Cape Town 277
career manager 56
categories of international capability 16
CEE 230, 231
Central and South America 133
Centre for Research in Employment and Technology in Europe 52
champions 69
checklist for performance management factors 184
Chevrolet Cavalier 199
Chile 116
China 36, 41, 42, 113, 115, 206, 245, 249, 254, 256, 258, 265
  the sleeping giant awakes 244
  People's Republic of 244
Chinese 118, 133, 251, 252
  bureaucracy 252
  labour law 249

Perceptions II – A Business Development Executive's Reflections 255
rules to be kept in mind when hiring staff 247
technicians and professionals 246
chrysanthemum throne 269
City University Business School 116
Clinton, President 257
co-determination Act (1979) 219
collective agreements 237
collective bargaining agent 159
Colombia 211
commercialize core capabilities 59
Common Market in Europe 286
company culture and values 239
company culture, internal 201
company-wide legitimacy for the 'new deal' 128
compensation solutions for local national employees and third country nationals 85
Confucius 264
consulting the right people 177
content and process in performance management system design 182
context for international performance management 181
continental European countries 113
conventional careers, end of 27
core capabilities, examining 25
core HR mechanisms 144
corporate
  'glue' 56, 129
  culture 276
  memory 58, 62, 77
  representative 173
  versus local market postures 108
cross-cultural 109
  dimension 46
  frameworks 182
  issues 192
  joint venture 223
  sensitivities 62
  tolerance 48
Crump 269
cultural
  achievements 74
  change 174
  cocktail 48
  contexts 116
  dimensions 117
  diversity 46
  dynamics 263
  factor 16, 263

Index

Index